Urban Sustainability through Environmental Design

What can architects, landscape architects and urban designers do to make urban open spaces, streets and squares more responsive, lively and safe?

Urban Sustainability through Environmental Design seeks to answer this question by providing the analytical tools and practical methodologies that can be employed for sustainable and long-term solutions to the design and management of urban environments.

In recent years there has been obvious success in smartening and repopulating our towns and cities; however, there are concerns that these responses to regeneration are capable of sustaining only a limited sector of the community through the creation of 'boutique' environments and 'cappuccino' culture. *Urban Sustainability through Environmental Design* discusses this approach, calling into question the capability of 'quick-fix' development solutions to provide the establishment of fixed communities and suggesting a more time-conscious and evolutionary approach. The book focuses specifically on the analytical side of this problem, presenting tools of urban analysis selected to frame long-term, sustainable urban design solutions.

Urban Sustainability through Environmental Design is the first significant attempt to draw together and publish a pan-European view on sustainable urban design with a specific focus on social sustainability. It presents an innovative approach that focuses on what sustains solutions rather than on the solutions themselves: on the tools of urban analysis rather than the interventions. With its practical approach and wide-ranging discussion, this book will appeal to all those involved in producing communities and spaces for sustainable living, from students to academics through to decision-makers and professional leaders.

Kevin Thwaites researches and teaches landscape architecture and urban design at the Department of Landscape, University of Sheffield, where he is director of Learning and Teaching. He has worked in private practice and, with Ian Simkins, is co-founder of elp:rdu, a research facility which explores experiential aspects of outdoor space use.

Sergio Porta is assistant professor in urban planning and design at the Department of Architecture and Planning of the Polytechnic of Milan, Italy, where he holds the 'Laboratory of Urban Design' course. He is adjunct professor at the King Fahd University of Petroleum and Minerals in Dhahran, Saudi Arabia.

Ombretta Romice is an architect heading the Urban Design Masters at the University of Strathclyde in Glasgow. She is actively involved in IAPS (International Association for People-Environment Studies).

Mark Greaves is a professional planner focused on the delivery of exemplary urban design solutions. He is currently working in local authority planning in the UK.

Urban Sustainability through Environmental Design

Approaches to time–people–place responsive urban spaces

**Edited by
Kevin Thwaites, Sergio Porta,
Ombretta Romice and
Mark Greaves**

LONDON AND NEW YORK

First published 2007
by Routledge
2 Park Square, Milton Park, Abingdon, Oxon OX14 4RN

Simultaneously published in the USA and Canada
by Routledge
270 Madison Avenue, New York, NY 10016

Routledge is an imprint of the Taylor & Francis Group, an informa business

Typeset in Frutiger by
Florence Production Ltd, Stoodleigh, Devon
Printed and bound in Great Britain by
TJ International Ltd, Padstow, Cornwall

British Library Cataloguing in Publication Data
A catalogue record for this book is available from the British Library

Library of Congress Cataloging in Publication Data
Urban sustainability through environmental design : approaches to time, people, and place responsive urban spaces/Sergio Porta . . . [*et al.*].
    p. cm.
    Includes bibliographical references.
    1. City planning. 2. City planning–Environmental aspects. 3. Sustainable development. 4. Public spaces. I. Porta, Sergio, 1964–
    HT166.U7453 2007
    307.1′216–dc22   2007019107

ISBN10: 0–415–39547–X (hbk)
ISBN10: 0–415–38480–X (pbk)

ISBN13: 978–0–415–39547–2 (hbk)
ISBN13: 978–0–415–38480–3 (pbk)

Contents

Notes on the authors

Editors

Mark Greaves is a planner currently working at a large metropolitan local authority in the UK. His planning experience in both policy development and application to project management has ranged from the strategic regional level down to town-centre strategies, area masterplans and small-scale site interventions. He has worked in the USA and the UK and is firmly committed to the tenets and delivery of exemplary urban design.

Glasgow City Council, Department of Regeneration and Services, mark.greaves@drs.glasgow. gov.uk

Sergio Porta, architect, has a PhD in territorial and environmental planning and is a lecturer at the Politecnico di Milano, Italy. He researches spatial analysis and sustainable urban design, with a special focus on the creation of lively human environment in cities. This involves the intersection of scientific areas as different as traffic management, urban sociology, architectural design, public policy and involvement, spatial analysis and others. He was visiting scholar at the Institute for Governmental Studies of UC Berkeley, California, in 1998, associate researcher at the Institute for Sustainability and Technology Policy in Perth, Western Australia, in 2001 and is currently adjunct professor at the King Fahd University of Petroleum and Minerals of Dhahran, Saudi Arabia. He is a founding member of the Urban Sustainability through Environmental Design (UStED) Network.

Department of Architecture and Planning, Polytechnic of Milan, sergio.porta@polimi.it

Ombretta Romice is a lecturer in the Department of Architecture, University of Strathclyde in Glasgow, UK. She is an architect actively involved with the International Association for People-Environment Studies (IAPS). Her work focuses on urban design, environmental psychology and user participation in design. She holds a PhD in architecture and psychology and a post-doctoral in housing and regeneration sponsored by the European Union. She is a founding member of the Urban Sustainability through Environmental Design (UStED) Network.

Department of Architecture, University of Strathclyde, ombretta.r.romice@strath.ac.uk

Kevin Thwaites, PhD, teaches and researches urban design and landscape architecture at the University of Sheffield, UK. His interests lie with the philosophy and theory of outdoor place-making, particularly the relationship between the routine experience of people and its spatial expression in the daily encountered outdoors. With Ian Simkins, Kevin is co-founder of elp:rdu. Kevin and Ian's book, *Experiential Landscape: An approach to people, place and space* (Routledge, 2007), synthesizes human-environment relations and aspects of place theory with practical methods and tools to help environmental design professions, such as landscape architecture and urban design, make socially beneficial and experientially rich outdoor places.

Department of Landscape, University of Sheffield, kevin.thwaites@elprdu.com

Contributors

Nastaran Azmin-Fouladi, BSc, MSc, PhD, is research fellow at the Cities Institute, London Metropolitan University, UK. She has been involved in design projects for hospitals, transport, sport and housing schemes. She is currently researching urban and street design for the Accessibility and User Needs in Transport (AUNT-SUE) project under the EPSRC Sustainable Urban Environments research programme.

Cities Institute, London Metropolitan University, n.azmin-fouladi @londonmet.ac.uk

Carole Després is full professor at the School of Architecture and director of the Planning and Development Research Center at Laval University in Quebec City, Canada. She holds a PhD in environment-behaviour studies. Coordinator of GIRBa, her main contributions to research focus on the uses and meanings of housing and neighbourhood in the context of urban sprawl, as well as on transdisciplinarity.

École d'architecture, Université Laval, Québec, carole.despres@arc.ulaval.ca

Professor Graeme Evans, MA, PhD, FCCA, is director of the Cities Institute at London Metropolitan University, UK. He leads the AUNT-SUE research consortium and is co-investigator on the VivaCity2020 SUE project, for which he has been investigating mixed-use and urban sustainability from social, economic and environmental design perspectives. He has served as an enabler and design quality facilitator for CABE and is currently developing a GIS-based national cultural planning toolkit with EDAW.

Cities Institute, London Metropolitan University, g.evans@londonmet.ac.uk

Jo Foord, BSc, PhD, is a human geographer researching and teaching city theory, retail consumption and production and the new 'creative' economy at the Cities Institute, London Metropolitan University, UK. She leads Cities Institute's GIS research unit and GeoKnowledge project (HEIF) and undertakes analysis of economic, social and amenity data for policy evaluation, including the AUNT-SUE and VivaCity projects. She is currently researching sustainable city growth in Canadian and UK cities.

Cities Institute, London Metropolitan University, J.foord @londonmet.ac.uk

Hildebrand Frey, a graduate of the school of architecture at Stuttgart University with a specialization in urban design and urban planning, is a retired senior staff member at the University of Strathclyde, UK. He has extensive experience in practice, research and teaching. His main research interests and fields of numerous publications are sustainable urban development, sustainable urban form and urban and regional network structures. He currently holds a three-year research grant from the EPSRC for the investigation of suburban areas and ways in which they could be transformed to become more sustainable integrated, mixed-use and socially inclusive urban areas.

Department of Architecture, University of Strathclyde, h.w.frey@strath.ac.uk

Barbara Goličnik specialized in landscape architecture at Edinburgh College of Art, Heriot-Watt University, UK. She is a researcher at the Urban Planning Institute of the Republic of Slovenia, working on multidisciplinary national and international studies and projects on design research and environment-behaviour issues in the context of urban planning and open public space design. She is a visiting lecturer in Slovenia and abroad.

Urban Planning Institute of the Republic of Slovenia (UPIRS), barbara.golicnik@urbinstitut.si

Florent Joerin is associate professor at the Planning and Development Graduate School of Laval University in Quebec City, Canada. He is the holder of the Canada Research Chair in Territorial Decision-Making. Co-director of GIRBa, he specializes in the integration of geographic information systems in decision-making processes.

École supérieure d'aménagement et de développement, Université Laval, Québec, florent. joerin@esad.ulaval.ca

Vito Latora is an assistant professor of theoretical physics in the Physics Department of Catania University. Italy. His main fields of research are statistical mechanics, non-linear dynamics and complex systems. Current interests include the study of the structure and function of complex networks based on a combination of empirical studies, mathematical methods and computer simulations; he applies physics to urban planning and design and statistical methods in biology and geophysics. He has authored over 100 scientific papers for international refereed journals and conferences.

Dipartimento di Fisica e Astronomia, Università di Catania, latora@ct.infn.it

Alice Mathers is a planner and landscape architect currently undertaking an ESRC-awarded PhD at Sheffield University, UK. She is an associate of elp:rdu specializing in the creation of visual communication methods to be used as a participation toolkit for the inclusion of people with learning disabilities in the experience of public open space. Alice's expertise lies in bridging the gap between disability and environment. She teaches Urban Design and Social Aspects modules at Sheffield University and is guest lecturer for the Disability and Research undergraduate course at Sheffield Hallam University.

Department of Landscape, University of Sheffield, alice.mathers@elprdu.com

Eugenio Morello is an architect with a PhD in environmental design and building technologies, and is contract professor at the Politecnico di Milano, Italy, where he is also research assistant in the Department of Building Technology. His research field is environmental design at the urban scale and the integration of sustainable building technologies into large masterplans. In particular he explores the role played by environmental indicators in defining the city form, for the effective environmental comfort and energy performance of human settlements.

Polytechnic of Milan, Department of Building Technology, eugenio.morello@polimi.it

Aurore Nembrini is a professional research consultant at GIRBa at Laval University, Quebec City, Canada. Trained as an environmental engineer, she specializes in geographic information systems and is involved in research concerning public participation.

École d'architecture, Université Laval, Québec, aurore.nembrini@arc.ulaval.ca

Peter Newman is professor of city policy and director of the Institute for Sustainability and Technology Policy at Murdoch University, Australia. In 2006–7 he was a Fulbright Scholar at the University of Virginia, Charlottesville, examining innovations in sustainability in US cities, regions and states. Peter moves between academia and government, applying sustainability to city planning.

Institute for Sustainability and Technology Policy, Murdoch University, P.Newman@murdoch. edu.au

Carlo Ratti, architect and engineer, teaches at the Massachusetts Institute of Technology, US, where he also directs the SENSEable City Laboratory, a new research initiative between the MIT Department of Urban Studies and Planning and the Media Lab which explores how technology is transforming urban design and living. Carlo is also founding partner and director of carlorattiassociati, a rapidly growing architectural practice that was established in Turin, Italy. He also taught at Harvard University and the École Nationale des Ponts et Chaussies and is junior fellow of the Aspen Institute.

SENSEable City Laboratory, MIT, ratti@mit.edu

John L. Renne, AICP, is an assistant professor of urban planning and transportation studies at the University of New Orleans, US and an associate director of the University of New Orleans Transportation Center. He is also a research associate at the Institute for Sustainability and Technology Policy at Murdoch University and the Planning and Transport Research Centre in Western Australia. Dr Renne's work focuses on transit-oriented development across the USA and Australia. He is a founding member of the Urban Sustainability through Environmental Design (UStED) Network.

University of New Orleans, jlrenne@gmail.com

Ian Simkins is co-founder with Kevin Thwaites of the experiential landscape place research and development unit (elp:rdu, www.elprdu.com), a UK-based research facility concerned with the development of experiential landscape. Ian practises as a chartered landscape architect and tutors urban design related subjects at the University of Sheffield, UK. He is a member of the core team of UStED and a member of the International Association for People – Environment Studies (IAPS). Ian is currently completing PhD research on the spatial experiences of primary-school-age children.
  Department of Landscape, University of Sheffield, ian.simkins@elprdu.com

Geneviève Vachon is architect and full professor of urban design and architecture at Laval University's School of Architecture in Quebec City, Canada. She holds a PhD in urban studies and planning from MIT. She is co-director of GIRBa, where she contributes in areas of urban morphology, architectural typology and collaborative design.
  École d'architecture, Université Laval, Québec, genevieve.vachon@arc.ulaval.ca

Acknowledgements

All of the ideas expressed in this book are a shared responsibility of the authors. Each of us has, however, taken a lead in, or has personally written, specific chapters as follows: Mark Greaves wrote chapter 6 in collaboration with Ombretta and contributed material to chapters 1 and 7. Sergio Porta wrote chapter 2 and in collaboration with Ombretta chapters 5 and 8; chapter 7 with contributions from Mark and Kevin; and with Kevin chapter 21. Ombretta wrote chapter 4, collaborated with Kevin and Sergio on chapters 3 and 5, and with Mark on chapters 6. Ombretta also contributed to chapter 8 and was responsible for all the editorial work on chapters 9 to 20. Kevin wrote chapter 3 in collaboration with Ombretta, and with material from Mark and Sergio, chapters 1 and 7. Kevin and Sergio collaborated chapter 21. All the material in chapters 9 to 20 is the responsibility of the named authors. Material for chapter 20 originates in Ian Simkins' doctoral dissertation, reaching the concluding stages at the time of publication.

We are indebted to Cherry Ekins for her dedication and skill during the copy editing stages and are grateful to Beth Helleur of LDA Design, Exeter for the main cover photography.

Base Mapping: Reproduction by permission of Ordnance Survey on behalf of HMSO, © Crown Copyright 2007. All rights reserved, Ordnance Survey Licence number 100045659.

Preface

Hildebrand Frey

In the thousands of years of urban development only one short period introduced layout patterns and volumetric forms that changed the structure and face of the city. New design principles of the modernist city were promoted by Le Corbusier, who in the early 1920s called for the replacement of much of our urban heritage of today's inner-city areas by free-standing towers and slabs. Unfortunately, during the 1950s, 1960s and early 1970s this is exactly what we did, and 'The evil that Le Corbusier did lives after him' (Hall [1988] 1990: 204).

Around the mid-1970s we started to understand the damage that had been done not only to the city but also to the citizens, and this rekindled our affection for the traditional (pre-modernist) city. People like Kevin Lynch, Jane Jacobs, Christopher Alexander and many others built the foundation for the renaissance of the 'good city' and elucidated its superior social, environmental and spatial/formal properties. The irony is that, regardless how hard we try to recreate these properties, we seem to be unable to succeed. There are many reasons for this, but only a few shall be spelled out.

The pre-industrial traditional city grew incrementally and, more importantly, very slowly as the result of the decisions of individual people, enterprises and local authorities. This meant that each new project had time to study its urban context and shape it such that it would be compatible with the existing morphology, construction systems, materials and facades to maintain continuity of urban structure and form. There was also time for each project to be specifically designed and adorned to generate architectural and functional variety within continuity. There was specifically also time to design and develop the public realm, and some of the most beautiful and popular public squares took hundreds of years to be completed to their present-day form.

Industrialization caused cities to grow, first also relatively slowly. However, when industrialization accelerated, population and housing demand grew enormously. Consequently, the building process had to be accelerated and this meant simpler details, cheaper materials and mass repetition of the same building types. Public squares and buildings during this period were still very carefully designed and landscaped, built by leading industrialists and councillors to express the pride in the city's economic and cultural growth. Most importantly, the original morphology of the city and the scale of buildings were maintained and expanded so that even poorly built urban fabric in workers' areas still had many of the characteristics we today classify as some of the keys to sustainable development: density, a mixture of uses, local facilities in walking distance and so forth.

After the Second World War much of the historical fabric in inner-city areas was demolished and the modernist city came into existence to provide decent housing for the masses. Prefabrication systems, adopted to speed up the process of construction, stereotype high-rise blocks and slabs with mass-produced and therefore endlessly repetitive facades and use zoning meant that the visual-formal variety and vibrancy of urban life of the earlier city vanished. Streets, no longer enclosed by buildings, had now only one function: to accommodate vehicular traffic. Most new towns and Comprehensive Development Areas were planned, designed and constructed in little more than 20–25 years. There was no time for thoughtful design and slow incremental development. It is at this point in the city's history that the qualities of the traditional city were largely lost.

Today we are part of a global economy and much of the development in the city is no longer locally promoted but the work of powerful transnational enterprises and companies, virtually uncontrollable by our planning system, with little if any knowledge of, or interest in, local urban qualities and conditions. Their architecture has become internationalized, and much of the shaping of the public realm is done for commercial benefits. Most importantly, the scale of development has increased considerably. Despite the fact that we today recognize again the necessity of urban blocks and a legible structure of streets enclosed by buildings at least in the inner area of the city, the built environment is plain, mixed use is reduced to a few shopping streets and the human scale of city streets has been largely lost as a result of over-scaled commercial development and under-scaled suburbia.

This conundrum attracted the attention of the authors of this book. In a collaborative process they developed an understanding of the problems we face, redefined the properties of a good city and developed a considerable number of 'tools' that help planners and designers to pursue and, hopefully, achieve these properties. The tools will provide answers to the following questions.

- What are the properties of the city that support a sustainable social, economic, land-use and temporal mix?
- What spatial, structural and activity patterns and what travel distance values of a city promote sustainable forms of transport?
- How can transport be made to respond to the needs of vulnerable groups and become more socially inclusive?
- To what degree does centrality and good accessibility of a place contribute to its attractiveness, safety and vibrancy of uses?
- How can social, economic and environmental outcomes of urban development be accurately measured?
- How can individual people and entire communities be actively involved in urban development from the initial briefing stage to design and implementation?
- How can participation and social inclusion in the shaping of the everyday spatial environment involve the under-represented sectors of society (e.g. children, people with learning difficulties) to become a truly inclusive process?
- How do the geometric patterns of urban spaces influence their environmental conditions (e.g. radiation exchange, energy consumption, wind porosity, visibility) and ultimately the well-being of people?
- What specific characteristics add a human dimension to an urban space and transform it into a people-friendly place?
- How do specific spatial characteristics and design details of public urban spaces influence people's behaviour patterns and the use dynamics of the space?

In view of the widely experienced difficulty of translating concepts of sustainable urban development and form into practically applicable action programmes, the combination of a theoretical underpinning of the notion of sustainable development with practical advice as to how to achieve it is one of the strengths of this book. Another one is that the authors and contributors – all interested in the planning and design of urban space – bring experiences to the discussion from a variety of backgrounds and disciplines: architecture, urban design, urban planning, landscape architecture, environmental design, environmental psychology, geography, urban transport planning and theoretical physics; this makes it possible to investigate urban issues and problems from different perspectives. The third strength of the book is the way in which the authors have worked together: rather than each of them writing a separate chapter, they collectively discussed all contributions to the book in internet conferences so that something like a 'concerted' and holistic view emerged to overcome the disciplinary fragmentation of much of the debate on the city and sustainability.

PART I
TIME-CONSCIOUS URBAN DESIGN

This order is all composed of movement and change, and although it is life, not art, we may fancifully call it the art form of the city and liken it to the dance – not to a simple-minded precision dance with everyone kicking up at the same time, twirling in unison and bowing off en-masse, but to an intricate ballet in which the individual dancers and ensembles all have distinctive parts which miraculously reinforce each other and compose an orderly whole.

Jacobs (1961: 50)

Section One

THE UNSUSTAINABLE LASTING OF TIME-UNCONSCIOUS URBAN DESIGN

1 Space and people: the case for socially sustainable urban design

Historic places should be assessed dispassionately for the practical lessons they offer to the present, and no more. Planners must be neither nostalgic like traditional architects nor ideological like the modernist ones; urbanism must remain dedicated to whatever works best in the long run.

Duany (2003: 121)

Since the advent of Richard Rogers's Task Force Report in 1999 (DETR 1999), a great deal of good has happened in our towns and cities. A cursory look at nearly any city skyline today reveals a plethora of cranes signalling a rush of construction which aims to regenerate neglected city quarters, often removing or reinventing now obsolete industrial usage and creating smart residential, retail, leisure and commercial attractions to repopulate urban areas. In far less than a decade many urban centres have been, and continue to be, literally transformed by this process. To the good, thanks to Rogers and his collaborators, we now know that 'quality of place' and its role in sustaining fulfilled lives matters to processes of urban regeneration just as much (if not more) than economic prosperity, functionality, etc. The jury is probably still out in terms of a full determination of what quality of place really means in this context, but Rogers has helped make it pretty clear that design, as well as economic, social and cultural factors, for instance, is key to its achievement. It must be a kind of design, however, that gives special attention to the needs, aspirations and experiences of urban inhabitants instead of just the kind that aims for superficial aesthetic goals.

In response, we can see implicit in much of the urban design guidance that followed the publication of the Rogers Task Force Report, much of it under the auspices of UK agencies including, for example, the Office of the Deputy Prime Minister, English Partnerships, the Commission for Architecture and the Built Environment, etc., a clear recognition of the value and significance of earlier research and theoretical development in urban design thinking that has sought to put people first. Among these we can cite a renewed appreciation for Jane Jacobs's (1961) insistence about the vitality and complexity of street life; Lynch's (1960) research about the way cities can and must be able to be subliminally read and understood; Cullen's (1971) concept of townscape as a sequential continuity of experience instead of a collection of static buildings and the spaces between; Alexander's (1977, 1979) ideas about the integral relationship of human functioning and its spatial context; Tibbalds's (1992) call for people-friendly towns; and other human-oriented approaches such as those of Oscar Newman (1973, 1996), William Whyte (1980, 1988), Allan Jacobs (1978a, 1978b, 1985), Raquel Ramati (1981), Peter Bosselmann (1987, 1998), Clare Cooper-Marcus (1986, 1998), Jan Gehl and Lars Gemzøe (1980; Gehl 1996), Peter Newman and Jeff Kenworthy (1999), Hildebrand Frey (1999) and many others. It is fair to say, and to a large extent true, that much of the essence of these theoretical contributions has influenced practical approaches to urban regeneration and design, and that this has made an important contribution to beginning a reversal of what some commentators see as the tyranny of modernism so that we can now, at least to some extent, be confident of moving towards more socially responsive solutions. City skylines are changing, dereliction and neglect are being transformed, people are returning to the city to work, to play and to live. There is evidence of fine design and civic pride expressed through new buildings, streets and open spaces. Those who once said that café society would never take hold in Britain because of the climate have, for the most part, simply been proved wrong.

One of the first examples of the kind of city quarter regeneration that typifies what is now taking place across the nation can be found in the south-east corner of Leeds, UK; a place known as The Calls. Once a semi-derelict and neglected backwater of past industrial and commercial use, The Calls has been brought back to life with a careful blend of conservation and imaginative new development and today appears a vibrant mix of retail, business, leisure and residential use. The Leeds Development Corporation's vision for The Calls, to create a thriving, characterful blend of conservation and innovation to encourage and support a working and residential community in an attractive environment, has largely been achieved. It is often cited in publications as an exemplar of quality urban regeneration, fulfilling many of the aspirations of Lord Rogers's Urban Task Force to breathe new life into towns and cities through generating a strong sense of place. That this has happened, and indeed continues to happen, probably owes much to the approach adopted by urban design consultants Llewellyn-Davies, who set out to produce a masterplan that emphasized spatial rather than merely planning considerations. As a consequence a template for regeneration emerged that paid careful attention to the quality of the streetscape and to enhancing the network of small spaces and squares implicit in the historic layout of The Calls. It is evident this has contributed to lifting a neglected part of Leeds into prominence, creating an attractive and popular place to live, work and socialize, and there is now a substantial residential population.

Places like The Calls are in many ways becoming models for the repopulation of cities, presenting to us a potential appearance for the new urban neighbourhoods. The question is, though, is this model the right one, or not? The Calls has many impressive features: sensitive architectural regeneration, relationship to the city centre, exploitation of its waterside setting, vibrant social opportunities, impressive visual character, for example, but questions remain about the extent to which developments like these are conducive to creating communities. The Calls has an increasing number of inhabitants, but like many city-centre developments that follow similar models these tend to be an often transient population of mainly young professional people who may not establish the kind of long-term roots in the area that will nurture and sustain a stable neighbourhood identity. One of the outcomes of an informal inquiry into the lives and habits of Calls residents and users began to reveal that The Calls was indeed locally regarded as a neighbourhood in the sense that it stood out or had special associations that set it apart from the wider city. What was perhaps unexpected, however, was that the rich visual and spatial qualities so evident within The Calls area did not appear to register more prominently in the routine of its users. People did not seem to be forging the kind of meanings and associations there that anchor a sense of belonging to a neighbourhood. The Calls presents an attractive, trendy backdrop, an appealing place to pass through and somewhere for a diversity of evening entertainment. But this does not seem to be sufficient definition for a socially sustainable neighbourhood. The mere presence of inhabitants does not in itself make a community: it does not make a place live in the sense that Jane Jacobs meant.

Why this is so is hard to pin down? Certainly the wealth of opportunity available in the central city draws people away from The Calls area, and indeed it could be argued that this is in fact a part of the appeal of city living. But this seems certainly exacerbated by an absence of neighbourhood supporting facilities: there are plenty of expensive bars and restaurants, but although a couple of local grocery stores have recently opened, there are no post offices, doctors or dentist, and certainly no school or community centre. Other influencing factors, though, seemed to relate more to a fundamental lack of understanding about how space can be encouraged to develop into place in a mixed-use setting. Unimaginative approaches to car parking make some office and residential courtyard spaces unavailable for better social uses. Some open spaces in newer residential blocks are at best ambiguous as to their intended purpose, encouraging haphazard storage of private cars, litter and an air of neglect and decay. The routing of a section of the Leeds city-centre loop road through the site has effectively destroyed the Development Corporation's hope for better pedestrian priority and new development here, a decision that flies in the face of Llewellyn-Davies's masterplan and completely compromises an obvious potential to create quality public squares in this key central location. It began to seem as though, hidden beneath the impressive veneer of The Calls regeneration, was a fundamental lack of confidence about how to optimize the place-making potential of its spatial infrastructure. In many places it is as though an attractive stage set had been sculpted with insufficient reference to the play that it was supposed to help express: in many ways an impressive container but too often devoid of clear meaning and significance, especially in relation to its residential purpose (Figure 1.1).

Another area that shares much in common with The Calls is the Merchant City in Glasgow. It recently won the 'Best Neighbourhood in Britain' award from the Academy of Urbanism, an esteemed collection of individuals with a wide range of expertise who support and promote good-quality urbanism throughout Great Britain and Ireland. The area has an agreeable location; it sits adjacent to the main city-centre area of Glasgow and abuts George Square, which is the symbolic and administrative heart of Glasgow. Strathclyde University is in close proximity, so student life is ensured. The Merchant City hosts numerous trendy bars and restaurants, and contains some niche market retailers and fashionable boutiques housed within some of Glasgow's most historic buildings. Many renovations display concern with both history and design quality, and much of the regeneration has been achieved through effective collaborations between public and private sectors. There have been some impressive streetscape improvements in the area, employing high-quality materials. More and more flats are being built in smart new buildings to complement the original warehouse conversions that kick-started the initial regeneration efforts. But does it actually function as a lively and liveable 'neighbourhood'?

Overall, while the area has no doubt benefited from substantial investment, improvements to the public realm and some beautifully refurbished buildings indicative of an area that has been successfully regenerated, on many levels it still does not really function as a 'neighbourhood'. For instance, the overwhelming majority of the amenities and services in the area are limited to bars and nightclubs, with a few cultural attractions thrown in the mix. However, the area is too functionally limited to be considered a successful neighbourhood, as traditional or even sustainable neighbourhood requirements such as doctors' surgeries, dentists, nurseries, schools, green space and even a butcher or baker are either non-existent or in short supply. If an urban renaissance means a lively bar scene catering to young urban professionals and students then the Merchant City can be considered a success. In a nutshell, a neighbourhood should provide for all your daily needs, but in this case unless your daily needs consist of an evening meal in a swanky restaurant followed by a pub crawl then the area does not really work (Figure 1.2).

A successful neighbourhood should also meet longer-term needs – the cycle of a lifetime in addition to daily needs. The area abounds in one and two-bedroom flats (predominantly buy-to-let) that suit the student and young professional market and satisfy investor demand. On the positive side there is no doubt that a significant measure of life has been brought back to a previously underutilised area of the city centre. However, there are few, if any, larger flats or family housing that would enable people who may enjoy the area to stay on and start a family. This limited range of housing subjects the area to a stream of transitory residents which seriously inhibits any sense of community that should be inherent in a quality neighbourhood. The Merchant City, on a

1.1 The Riverside and Calls, Leeds

surface level impressively regenerated, does not function as a neighbourhood and leaves one to question if it really deserves an award from a body promoting the qualities of good urbanism.

Clearly these are only two examples, but the comparative longevity of The Calls regeneration project, begun over 20 years ago, might allow us a glimpse of what may lie ahead for younger redevelopment projects and those yet to come that follow similar patterns. It is not that The Calls project is unsuccessful: in many important ways it is highly so. We can confidently say, for example, that an approach like this succeeds in attracting people to cities, but the questions remain: will they stay there, will they feel able to put down roots, to raise their families, develop and sustain neighbourhoods? If they do not or cannot then in what way can we say that this approach is socially sustainable? And if we cannot say this then why are we doing it? Indeed, it could be argued that the sustainability of these new residential environments is more or less solely dependent on a continuous supply of well-paid, largely transient professional people, attracted by exclusive 'boutique' environments marketed primarily for lifestyle opportunities. If the city economic bubble were to decline or at worst burst, what then for these urban utopias? Indeed, questions like this were central to a recent BBC TV programme which featured architect and broadcaster Maxwell Hutchinson challenging the seemingly insatiable appetite for stylish apartment blocks as a central feature of city regeneration. Hutchinson provocatively argued that such environments were often sterile and experientially vacuous, and could be gradually abandoned to become the slum developments of tomorrow. When industrial decline happened in cities at least it left us a legacy of robust structures that, when the circumstances were right, lent themselves relatively easily to a change of use,

1.2 Glasgow's Merchant City

reinvigorated for dwelling, retail and leisure and new forms of enterprise. Can we be sure that the same can be said for the riverside apartment blocks and their spatial infrastructure that now proliferate in urban centres? If not then we must question again how sustainable such places really are.

Despite their evident success, is this as yet a partial or provisional success? Or, in short, is this a success in terms of social sustainability? Might we have gone slightly off track in our response to modernist principles, and if we have how might we recover our sense of direction? We began by alluding to the fact that lessons from theoretical resources generated over the past four decades have undoubtedly helped to develop an alternative, more humane, approach to urban design, and that this is showing signs of success. However, one of the arguments we want to extend here is that our reading of these resources may have been selective and there may be important messages that we have yet to comprehend fully and embed in our approaches to urban regeneration and design. Central to this may be a body of knowledge that relates to the way we understand the nature of urban order, and particularly the concepts of space and place implied by it. Returning to Jane Jacobs and the quote at the head of this part of the book about the way she believes order in cities is manifest, it is clear that this is not an order composed of material components and the spaces in between, but an order apparent in the collective actions of people as they go about their daily routines. It is not a static, sculptural kind of order, but like music and dance characterized only by movement and change: dynamic activity that comprises an orderly whole.

Such order can never be static, fixed and determined; instead it evolves in continuous flux, through time, according to what happens there and according to the meanings and associations that people project there. This unfolding life is the way order in place rises and falls, ebbs and flows through time and location in a rhythmical and symbiotic dance of situated human action and emotional expression. An important implication is the role of time here: the need to allow human situations to settle, develop, evolve and change as they will. Possibly one of the problems we have with our current approaches is that, in the rush for instant solutions, we think that urban order can be imposed, specified, made and delivered to specification. Maybe we have overlooked a central message implicit in Jacobs and others that an urban order defined mainly in terms of the dynamic actions of human subjects must be allowed space and time to unfold gradually, to grow and evolve, to mature and to settle. The quick-fix injection of large new urban populations in one place at once brings to mind more of a process of industrial manufacture, an imposition rather than a growth and evolution.

References

Alexander, C. (1979) *The Timeless Way of Building*, Oxford University Press, New York.

Alexander, C., Ishikawa, S., Silverstein, M., Jacobson, M., Fiksdahl-King, I. and Angel, S. (1977) *A Pattern Language*, Oxford University Press, New York.

Bosselmann, P. (1987) *Experiencing downtown streets in San Francisco*, Institute of Urban and Regional Development, University of California at Berkeley, Reprint n. 217.

Bosselmann, P. (1998) *Representation of places: reality and realism in city design*, University of California Press, Berkeley CA.

Medium-Density Family Housing, University of California Press, Berkeley CA.

Cooper-Marcus, C. (1998) *People's Places: Design Guidelines for Urban Open Space*, Van Nostrand Reinhold, New York.

Cooper-Marcus, C. and Sarkissian, W. (1986) *Housing as if People Mattered: Site-Design Guidelines for*

Cullen, G. (1971) *The Concise Townscape*, Architectural Press, Oxford.

DETR (1999) *Towards an Urban Renaissance: Final Report of The Urban Task Force*. Taylor & Francis Group, London.

Duany, A. (2003) 'Neighbourhood design in practice', in Neal, P. (ed.) *Urban Villages and the Making of Communities*, Spon Press, London.

Frey, H. (1999) *Designing the City: Towards a More Sustainable Urban Form*, Spon Press, London.

Gehl, J. (1996) *Public Spaces, Public Life*, Arkitektens Forlag, Copenhagen.

Gehl, J. (2001 4edn.) *Life Between Buildings: Using Public Space*, The Danish Architectural Press, Copenhagen.

Jacobs, A. (1978a) *Great Streets*, The MIT Press, Cambridge, MA.

Jacobs, A. (1978b) *Making City Planning Work*, The American Society of Planning Officials, Chicago.

Jacobs, A. (1985) *Looking at Cities*, Harvard University Press, Cambridge, MA.

Jacobs, J. (1989 [1961]) *Death and Life of Great American Cities*, Random House, New York.

Lynch, K. (1997 [1960]) *The Image of the City*, The MIT Press, Cambridge, MA.

Newman, O. (1973) *Defensible Space: Crime Prevention Through Environmental Design*, Collier Books, New York.

Newman, O. (1996) *Creating Defensible Space*, U.S. Department of Housing and Urban Development, Washington, D.C.

Newman, P. and Kenworthy, J. (1999) *Sustainability and Cities: Overcoming Automobile Dependence*, Island Press, Washington, D.C.

Ramati, R. (1981) *How to Save Your Own Street*, Doubleday, New York.

Tibbalds, F. (1992) *Making People Friendly Towns: Improving the Public Environment in Towns and Cities*, Longman, London.

Whyte, W. (1980) *The Social Life of Small Urban Spaces*, The Conservation Foundation, Washington, D.C.

Whyte, W. (1988) *City: Rediscovering the Center*, Doubleday, New York.

2 Three core messages, or what we mostly should do

Urban design will be a key element of the renaissance of cities, to break down the isolation between parts of the city and to achieve retention and continuity of character, in the face of the impersonal trends of homogenisation. There will be a number of policies, measures and interventions, in which the planner will play a key role. They will include: the revival of urban design to protect and enhance streets, squares, footpaths and other thoroughfares as key linkages in the urban framework; the rehabilitation of degraded or inhumanly planned pieces of the urban fabric; measures to facilitate personal contacts and opportunities for leisure and recreation; measures to ensure the individual and collective feeling of security, as it is a key element to guarantee urban well-being; efforts to create memorable urban environments derived from specific genius loci, thus enhancing diversity and character; maintenance and cultivation of a high level of aesthetic excellence in all parts of the urban networks; conservation through planning of all significant elements of natural and cultural heritage.

Conseil Européen des Urbanistes (2003: 9 – 10)

Against this background of questions about the way in which people-space relations have been, and continue to be, interpreted and applied in urban regeneration and design, we have three core themes in this book that we wish to explore. These are outlined here before moving on to look at how human-environment relations have underpinned the embedding of modernist principles in contemporary urban design and how this has more recently been countered by movement towards the sustainable compact city. We suggest that, beneficial though this has been, in its present form it may be contributing to the development of what has been described in a recent edition of the *Harvard Design Magazine* (Saunders 2007) as 'cappuccino urbanism', a form of urban regeneration in danger of reducing the humanist reaction against modernism to its own kind of exclusive, lifeless and shallow formula. We conclude this section with some thoughts about how we might fine-tune this with ideas about 'time consciousness'.

Adjusting the bourgeois city

Recent reflection on whether compactness (what level of compactness, in what relation with functions, activities, local culture and environmental conditions) is conducive to sustainability in cities builds on an understanding which should be considered a general achievement in contemporary urban design (Jenks 2005): put simply, the compact city has proved successful as an urban form in saving land, mixing activities and social groups, enhancing human relationships and local communities and allowing evolution, change and innovation to emerge, while the 'dispersed' city has proved a failure in terms of environmental balance, social equity and cohesion and local economy support. While different urban forms, including low-density detached agglomerations, might successfully cope with settlements of limited size, the future of large cities is strictly linked with the traditional compact bourgeois city model and our capacity to update, reframe and adjust it to the emerging scenarios. The bourgeois city, the industrial city, the 'city of stone', came to the forefront of history just yesterday; if the compact, walkable, pre-industrial settlement constituted the way human beings have been gathering in stable shared environments for almost 6,800 of the 7,000 years of city history, beginning in the late eighteenth century the bourgeois city interpreted a brand-new kind of physical, social, environmental and economic realization: the large city of the new industrial era. Figure 2.1 is an authors' elaboration from Newman and Kenworthy (1999): the impressive acceleration in the speed of historical change does not alter the fact that human coexistence in cities has never been like ours from the beginning of times to just yesterday. An immense innovation in almost all fields of human life, the bourgeois city appears as one of the most terrific realizations of humanity, so much so that it parallels that sort of 'great and terrible' realizations which changed the course of human evolution – like, following Michel Serres (1993), the appearance of the thought of God, agriculture or geometry. Everything seemed to change in the bourgeois city, with the aim of making the coexistence of millions of humans possible and convenient on a large scale: new technological devices (siphons and domestic toilets, gas and electricity, public transport, street pavements and illumination, hospitals, slaughterhouses, lifts. . .), new social classes and actors (a growing bourgeois middle class, as well as factory workers, trade unions, organized women associations. . .), new kinds of urban environments (periphery, industrial areas, urban greens and parks, boulevards. . .), new medical practices and discoveries (vaccination, X-rays, advancements in microbiology and surgery. . .), all contributed to that massive realization. But the point here is that, despite all such novelties, the essential *spatial* substrate of the pre-industrial city persisted in the way the basic elements of space were put in relation one another: streets were still the scene of social life, buildings still

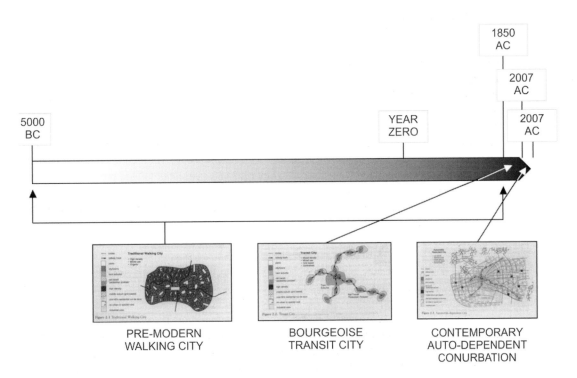

2.1 From the walking city to the contemporary automobile-dependent conurbation

faced that scene, the city – especially along main streets and central areas – was generally mixed in the type of activities and people, the physical as well as social organization of the community were focused around centres and sub-centres mostly linked to public transport, the density of the city was supportive of such organization. The pre-industrial city was adjusted in order to deal with the new needs by means of countless gradual changes and betterments without any real theoretical basis or central control (Peterson, 1976), to the point that a massive innovation took place on the basis of a continuity in the fundamentals of the spatial structure. All technological differences apart, in fact, pre-industrial towns and cities and the large bourgeois cities of the new industrial era shared the same basic spatial substrate which constituted the line of continuity of urban life through centuries and millennia.

That line got broken with the first decades of the twentieth century, the cradle of the modern city. Among the many, two factors counted in making that major shift: the first was a *technological innovation*, the appearance of the automobile as the principal mode of transportation for the general masses of urban (and ex-urban) inhabitants, which happened in the early 1920s in the USA and just after the Second World War in Europe; the second was a *cultural innovation*, the emergence of modernism as the mainstream attitude of the emerging discipline of city planning and design between the first and third decades of the twentieth century (see Chapter 3). The combination of these factors drove to the actual subversion of what we called the persistent 'spatial substrate' of city life: the attack was brought to the very core of the city as it was known so far, by dividing the interwoven fabric of activities and uses in specialized 'functional' districts, breaking the relationship between the street and the city, spreading urbanization all around with no reference to any pedestrian coverage limit nor public transit organization, systematically demolishing all pre-existent public transit features and plants, dramatically lowering the density of the now 'diffused' or 'sprawled' agglomerations, thus increasing the need for more car ownership and use and leading to the 'automobile-dependent' city of today (Newman and Kenworthy 1998). The impact of this cultural blame on the way all cities have been built in the twentieth century was enormous. The idea of the masters, standing astonished right in front of the great spectacle of the Western world's massive urbanization of those times, was that the great city of the twentieth century was to be entirely new stuff, and therefore needed entirely new ideas – order against disorder, geometry against supposed 'chaos', specialized streets and public spaces against multifunctional streets and public spaces – for the age of the automobile and city planning.

One of the many ironies of history is that the modern city of the masters has never really worked in the large cities for which it was conceived. When it worked, it was in small rural villages where low density was not a problem, or in ghettos of well-paid people who did not need, nor searched for, any real complexity in their daily life. Of course the huge simplification brought to the world by the modern gospel proved to match perfectly the new processes of massive land development based on the creation of real estate revenues, but in social, environmental and broader economical terms it resulted in a generalized disaster of enormous proportions.

So here is where the real specificity of large cities emerges: that, at a deeper level, they have no real specificity at all; that, after all, it is always the old story of living together and making the best of our ecological attitudes (the attitudes that link human beings with their spatial environment), but at a larger scale; and that this jump in scale implies a huge work for adjusting and bettering the urban environment and heritage, which has nothing to do with subverting it (and is actually the opposite of subverting it).

In conclusion, we clearly see now that contemporary cities are mostly large and increasingly globalized. As one of its side-effects, globalization strengthens both the existence of, and the claim for, sense of place and localisms. Because our investigation on the form of settlements is mostly oriented to the large city, we find that the generalized failure of the so-called 'detached – low density with CBDs – tower in the park – car dependent' conventional model (along with its later evolutions towards more varied constitutions like edge-cities around denser business/commercial nodes, gated well-done elderly 'sun' cities, ethnic ghettos and so forth) in building the large city must be acknowledged as a relevant starting point. We also recognize that many of the arguments which backed the dispersed 'garden' city in its early stages at the beginning of the twentieth century, which were all about social hygienism and public health, are now outdated due to an almost unbelievable development of technology and scientific knowledge in all fields, from microbiology to epidemiology, from industrial planting to waste treatment (organic and inorganic), from micro-climate management (heating-cooling) to public transport and communication.

So, here we go with the first message of this book: large compact cities are much more feasible in our times than they used to be when they emerged at first at the dawn of the industrial age. They now represent an opportunity as they have never been before. Therefore we should look backward to the large bourgeois compact city model in order to adjust it in view of the info-city of the future.

Overcoming the cultural brake

Architects and city planners have the greatest responsibility for the failure of the large city as a social product. If the performance of a complex system (its overall resulting behaviour) cannot be reduced to being determined by any of its constituent factors alone, then how cities were designed is not the only force that counts when it comes to the overall behaviour of cities or city spaces. Nevertheless, it is important to acknowledge that many of the most influential modern architects and city planners have contributed to the justification, legitimization, design and construction on a massive scale of many of the most inhuman and anti-social urban places on earth.

The emphasis, as for the artists of the new avant-garde 'art-compounds', as Tom Wolfe (1981) called them, was on 'starting from zero': the 'city of asses', as Le Corbusier dared to term the European urban heritage as a whole, was declared outdated. The old city was no longer to be bettered or adjusted: it was to be demolished to make room for the new one, the one that so delighted Le Corbusier and his bunch of fellow modernists. They actively contributed as much as they could directly, as operators, and indirectly, as cultural agents and opinion leaders, to the systematic destruction of the city as a global phenomenon in the last 70 years or so in the Western world. As much of their ideology and practice is currently quite embedded at the core of many of the subjects and structures that still govern most of the process of city building today, with tremendous impacts at a huge scale in the developing countries, it is perhaps worth repeating: they were not the epigones, the pupils, they were the celebrated masters, the awarded leaders of the discipline, the barons of university departments, the chairs of faculties and colleges, the editors of leading journals; they were what constituted – and to some extent still constitutes – the mainstream in the field of city planning. In terms of building good places for the urban living of our people and future generations, what they did was to create disaster after disaster in a surreal and growing detachment of culture from real life, where the larger the failure the higher the honour.

Certainly, this was not due to any bad intention. The culture of architectural and urban planning and design faced a major paradigm shift between the first and the third decades of the last century; that shift led to what we call 'modernism', a blend of ideas and attitudes that, in terms of spatial planning, can be reduced to a bunch of simple ideas (see Box 2.1).

Coded and slowly refined and adjusted throughout the most impressive process of urbanization in history, that of the past century, such ideas have deeply permeated city building not just in terms of planning visions, but also in terms of organizations (professional, academic, of the public administration), careers, technical resources (technical handbooks and manuals, analytical tools, software devices) and of course norms and guidelines, so much so that they still dominate, by an extremely powerful, monumental 'inertia', current practices and thoughts: nothing 'strange' happening, everything still goes that way. And it does.

Box 2.1 The modern city list

1. A city of specialized districts: because the city is a mechanism, it would profit from the ordered distinction of each part based on one function. The rationale behind this is twofold: on one side, it enhances the possibility of planning and realizing the functioning of each part in a proper (rational) manner, responding to the needs that are primarily associated with that function; on the other side, the assembly of all such parts can be approached with a clear understanding of all reciprocal relationships, again based on the functions involved.

2. Buildings independent from streets: buildings should be independent from streets in order to break the closure of the streetscape, favour the construction of healthier residential environments and avoid the intermingling of the buildings' ground-floor activities with vehicle movements that take place in the street. Moreover, the longitudinal axes of buildings should be oriented along the north-east south-west axis to maximize the exposure of residential façades to the sun's rays.

3. Open disposition of buildings in parks and super-blocks: the traditional urban block must be set in an open layout where possibly high-rise buildings are built up freely in a green area that constitutes a defensive facility against problems coming from the streets (danger, noise, pollution). That green area should be designed to be as large as possible in order to form a mainly self-sufficient pedestrian super-block bordered by arterial streets and off-street car-park areas and provided with basic facilities and services in the middle. That allows nature to come into the city and save it from its malign character.

4. Parks and greens will save our cities: cities are bad, nature is good. In order to save our cities, we should fill them with parks and greens as much as possible.

5. Community centres and main streets should be located as far apart as possible. The heart of the community should live in safe pedestrian environments with no exchange with dangerous traffic. In a hierarchical configuration, streets from higher to lower rankings should serve communities from lower to higher levels of density, following a rule of inverse correlation.

6. Hierarchy of specialized streets: beside several categories of public spaces that must be left to the un-programmed utilization of a variety of end-users (like parking areas or playgrounds), all open areas and especially all streets must be designed for just one type of user. Interconnections between streets and spaces for different users should be carefully designed in order to avoid contacts as much as possible.

7. A top-down all-at-once process: like every machine, the good city is designed once and forever by means of the application of knowledge and talent by trained scientists and leading intellectuals. In that sense, the city is a piece of art, where changes that might intervene between the final conception and the realization, not to mention those happening after the realization, are to be considered offensive to the purity of the original plan which embeds the creators' intentions. Like hammer blows on a beautiful statue, every modification of the city is for the worse.

At a philosophical level, however, the foundations of modernism in city planning and design are seriously put in question by a second major shift, a 'neo-traditional counter-revolution' (Marshall 2005) that we can better interpret as an outcome of the large claim for more sustainable urban communities. This second paradigm, the sustainable compact city, is based on some other key principles that, when listed, reveal an almost literal opposition to the previous ones (see Box 2.2). While a quick sketch of this opposition in the history of urban design will be detailed in Chapter 5, it is worth noting here that such shift towards a more human and environmentally conscious city is not just a matter for architects or urban planners: rather, it is an expression of a much deeper conflict between a mechanistic and an organic interpretation of the world, which involves disciplines

Box 2.2 The compact sustainable city list

1. A mixed-use city: because the city is a living organism, it is complex. As such, we will never be able to plan the city, but rather, at best, grasp several clues as to how it works in a condition of prevailing uncertainty. The complex character of the city is not a problem, it is its higher gift. The reason people meet in cities is exactly to take advantage of the unplanned and the diverse. Therefore the city should never be planned in specialized areas but, on the contrary, the ability of the urban environment to favour a mix of uses and users should be enhanced as much as possible in every case. The emergence of clusters of activities and human types should be left to the 'natural' evolution of the urban body to the extent that it does not damage the social and environmental balance of the system as a whole. Still, although it is recognized that mixed uses are beneficial, little guidance is available on what constitutes appropriate mixed uses, the scale of mixed use, and the location and visibility of mixed uses and the mass of the supporting population. See Evans and Foord in this volume.

2. Graded density: in the context of mixed land use, density policy relates not only to housing but to other urban activities as well. Levels of 'use intensity' should vary in relation to the level of public transport accessibility and closeness to prime pedestrian focuses, graining from high-intensity uses near central high streets and transport nodes to low intensity near open country, open space wedges or major roads. See Newman, Renne and Porta and Latora in this volume.

3. Compact communities: compact cities are made of compact communities: well-designed, higher-density, medium-rise housing and mixed-use developments focused on town and local centres and other public transport hubs, large enough to offer a range of social and economic amenities within walking distance of people's homes. For compact communities to function well, it is important that, within residential areas, concentrations of single income groups and single types of housing tenure are avoided. A balanced, mixed community can prevent the growth of extensive areas of deprivation which support few amenities and local facilities. See Azmin-Fouladi in this volume.

4. Representation and participation: the future welfare of humanity requires people to be considered both as individuals, with specific freedoms of choice to be maintained, and also as communities connected to society as a whole. This is an important goal for the connected city, which is responsive to the interests of society as a whole while having regard to the needs, rights and duties of various cultural groups and individual citizens. In the connected city, new systems of representation and participation will be developed, making full use of easier access to information and the wider involvement of active citizens' networks, thus giving them all – residents and users – a voice in the future of their urban environment. See Romice and Frey and Vachon *et al.* in this volume.

5. Local identity: although the design of the built environment alone cannot turn inhabited spaces into communities, it can create the conditions where a sense of neighbourliness and belonging is more likely to develop. This can be done by involving the existing community in the design and development of schemes affecting districts; through the reuse of existing buildings and structures, materials and elements and land form, by designing spaces that respond to human needs of appropriation and the identity of both mainstream groups and minorities. See Goličnik, Mathers and Simkins and Thwaites and Simkins in this volume.

6. The flourishing of city life: cities are a major realization of human civilization. Cities are where people have always gone to find civic values, feel safe under a common law, sing the glory of God, profit from interaction with other human beings, free their deeper talents and meet opportunities to be elevated over a condition of wilderness. Good cities have their own rules, which include a certain amount of parks, greens, rivers and all natural benefits: in order to work well in a city, such natural resources should be carefully located, shaped, connected and integrated in city life. If badly or poorly designed, nature in the city can work to the detriment of the environment and urban life, fostering anti-social behaviours, enlarging the city fabric, creating physical barriers to the collective use of spaces or adding abandoned lands. The green network of green spaces is the essential backcloth to urban life, helping to maintain the neighbourhood ecosystem in equilibrium. The value of green spaces is greatly enhanced if they are interlinked and if users are accustomed to them from early ages. Furthermore, landscape design ought to be based upon an understanding of its effects on people. See Thwaites and Simkins in this volume.

7. Buildings should form closed blocks: very often, the highest volume of accommodation in the lowest number of storeys can be achieved by locating development in a lineal form around the periphery of the site. Buildings of three to five floors should be assembled such that they form closed blocks that define street canyons. Such blocks should be of limited size in order to enhance the connectivity of the overall street layout, foster choice in navigating the urban fabric and multiply corner locations that are essential to the vitality of commercial retail. Blocks must moreover be oriented and shaped to maximize the overall environmental performance at the neighbourhood scale (penetration of sunlight and wind, control of humidity and comfort). See Morello and Ratti in this volume.

8. Buildings that line the streets: the alignment of building facades on the street is essential for providing acceptable levels of self-surveillance (eyes-on-the-streets), diversity and intimacy to the streetscape. Entrances should open directly on to the sidewalks and car parking should be mainly designed on-street (Porta and Renne 2005).

9. Community centres must be served by main streets: the heart of the community only lives if the wide range of service and commercial activities that are related to the movement of people can flourish, which only happens in close proximity with streets that, in structural and functional terms, are principal. This means that such principal streets simultaneously carry significant amounts of motorized traffic and an equally relevant social functionality for pedestrians and human exchange: the coexistence of such conflicting sets of users has to be managed by means of traffic-calming techniques. See Porta and Latora in this volume.

10. Traffic tamed but not forbidden: along and around mixed-use areas and centres, streets should act as a series of casual meeting places where the interest of conviviality should take precedence, but vehicles contribute a sense of bustle and assist in natural policing of the streets after hours. See Newman and Renne in this volume.

11. Networks of shared streets: the spatial organization of the connected city will include full integration of transportation and town-planning policies. They will be complemented with urban design and easier access to information, thus minimizing the need for unnecessary travel. Ease of movement and access will be a critical element of city living, together with greater choice in the mode of transport. Beside several categories that must still be dedicated to special users (like pedestrian streets, bike lanes and highways), in most cases the street space must be designed for being shared – as much as possible depending on the level of the street and the kind of urban environment that it serves – by a variety of different human types, including both vulnerable and strong road users. Traffic-calming techniques are suggested to reach and maintain a positive balance in the competition between strong and vulnerable road users on both local and – especially – arterial streets. Such a system of streets should be designed to maximize the interconnectedness in an organic whole, avoiding cul-de-sac and hierarchical 'dendritic' layouts. See Newman and Azmin-Fouladi in this volume.

12. A piecemeal, fine-grained, bottom-up process: like every organism, the city evolves as time passes. Although a certain amount of programming might well operate, especially at the lower scales, the evolution of the city is basically unplanned and good cities are basically self-organized. Good city planning and design should be conceived in order to favour, accommodate and ensure, side by side with the protection of natural resources and past heritage, all changes that might emerge from the unforeseeable interaction of millions of individual and associational initiatives as well as from the external environment. As with a little child, the robustness of the city fabric depends on its capability to change, grow and evolve properly. See Romice and Frey and Vachon *et al.* in this volume.

as much as attitudes and values that are deeply enrooted in how we think and live our lives every day.

Resistance to the actual search for and construction of a sustainable city mainly comes from this sort of inertia, which leads us to the second message of this book: in order to approach the sustainable city of the future and reframe the traditional compact city model in a sound and feasible way for the contemporary information age, the crucial battlefield is not primarily economic, politic or social: it is *cultural*. There are lessons that have not been understood enough, others that still have not been dismissed enough, and all this can be drawn back to a deeper understanding of the relevance of *time* in its multiple manifestations, which, in turn, leads to what order is or is not.

Approaching time-conscious urban design

By comparison with approaches based on modernist principles, the 'new generation' compact developments seem to run in the right direction, but still they miss the point. It looks like a minor problem, it seems a side-effect of a largely positive stream of experiences, but it is actually an 'all-or-nothing' question, something that can turn the whole thing in a new failure. The problem is, again, mainly cultural, but it is so deeply embedded at the root of our contemporary essence that, in order to be solved, it will require an extraordinary effort which will challenge organizations, traditions and habits in many fields of our social and economic life.

Sustainability is not just about repopulating urban deserts in economically viable ways: it has to do with repairing the organism. When a living organism is broken, it can only begin to heal when life has begun to flow again through all its parts and the evolution of the larger system has been ensured. This is often not the case with such new compact city redevelopments. Large parts of the social body of the local urban community are not expected to take advantage of such redevelopments: they are actually excluded. In short, we too often witness the rapid deportation of significant amounts of people and activities that previously populated the place, which results in a loss of precious human relations, a waste of 'social capital' and finally a lack of community. Too often large infill developments or the rejuvenation of central 'downgraded' urban areas take the well-known taste of 'project planning' in the sense that Roberta Brandes-Gratz proposed (see Box 2.3). Sustainable urban renovation cannot be based on social exclusion. This may or may not have to do with gentrification, i.e. the process by which new middle-class people flow into previously deprived areas in the context of large interventions of urban renewal: gentrification as a process of investment and amelioration of a place is nothing bad for the wealthy people, but rather for the poor. The problem is the displacement of the poor, not gentrification, and there is no necessary causal relationship between the two that cannot be overcome by simple appropriate financial policies and strategies of social protection (Whyte 1988).

In realizing the new generation of compact urban mixed-used developments we have produced a major shift from modernism, we have oriented the arrow almost in the right direction (Figure 2.2), we have done a lot of good stuff, but we are still not to the point. The social accountability of the whole thing is mostly far from being achieved. That is not a secondary issue: it is actually the core, it is the heart, it is the real thing, it is all what we strive for, speak of and discuss. Either we get it, or we get nothing. We are almost there, we are in sight of the destination, but we still are on this side of the river. There is a bridge that still has to be raised up to overcome an obstacle; no matter how close we feel we are to the realization of sustainable human environments, we will actually remain far away from it until the bridge is built and the obstacle overcome. Without that bridge, the sustainable city will remain a mirage on the horizon. So what is the nature of that obstacle? It does not seem anything new. It is rooted at the very core of the cultural impediment; it certainly has to do with something that deeply differentiates the two approaches (modernism and sustainability) and has been abandoned on the way. This obstacle has to do with order and chaos, and it definitely has to do with time.

Box 2.3 The time-conscious quotation list

Jane Jacobs (1961). Cities need old buildings so badly it is probably impossible for vigorous streets and districts to grow without them. By old buildings I mean not museum-piece old buildings, not old buildings in an excellent and expensive state of rehabilitation – although these make fine ingredients – but also a good lot of plain, ordinary, low-value old buildings, including some rundown old buildings. If a city area has only new buildings, the enterprises that can exist there are automatically limited to those that can support the high costs of new constructions. [. . .] Chain stores, chain restaurants and banks go into new constructions. But neighbourhood bars, foreign restaurants and pawn shops go into older buildings. Supermarkets and shoe stores often go into new buildings; good bookstores and antique dealers seldom do. Well-subsidized opera and art museums often go into new buildings. But the unformalized feeders of the arts-studios, galleries, stores for musical instruments and art supplies, backrooms where the low earning power of a seat and a table can absorb uneconomic discussions – these go into old buildings. Perhaps more significant, hundreds of ordinary enterprises, necessary to the safety and public life of streets and neighbourhoods, and appreciated for their convenience and personal quality, can make out successfully in old buildings, but are inexorably slain out by the high overhead of new constructions. As for really new ideas of any kind – no matter how ultimately profitable or otherwise successful some of them might prove to be – there is no leeway for such chancy trial. Error and experimentation in the high-overhead economy of new constructions. Old ideas can sometime use new buildings. New ideas must use old buildings. [. . .] Flourishing diversity anywhere in a city means the mingling of high-yield, middling-yield, low-yield and no-yield enterprises. [. . .] We are dealing here again, as we were in the case of mixed primary uses, with the economic effects of time. But in this case we are dealing with the economics of time not hour by hour through the day, but with the economics of time by decades and generations. [. . .] Indirectly through the Utopian tradition, and directly through the more realistic doctrine of art-by-imposition, modern city planning has been burdened from its beginnings with the unsuitable aim of converting cities into disciplined works of art. [. . .] To see complex systems of functional order as order, and not as chaos, takes understanding. The leaves dropping from the trees in autumn, the interior of an airplane engine, the entrails of a dissected rabbit, the city desk of a newspaper, all appear to be chaos if they are seen without comprehension. Once they are understood as systems of order, they *look* different. [. . .] It is fruitless, however, to search for some dramatic key element or kingpin which, if made clear, will clarify all. No single element in a city is, in truth, the kingpin of a city. The mixture itself is kingpin, and its mutual support is the order.[. . .] A city is not put together like a mammal or a steel frame building – or even like a honeycomb or a coral. A city's very structure consists of mixtures of uses, and we get closest to its structural secrets when we deal with the conditions that generate diversity. [. . .] Cities happen to be problems in organized complexity, like the life sciences. They present 'situations in which a half-dozen or even several dozen quantities are all varying simultaneously *and in subtly interconnected ways*'. Cities, again like the life sciences, do not exhibit *one* problem in organized complexity, which if understood explains all. It can be analysed into many such problems or segments which, as in the life sciences, are also related one another. The variables are many, but they are not helter-skelter; they are 'interrelated into an organic whole'. Jacobs, J. (1989 [1961]: 187–189, 375–376, 433).

Christopher Alexander (2002). The structure we know as living structure, is just that kind of structure which has unfolded smoothly and naturally, arising step by step from what exists, preserving the structure of what exists, and allowing the 'new' to grow in the most natural way as a development from the structure of 'what is'. This startling view provides us with a view of ethics and aesthetics that dignifies our respect for what exists, and treasures that which grows from this respect. It views with disfavour only that which emerges arbitrarily, without respect for what exists, and provides a vision of the world as a horn of shimmering plenty in which the 'new' grows unceasingly from the structure that exists around us already. That this horn of plenty is inexhaustible, and that we may conceive an everlasting fountain of novelty without ever having to beat ourselves over the head for the sake of novelty per se – that may perhaps be one of the greatest potential legacies of this new view of the world. Alexander, C. (2002: 84).

Richard Sennet (1970). The line between slavery and freedom in rich communities depends on the character of the transition it is possible for men to make from adolescence to adulthood. [. . .] There appears in adolescence a set of strengths and desires which can lead in themselves to a self imposed slavery; that the current organization of city communities encourages men to enslave themselves in adolescent ways; that it is possible to break through this framework to achieve an adulthood whose freedom lies in its acceptance of disorder and painful dislocation; that the passage from adolescence to this new, possible adulthood depends on a structure of experience that can only take place in a dense, uncontrollable urban settlement – in other words, in a city. [. . .] The jungle of the city, its vastness, its loneliness, has a positive human value. Indeed, I think certain kinds of disorder need to be increased in city life so that men can pass into a full adulthood and so that, as I hope to show, men will lose their current taste for innocent violence. [. . .] It is in the building of purposely diverse cities that society can provide men the experience of breaking from self-slavery to freedom as adults. I believe that freedom to accept and to live in disorder represents the goal which this generation has aimed for, vaguely and inchoately, in its search for 'community'. Sennett, R. (1970: 17–18).

Roberta Brandes-Gratz (1998). Two approaches invariably conflict in each story of downtown change. The first and most prevalent is the project approach to rebirth, what I call *Project Planning*. [. . .] This approach assumes that a void exists that can be filled with a project. The planning process is designed to achieve the project, market it, sell it, and involve the public in selecting a predetermined solution – in other words, the project. The Project Planning process should not be confused with a problem-solving process. A problem-solving process may or may not involve a project. Project-based Planning does. The problem, if there was one, remains unsolved. Under Project-based Planning a project must be big to be meaningful. [. . .] Under this Project-based Planning the new is added at a large enough scale to overwhelm and alter what exists. What exists may be wiped out entirely, as with urban renewal. Something radically replaces it. Few clues are left as to what has been lost and what alternative strategy has been missed. [. . .] Urban Husbanders assume that assets are already in place to be reinvigorated and built onto in order to stimulate a place-based rejuvenation that *adds* to the long-evolving, existing strengths, instead of replacing them. Planning is meant to be about problem solving, relying heavily on the expertise of citizen users, the accumulated experience and wisdom of the community. Building on resources to diminish or overcome problems is the chosen route, instead of projects that obliterate those worthy resources. Urban Husbanders advocate introducing change incrementally and monitoring it carefully, providing a great opportunity to learn from each step.[. . .] Proponents of Urban Husbandry strengthen what exists before adding anything new. They involve many entrepreneurs of various sizes, not just one big developer. [. . .] They work to add a layer of organic urban growth, rather than replace what has taken decades to grow. Brandes-Gratz, R. (1998: 59, 61–62).

European Council of Town Planners (2003). The future is built at every moment of the present through our actions. The past provides invaluable lessons for the future. In many respects, the city of tomorrow is already with us. There are many features of present city life which we cherish and value, and which we hope to bequeath to future generations. What is the basic problem with our existing cities? In our view, it is the lack of connectivity, not only in physical terms, but also in relation to time, which affects social structures and cultural differences. This does not just mean continuity of character in the built environment, but also continuity in identity, which is in our view an important value to be fostered in a dynamic world. For the future, the notion of the network city needs to be stressed, a series of polycentric urban networks, many of which transcend national boundaries within the new Europe. ECTP (2003: 3).

Michael Hough (1990). The pressures (that come from educational conditioning) to do as much as possible in making changes to places often appear endemic to the land design disciplines. In the absence of a basic ecological foundation on which design can rest, this is to be expected. Doing as little as possible, or economy of means, involves the idea that from minimum resources and energy, maximum environmental and social benefits are available. The greatest diversity and identity in a place, whether a regenerating field or urban wetland, or a cohesive neighbourhood community, often comes from minimum, not maximum interference. This does not mean that planning and design are irrelevant or unnecessary to a world that if left alone would take care if itself. It implies rather, that change can be brought about by giving direction, by capitalising on the opportunities that site or social trends reveal, or by setting a framework from which people can create their own social and physical environments and where landscape can flourish with health, diversity and beauty. Hough, M. (1990: 179–180).

Jan Gehl (2001). Among the three distinct categories of people activities – necessary activities, optional activities and social activities – the optional and the social activities are the important keys to city quality. In poor quality city areas one will only find necessary activities i.e. people doing things they have to do. In good quality city areas one will find not only necessary activities (carried out under decent conditions) but also a multitude of recreational and social activities people love to do while in cities. However these activities will only happen if the circumstances are right; i.e. if the city offers tempting, good quality spaces. This is why a good city can be compared to a good party – people stay for much longer than really necessary, because they are enjoying themselves. Gehl, J. (2001: 13).

Guy Briggs (2005). References to 'city intelligence' should measure how effectively the city (fabric, networks and systems) facilitates the functioning of human socio-cultural and economic systems, and allows their evolution. [. . .] In a world in constant change, the basis for a city's long-term success, and therefore maintaining its intelligent status, lies in the adaptability of its fabric, processes and systems. It is this aspect that makes city intelligence and urban sustainability mutually dependent concepts. [. . .] The city is not static; it is a dynamic system in which the key to its long-term health and success, or its intelligence, will be its capacity to adapt to change. Like any ecological system, the key to this capacity is diversity. [. . .] The Darwinian concept of adaptability is the primary link between these two concepts. City intelligence will measure the capability of a city through the adaptability of its systems (its fabric and processes) to fulfil its fundamental role, ensuring that its citizens are capable of carrying out their transactions and living in freedom. Sustainability will measure the extent to which the city is capable of doing so without negatively affecting the wider environment, or the future capacity of the city to continue to fulfil its role in the same way. [. . .] The cities that thrived and prospered into the modern age (incidents of politics or war aside) were those that best facilitated expansion through trade and expression, and that were able to adapt continually to changing economic or socio-cultural circumstances; that is, those that were most 'intelligent'. Intrinsic to this definition of intelligence was urban competition; in other words, competition for resources, people and trade. [. . .] If cities are to strive for sustainability, urban governance and policy should be directed at achieving urban intelligence. This will require a major shift [. . .] so that these two aspects, process (governance) and tools (policy), become more strategic and more integrated, with the aim of being facilitatory rather than directive. Briggs, G. (2005: 39–41).

William H. Whyte (1980, 1989). It is significant that the cities doing best by their downtowns are the ones doing best at historic preservation and reuse. Fine old buildings are worthwhile in their own right, but there is a greater benefit involved. They provide discipline. Architects and planners like a blank slate. They usually do their best work, however, when they don't have one. When they have to work with impossible lot lines and bits and pieces of space, beloved old eyesores, irrational street layouts, and other such constraints, they frequently produce the best of their new designs – and the most neighbourly.

Five feet added to most sidewalks would more than double the effective walkway width. So it can be with other kinds of spaces – small parks, arcades, sitting places. In high density core areas, they can be a very efficient use of space. In New York the most heavily used and yet pleasant and amenable of spaces are among the smallest; the two best measure 42 by 100 feet and 65 by 100 respectively. In Tokyo, similarly, the spots where people like to tarry are small busy places – a sidewalk with shoeshine people, the benches alongside a store, a meeting place outside a station. These are the kind of bits and pieces usually scorned in orthodox planning, with its emphasis on order and structure. But in them is the genius of place; and with just minor reallocation of space many more can be created. Whyte, W. (1980: 1–18; 1989: 93).

Kevin Lynch (1966). We are faced with still another problem, in addition to those of the multiplicity of objectives and alternatives. Plans have traditionally been conceived as targets, that is, as states to be achieved after a given length of time. [. . .] This conception is appropriate to the architectural or project scale, where development is episodic: a revolutionary period of construction is followed by a longer period of physical conservation. However, it is not appropriate to the constant cyclical and secular change of a city. In an unsophisticated city plan, the recommended solution is thought of as a final state, which is impossible. Even a designer who is aware of the continuous flux of the city must unfortunately use a static graphic device to indicate a momentary state, a slice of future time. Sometimes the plan will include several successive slices: it will be a staged plan. [. . .] What we require instead is easy to describe but most difficult to develop: a technique of preparing and evaluating a set of continuous alternatives, presenting processes of development much as motion pictures might do it, judged for the way they satisfy a changing set of criteria throughout an entire time period. Even more, these plans should change their precision as they proceed further forward in time, as a result of the increasing uncertainty of prediction. For the time being, lacking such a technique for dynamic planning, we use the substitute method of staging, making future stages more diagrammatic, and perhaps developing a limited number of possible future branches for each basic alternative. This requires constant reminders that these are approximations to reality. One corrective is to add to each stage symbols that describe the process of change going on at the moment. Another corrective is to generate the stages in many ways: not only from a key point outward, but also from the immediate present forward, and from the distant future backward. Solutions can also be visualized as a general 'shape' of development process: crescendo, pulsation, cataclysm. [. . .]

A general theory of city form, today nonexistent, would deal with the interaction between city form and human behavior: how a city is shaped by social events and conditions, and how in turn it modifies them, in constant interchange. There are contributing streams which have begun to prepare the way for such a theory: ecology and cultural anthropology, urban history, locational economics and the recent attempts at the simulation of urban growth, various ideas from utopians and innovative design, plus a scattered literature on the result of certain forms of changes or conditions (on such various topics as perception, mental health, social relations, climate, cost and transport efficiency). Not only is this material scattered, but we lack organizing concepts with which to bring it into one structure. Studies of the planning process are further advanced, since these are of interest to other fields intellectually more mature than city planning. Here we are dealing with such questions as how objectives are formulated, the role and limits of intelligence, the process of generating and evaluating alternatives, decision making, implementation, the role of irrationality, the presence of multiple planning and decision systems, and how all these processes are interlocked in a constantly interacting whole. For our purposes, both these lines of thought should be brought together in a single body of knowledge, explaining how the various imperfectly informed actors in the city seek to realize their objectives by using or changing city forms, how city form changes as a result, how both objectives and constraints shift accordingly, and how the process continues in constant cyclical interaction. This is the theoretical base we would like to have. What we have been discussing is only one event in the process: the actions of the designer in a single planning system that can bring considerable weight to bear and can afford to hold comparatively long-range, community-oriented goals. If this community-oriented planning system is to be effective, the planning designer must be engaged in what might be called 'continuous design'. Ideally there will be continuous revision, an ever-developing basis for current decision. Practically, because of the same technical limitations that constrain us to use the staged plan, the general set of alternative is more likely to be overhauled episodically, part by part, or level by level. Lynch, K. (1966: 447–449).

Donald Appleyard, Allan Jacobs, Peter Bosselmann and the UC Berkeley group of environmental design (1982). People must be empowered to control and be responsible for the design, construction, use and maintenance of their spaces. Mere participation is not enough. Designers must open up design to all those affected in a shared process of goal-setting, problem analysis, creation and evaluation. Far from inhibiting design, the direct participation of people in the design process will enrich environments with the diversity of many different ideas. When the future users of environments are unavailable, indirect participation is still possible. The knowledge that has been accumulated in the last twenty years about people's needs, desires, perceptions and behaviours is now available in useable form, but designers ignore it. To draw on this knowledge requires a commitment. Where is it? Environmental designers should support the emergence of community and enhance public life through the sensitive creation of shared and public spaces, and settings conducive to community self-reliance. With the spread of privatization, insecurity, alienation and loneliness, designers have an obligation to enhance social interaction, cohesion, neighbourliness, and mutual aid, between different groups as well as similar ones. Designers cannot create community, but they can design physical settings where people can come together and develop design processes which themselves nurture communities.

Large scale environmental change is inherently damaging: it is insensitive to local needs; it denies personal identity and participation; and the consequences are impossible to predict. Furthermore, big designs are based on highly dubious 'economies of scale' that mainly serve corporations and bureaucrats, ignoring the far costlier effects of ecological imbalance and human alienation. Big design tasks must be broken down to human size whereby user involvement is possible; the complexity does not overwhelm; and the consequences of errors are not devastating. Every designed place must be thought of as an hypothesis to be tested. After occupancy, evaluation in terms of functional-effectiveness and user satisfaction should be a mandatory, periodic component of a continued design process. To perceive the design process as completed at the point of construction is to treat people – their use of, feelings about and modifications to the environment – as inconsequential.

Effective design is a two-way process and it involves far more than just visual form. For too long designers have relied on one-way visual communication skills, showing drawings to clients. A willingness to listen is not enough. The ability to listen entails a commitment to learn the appropriate language of the user group. Interpersonal communication skills are not optional extras, no designer should graduate without them. Environmental design is a craft, not a fine art. Everyone's taste is holy; the numerous aesthetics which abound in our communities are all legitimate. Designers must foster human fulfilment by providing opportunities for all people to create and affirm their emergent identities in new or adapted places. More diverse and joyful, better loved and cared-for environments will result. The monopoly of private aesthetic dialog among designers creates fine-tuned static and essentially alienating places which paralyze the personal expression of everyone else. The designer's prize is the user prison. Appleyard *et al.* (1982: 3–6).

Raquel Ramati (1981). We hope that this book will inspire you to look at streets with a fresh eye and make them a vital, inviting factor in your daily life. The thrust here is not the creation of new streets, but the rekindling of existing ones; not the instant implementation of huge urban renewal projects, but carefully planned, incremental steps, that can be taken right now – steps that can lead to improvements that are visible, affordable, and sustain community input. Such modest improvements, if they are strategically located and timed, can lead to other, larger improvements – finally more meaningful because they will have been rooted in such community spirit. Street saving is a journey that must be taken within a broader environmental, social and economical context. But in this framework, a small scale and incremental approach will help destine this journey to succeed. As Dostoyevsky put it, the most lasting forms of revolution take place one man at a time, and the same can be said of urban and community revitalization – one street at a time. Ramati, R. (1981: xv).

David Grahame Shane (2005). There is no one person in charge of the post modern city; the age of the single authority in absolute charge of a vast city is over. There is no longer one logic, voice or time-clock that can decree or coordinate comprehensive changes. Designers must work with multiple actors and multiple clocks. Change occurs piecemeal, in incremental fragments ranging in scale from the minute to the partial. [. . .] Given the absence of a single centre of control the old codes of single-function zoning will inevitably give place to a heterogeneous and flexible system that accommodates multiple actors more easily. [. . .] Designers will therefore have to work in an increasingly 'irrational' situation and incorporate the irrational into their work. [. . .]

As net importers of energy and people, cities have always existed in a state of imbalance and disequilibrium. To propose a city that exists in a state of perfect equilibrium, ecologically or socially, is to propose an impossible utopia. Jane Jacobs highlighted the dynamic nature of cities in her work from the

1960s onwards, showing that it is based on urban actors' need to measure and mediate differences in contested spaces. For Jacobs this is a good thing: insofar as cities become uniform and homogeneous they become stagnant, fixed, inflexible, incapable of change, dead. Through conflict, contestation, and the negotiation of differences, urban actors create new knowledge and new products, which aids human survival. Grahame Shane, D. (2005: 8).

Time is needed for persons associated in the same spatial context to develop capitals of trust, share ideas, sustain each other, obtain loans, run businesses, adjust the environment, produce pressures on the external systems and request attention from the higher levels of the political game. Time is needed for buildings to pay off the construction investment and downgrade to a lower level of financial accessibility in order to become affordable for start-up businesses. Time is everything for good ideas to find their way and be acknowledged. Time is a key factor for new entries to be accepted and adapt to a social/physical environment that has to adapt to them in turn. No matter how good the idea, it will most probably result in disappointment if it is implemented all at once over a living complex system like a city, a neighbourhood or a street. And that is not really anything new for urban design theorists: one need only note what has previously been said about this point (see Box 2.3). But this idea is not present even in our best-designed compact sustainable developments, which still share with their modernist ancestors a sort of virile attitude: to bring the thing together and fix it all with a brave punch. If we promote sustainable communities, we cannot think of imposing them on the ground directly from the skies of our ideas: that would mean replicating the fundamental modernist 'heroic' attitude – to interpret the design of cities not as a service to people and urban life but rather as a service to the designer's ego or an artistic adventure. That, in short, would not be sustainable. Sustainable communities are not created, they emerge and evolve. And this again has to do with order and chaos.

If social and functional mix are widely recognized to be among the pillars of any sustainable urban community of the future, there is a third mix that we still have not put into being. That third mix, which actually belongs to the original ideas of the founding leaders, has to do with the graduality of developments, the incremental implementation of plans and programmes, the multiplicity of actors and stakeholders involved and represented in such an incremental process, the preservation of existing ordinary buildings and resources, the valuation of cultural heritage, so that the resulting environment presents a large variety of contents regarding time: as a consequence, we can name the missing thing 'time-mix'. Is that a little thing? Unfortunately, it is not. It would be more comfortable to conclude that putting time-mix into our well-established practices for last-generation compact sustainable communities will not affect those practices greatly, but everything seems to lead to an opposite conclusion.

Time-conscious urban design can be portrayed as at least a threefold concept which includes and merges together *architectural heritage preservation*, *ordinary old buildings' preservation* and *incremental multi-actorial change*. Each of these three contents requires a different level of innovation at a different level of depth and diffusion into the city-building process. While architectural heritage preservation, which means the protection of monuments and buildings of excellence that have been associated with an artistic and historical value as a resource for the common good, is already widely recognized as a public policy in favour of the conservation and enhancement of a sense of identity and rootedness for the community, the idea of defending and transforming ordinary old buildings is much less acknowledged all around the world, and formal declarations have been generally failing in overcoming the academic boundaries and actually shaping public policies on the ground. The two issues might appear close to each other, but in fact they stand at the opposite corners of our culture: assigning a value to a monument which is recognized as a piece of art or a major historical monument means to stress the ideals that the community associates

2.2 The three arrows: the shift from modern dispersed to sustainable compact developments, then to the next stage of urban sustainability around time-conscious urban design

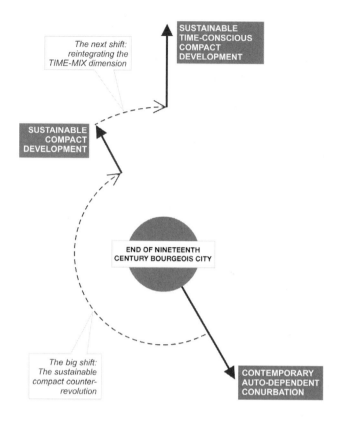

with such qualities, which is mainstream in our idealistic Western tradition; quite differently, the value that we might assign to an ordinary good old neighbourhood has to do with notions like 'environment' and 'system', which are very new concepts. It means to assign a value not to the single components of a whole but to the whole itself. It means to recognize that some places embed an added value which belongs to how things are put together rather than how they are constituted in themselves, and that such value has not primarily to do with 'beauty' but with 'liveability' and 'sense of place'; or, better, that the beauty of such places is not made of idealistic aesthetic canons but of popular sentiments like 'wholeness' and 'attachment'. That is a gigantic cultural jump, not far from the jump from a positivistic to a post- (or late) positivistic age. It should be no surprise, then, that we have few examples in the world where policies for the preservation, revitalization and respectful reuse of ordinary old buildings and fabrics have found their way in the daily practice of city planning. One of the most noticeable of such cases can be found in Italy.

Probably because of the incomparable cultural heritage of historical remains and dense built and open environments, Italy has been dealing with the problem of the environmental and architectural impact of industrialization and urbanization since its very beginning, which can be dated back to the late nineteenth century. Significantly, while a national law on the protection of prominent single buildings and areas of prominent historical, monumental or archaeological interest was coded in 1939, it took some half a century to realize a law for the protection of entire urban environments and open landscapes, which was done in the year 1985. It was not until the early 1960s, in fact, that an intellectual and even popular movement for the preservation and reuse of the countless historical centres of the country emerged, in the context of a new environmental awareness and the achievements of the global debate on the role of cultural heritage in contemporary cities (significantly, the Venice Charter for the Conservation and Restoration of Monuments and Sites was drawn up in Italy in the year 1964). Since then, especially by means of general regulatory plans – mandatory documents that rule environmental and urban development at the scale of the municipality – a whole stream of experiences of urban fabric investigation and preservation has been initiated and has determined the gradual stratification of concepts, practices, analytical tools, strategies and policies especially aimed at the maintenance and reuse of whole urban environments. The value of these environments was recognized in the particular consonance of materials, proportions, typologies, architectural languages and open spaces' characteristics incorporated in the dense fabric of ordinary buildings.

The rationale that backed this movement was mainly about cultural identity and historical roots, but in recent years, parallelling the endless degradation of urban fringes overwhelmed by auto-oriented transformations, it has appeared increasingly evident that such historical settlements are the only places that really still work in cities today. In contrast to the timeless fascination of small medieval villages, where automobile access is strictly limited and the local economy is in many cases based on special opportunities, like art-city tourism, the real point is in how urban historical environments – that belong to huge metropolitan systems with millions of inhabitants and city users and powerful pressures – turn out to be supportive of some of the most successful balances between quality of places, sustainable mobility, social safety and cohesion and economic vitality. That kind of balance is in such places at least favoured by the very spatial structure ensured by the historical basis of the urban fabric, in terms of both the topology of the spatial networks and the constitution of the streetscape, where the limited width of the carriageway, the presence of ground-floor activities, the preservation of historical pavements, the curving footprint of street routes, the lack of visibility at crossings, the sudden bottlenecks and, last but not least, the vibrant density of uses and people (in short, everything that might cause a heart attack to any good traffic engineer on earth) act as a 'natural' traffic-calming policy.

If architectural heritage preservation is increasingly a common policy in city-planning practices and ordinary old buildings' preservation is a policy that in some places, under favourable conditions, has matured into a long tradition as well as an advanced technicality, incremental multi-actorial change is by far the least tried and most challenging item of time-conscious urban design. Implementing such a kind of incremental culture, visions and practices would mean experimenting with deep changes in the current city-planning context as it counters some of the foundations of the modernist disciplinary core. In order for the process to assume an incremental shape, for instance at the scale of the neighbourhood, changes should involve planning norms which are currently geared to the idea that one general *project* is needed both to verify the delivery of benefits to the public interest and to structure the process of political and technical evaluation: in this case performative rather than prescriptive codes should be implied at all scales and in all steps. Changes should also involve urban design codes, in order to redefine the watershed between what is shaped in the masterplan and what is left to successive stages of implementation and different actors, but of course the same concept and role of a masterplan should be put in question in view of more radical scenarios where an incremental stepping is animated by multi-actorial decision-making. In this latter case, time-conscious urban design would reach a real participative and evolutionary dimension, where city planning and design covers only a limited area of the city-building process – an area that certainly would include the preservation of natural resources and cultural heritage, the protection of relevant old urban areas and buildings and the programming of larger-scale or longer-term decisions, but where much is left to the participative manifestation of local interests and conditions.

Therefore this is the third message that we wish deliver in this book: to the extent that we will be able to rethink lessons coming from the bourgeois compact city model incorporating practices of architectural heritage preservation, ordinary old buildings' preservation and incremental multi-actorial change, we will be approaching a concept of *time-conscious urban design* that appears to be crucial to any vision of sustainable urban communities for the future.

References

Alexander, C. (2002) *The Nature of Order: An Essay on the Art of Building and the Nature of the Universe. Book Two: The Process of Creating Life*, Oxford University Press, New York.

Appleyard, D. and Jacobs, A. (1987) 'Towards an urban design manifesto', in Larice, M. and MacDonald, E. (eds.) *The Urban Design Reader*, Routledge, London.

Appleyard, D., Bosselmann, P., Cranz, G., Dovey, K., Ellis, R., Goltsman, E., Hester, R., Iacofano, D., Liebermann, E., Lindheim, R., Lloyd, R., Cooper-Marcus, C., Priestly, T. and Whitman, F. (1982) *A Humanistic Design Manifesto*, Berkeley, CA.

Banerjee, T. and Southworth, M. (eds.) (1990) *City Sense and City Design: Writings and Projects of Kevin Lynch*, The MIT Press, Cambridge, MA.

Barton, H. and Tsourou, C. (2000) *Urban Villages and the Making of Communities*, Spon Press, London.

Brandes-Gratz, R. (1998) *Cities, Back from the Edge: New Life for Downtown*, John Wiley and Sons, New York.

Briggs, G. (2005) 'The intelligent city: ubiquitous networks or human environment?', in Jenks, M. and Dempsey, N. (eds.) *Future Forms and Design for Sustainable Cities*, Architectural Press, Oxford.

European Council of Town Planners (2003) 'The new Charter of Athens. The European Council of Town Planners' vision for cities in the 21st century', Lisbon, available at: www.ceu-ectp.org/e/athens/charter2003.pdf.

Gehl, J. (2001 4edn.) *Life Between Buildings: Using Public Space*, Danish Architectural Press, Copenhagen.

Hough, M. (1990) 'Restoring identity to the regional landscape', in Larice, M. and MacDonald, E. (eds.) *The Urban Design Reader*, Routledge, London.

Jacobs, J. (1989 [1961]) *The Death and Life of Great American Cities*, Random House, New York.

Jencks, C. (1995) *The Architecture of the Jumping Universe*, Academy Editions, London.

Lynch, K. (1990 [1966]) 'Quality in city design', in Banerjee, T. and Southworth, M. (eds.) *City Sense and City Design: Writings and Projects of Kevin Lynch*, The MIT Press, Cambridge, MA.

Lynch, K. (1997 [1960]) *The Image of the City*, The MIT Press, Cambridge, MA.

Marshall, S. (2005) *Streets and Patterns: The Structure of Urban Geometry*, Spon Press, New York.

Newman, P. and Kenworthy, J. (1999) *Sustainability and Cities: Overcoming Automobile Dependence*, Island Press, Washington, D.C.

Peterson, J. (1976) 'The City Beautiful movement: forgotten origins and lost meanings', *Journal of Urban History*, 2(4): 415–434.

Porta, S. and Renne, J. (2005) 'Linking urban design to sustainability: formal indicators of social urban sustainability field research in Perth, Western Australia', *Urban Design International*, 10(1): 51–64.

Ramati, R. (1981) *How to Save Your Own Street*, Doubleday, New York.

Saunders, W. (2007) 'Cappuccino urbanism, and beyond', *Harvard Design Magazine*, 25, Fall 2006/Winter 2007. Available at: www.gsd.harvard.edu/research/publications/hdm/current/25_Sanders.html

Sennett, R. (1970) *The Uses of Disorder: Personal Identity and City Life*, W.W. Norton, New York.

Shane, D.G. (2005) *Recombinant Urbanism: Conceptual Modeling in Architecture, Urban Design and City Theory*, Wiley-Academic, Chichester.

Serres, M. (1993) *Les Origines de la Géométrie*, Flammarion, Paris.

Wolfe, T. (1981) *From Bauhaus to our House*, Farrar, Straus and Giroux, New York.

Whyte, W. (1980), *The Social Life of Small Urban Spaces*, The Conservation Foundation, Washington, D.C.

Whyte, W. (1989) *City: Rediscovering the Center*, Doubleday, New York.

Section Two

A COMMON GROUND – SPACE AND PEOPLE

3 The knowledge of order and complexity

We are witnessing a fall in the social acceptance of the scientific representation of urban realities and a generic claim for more human environments. This section is concerned with trying to get to the roots of why we seem to have found difficulty accommodating authentic, routine human life and experience into the way that we shape our urban environments and making some suggestions about how things might be improved. We will first try to do this by taking a look at the conception of human-environment relations that underpins the prevailing Western view of how we see ourselves in relation to our urban surroundings. The central claim here is that in Western culture we remain in the grip of a world view that has brought about a largely subconscious acceptance of a particular concept of human-environment relations that has tended to privilege a rational and instrumental attitude to the environment as a primarily technical and aesthetic product. Whatever benefits they have undoubtedly brought in terms of technological advance and economic prosperity, for example, the dominant influence of the doctrines of positivism and its Enlightenment origins is now widely thought to be at least partly responsible for a preoccupation with rationalizing modes of thinking, a bias towards quantitative considerations and a subjugation of experiential and emotional dimensions of place experience. This can be overcome, however, and we will talk about some of the philosophical, theoretical and methodological implications to support our argument for a humanistic and socially inclusive approach to urban design where the emotional expression and psychological functioning that make up the life patterns of individuals and communities have primacy.

What has become known as the Scientific Revolution had by about 1700 transformed the way we thought about ourselves and the world around us, from a predominant concern with understanding the meaning of things to an awareness of the potent possibilities of prediction and control. Copernicus, Kepler and Galileo laid the foundations for the subsequent Enlightenment period by overturning the long-held view of the earth as the centre of the universe and the mechanistic interpretation of observations of celestial phenomena. Galileo was one of the first to approach the acquisition of knowledge through developing methods of scientific experimentation and communicating his findings via the language of mathematics. Access to truths needed no longer to be a matter of faith but a matter of rational and systematic enquiry, and this gradually began to raise the significance of measurable and quantifiable properties like movement and shape and diminish the significance of subjective properties like colour, taste and smell, for example. This has remained a cornerstone of scientific theory and practice ever since, and according to Caroline Merchant (1980) explains why an attitude toward the environment as an entity to be tamed and enslaved rather than respected for its organic, nurturing and spiritual qualities gradually took hold, fuelling the development of a mechanistic world view in which human self-confidence in its ability to transform and control the environment would eventually predominate.

This confidence in the potential of the rationalizing mind is perhaps most evident in the work of René Descartes, who elevated a belief that the only reliable truth came from scientific enquiry to the status of a scientific philosophy. In this respect Descartes is a significant influence on the conception of human-environment relations predominant in today's Western cultures. Descartes believed the power of the mind allowed access to certain knowledge through processes of intuition and deduction: an analytical method of reasoning which involved breaking down complex problems and thoughts into smaller fragments and placing them in logical order. For Descartes, mind was more certain than matter, and this brought him to certain conclusions about the structural relationship between the mind and the body. Almost in a single stroke of philosophical insight it became possible to think of the human self as a dualistic entity: a rationalizing mind contained within a material body comparable with the material components from which the rest of the world was made. If mind and matter were indeed conceptually separate, then it is logically consistent to believe that humans are separate from the environments they inhabit. Descartes's dualistic philosophy and the general world view to which it contributed were further strengthened in their potency through Newton's mathematical achievements, which appeared to confirm his concept of nature as a mechanical system capable of being understood in all its detail through scientific scrutiny. This has dominated Western scientific thinking and cultural development ever since, underpinning the Age of Enlightenment and embedding a world view in which, according to Lincoln and Guba (1985), there is a reductionist attitude to analytical procedures leading to fragmentation in thinking – a belief that complexity can be understood through analysis of its parts alone, and that quantitative criteria are raised above qualitative criteria as the measures of truths and reality. Civilization had become synonymous with the acquisition of reason and knowledge within a conceptual framework characterized by dualistic separation of mind from body, human from environment, individual from society, thought from deed; and a view of nature as a machine, determined by mathematical law and open to rational investigation (Capra 1982).

Descartes's philosophical principles not only laid the foundations for the conceptual separation of humans from their surroundings, but also had a profound influence on the way in which the surroundings should be arranged.

> There is often not as much perfection in works composed of several pieces and made by the hands of diverse masters as in those on which one individual alone has worked. . . Thus those ancient cities which, having been, in the beginning, only villages, have become, with the passage of time, great towns are ordinarily so badly put together, compared with those regular places which an engineer traces out on a plan according to his fantasy. . .
>
> Descartes (1994 [1637]: 27)

This remarkable statement had, as early as 1637, effectively declared that city building ought to be the responsibility of a single rational mind. The layout of ancient towns was, as far as Descartes was concerned, undesirably disordered, a random arrangement of buildings and crooked streets: 'look at how they are arranged, a big one here, a small one there, and how they render the streets crooked and unequal, one would say that it is chance, rather than the will of a certain man using reason, that has placed them thus' (ibid.). The purpose of man was now to impose order on a disorderly environment, unbend the bent, straighten the crooked, regularize and discipline towns and cities into temples of rationality. At the dawn of modernity, in pursuit of this particular utopia, Descartes firmly defined Euclidean geometry as the sole kind of order acknowledgeable by the eyes of the rational man for dealing with the form of environmental configurations like gardens, landscapes, streets and cities. Some three centuries later, Le Corbusier brutally reacted against Sitte's recall to the social aesthetics of medieval windy patterns with his well-known invective: 'The windy street is the path of asses, the straight street is the path of men' (Le Corbusier 1994 [1925]: 5). Only asses, the master went on, could have designed the historical cities of Europe with all that mess of narrow streets and that horrible, chaotic puzzle of intersections and squares. The power of Euclidean geometry remains immensely influential for architects and urban designers, almost an axiom when it comes to the design of streets, towns and cities. Old neighbourhoods and townscapes attract interest for their picturesque appeal, but in many ways their fundamental structural value is very often still underestimated. Later, in Part II, we will show that the status of Euclidean geometric principles is increasingly challenged, particularly by those concerned with the phenomenology of place experience, and crucially limited as an ordering mechanism for developing places rich in experiential potential.

Enlightenment thinking brought about a world view where the acquisition and application of knowledge became increasingly displaced from the world as lived, as the drive for empirical clarity replaced faith in experience. In architecture this was manifest in the establishment of the Ecole Polytechnique in the late eighteenth century, heralding an architectural theory based on scientific rationality derived from pure methodology and technical knowledge. The imperative for approaches to architecture, and later landscape architecture and urban design, which could claim equivalent levels of methodological certainty to those in the sciences eventually led to another dimension of duality where the act of creativity and design became divorced from the act of making. Shorn of its connection to craft, design became seen as an end in itself. Good environments could then be rationally prescribed through design, independent of users' personal, social or cultural variations. The people who actually used the built environment, those whose lives were inextricably woven into its form and fabric, were effectively excluded for reasons of ignorance or lack of taste, and in this context human well-being effectively became reduced to a by-product of design processes and their operationalization by specialist professionals.

The designed environments that resulted from this positivist attitude are, for some, thoroughly unsatisfying: 'deserts of quantitative reasoning' (Corner 1991: 118); 'mathematically efficient and economically profitable while the poetries of place have been blindly erased' (ibid.). What James Corner means in essence here is that rationalizing methodologies had in effect sucked out the life from designed environments so that they were lifeless shells of space. That such a thing was possible at all is, as far as Corner and others are concerned, rooted in the conceptual removal of people from their surroundings, as required by Cartesian dualism, coupled with an enduring faith in the certainty of Euclidean geometry that enabled space to be defined and then manipulated as a set of numerical dimensions. These ideas found their way into Bauhaus enquiries into the nature of pure form and geometrical space as part of a quest to identify the elements of a universal language of form. The concept of space arising from these ideas embodied no values other than those derived from mathematical and geometric properties. These principles were explored in architecture at the time, most notably through the work of Mies Van Der Rohe and later in landscapes by Eckbo, Burle-Marx and Barragan. Space understood in this way widens still further divisions between the making of places and the human lived experience. In these circumstances what was tasteful and beautiful was placed firmly in the hands of specialist experts.

As a fervent and lifelong opponent of what he considered to be the dehumanizing impact of some modernist approaches to architecture and built environment, it is ironic to say the least that one of the most influential forerunners of the academic study of design methodology was the mathematician, architect and town planner Christopher Alexander. Alexander's explorations were a well-intentioned attempt to link the generation of environmental form with how people lived. As a consequence of observing the way primitive people organize their surroundings, Alexander came to see form as the physical manifestation of underlying forces – natural, social or forces of association, for example – linked with the lives and habits of people. Drawing from his mathematical background, Alexander tried to conceptualize human action in relation to its spatial expressions. He thought that, just as arithmetic convention allows complex numerical problems to be solved easily, an equivalent ought to be possible for complex design problems (Alexander 1964). Appealing to the logic of arithmetic was supposed to provide designers with a means to validate solutions in a scientifically analogous manner, reducing over-reliance on formal rules derived from history or the wilder excesses of artistic individuality. With the publication of *Notes on the Synthesis of Form* in 1964, Alexander inadvertently spearheaded an outbreak of interest in the academic study of design and problem-solving methodology, further influencing approaches to architecture, engineering and landscape architecture that were increasingly rationalistic and more analytical, systematic and open, externalizing the design process and exposing the hitherto private thinking of the designer (Kelsey 1970; Jones 1980; Parnes 1992).

Alexander had never intended that human intuition should be removed from the activity of design, simply that it should be made accountable. But some of the subsequent interpretations of design methodology developed the flavour of an industrial production line: controlled procedures for divergent and convergent thinking where creative thought is replaced by logical deductions towards the production of plans which seem regarded as an end in themselves. John Kelsey's *A Design Method* for landscape architecture, in particular, is a triumph of Cartesian rationality, setting out a nine-step method out of which, at step nine, 'The landscape based plans should arrive as no surprise to anyone' (Kelsey 1970: 428). As John Tilman Lyle (1985) later pointed out, methods like this often appear to have more to do with meeting the demands of productivity and efficiency in professional practice than with making high-quality landscapes. Seven years after the publication of his *Notes on the Synthesis of Form*, Alexander rejected the idea of design methods as a subject of study because he realized the absurdity of separating the study of designing from the practice of design. This was echoed later by Christopher Jones in his books *Design Methods* (1980) and *Essays in Design* (1984), in which he too highlighted the interdependence of problem and solution in criticisms of design methodology. Designing as problem-solving alone is 'a dead metaphor for a living process' (Jones 1980: xxiii). Examination of Jones's criticisms in this respect can be seen to focus strongly on philosophical assumptions rooted in Enlightenment thinking, including, for example, a spurious justification for splitting intuitive and rational thinking; the removal of the method from the design situation; and the development of an attitude towards method as a process of control rather than creation and for its use in a search for certainty in design when design is about uncertainty.

Despite this crisis of confidence in design methodology, rationalistic problem-solving methods continued to become a defining characteristic of the environmental design professions during the second half of the twentieth century. The value of human experience, intuition and imagination diminished in the face of allegations of subjectivity, idiosyncrasy and romantic individualism. However, fuelled by increasing criticisms that the buildings, landscapes, town and cities which result from approaches built from this inheritance are unsatisfying, a desire for change in direction is becoming increasingly evident. Indeed, a whole stream of counter-arguments against modernist stigmatization has been raised since the early 1960s in the name of the 'magic' of old cities. The claim is not at all about aesthetics, the picturesque value of old towns, nor is it a call for a return to pre-modern ideas about style: it is about the liveability of our built environment. The modern city, conceived with Cartesian certitude, is increasingly seen to be hard to live in. The social successes of an urban settlement conceived as the unpredictable outcome of safety, trust, economic vitality and diversity sprout from the complex, unplanned interactions of countless different routes and experiences in a suitable environment. Calls for new approaches, processes, methods and paradigms appear to emphasize the resuscitation of the primacy of human experience as the basis for making new landscapes (Thwaites and Simkins 2007). The importance of the design situation is emphasized as having intrinsic value and uniqueness, and there is an acceptance of uncertainty and variety as qualities to be celebrated and encouraged instead of sterilized or hidden. The desire for new approaches appears to focus on a more complex conception of the environment and the role which individuals and groups play in the definition of its qualities and meaning. Social and cultural aspects are emphasized, in addition to the physical fabric, in an equal partnership of dynamic, interconnected and interrelated influences. These essentially human-oriented, qualitative and experiential principles do not easily correspond with the positivistic and techno-scientific roots from which the mainstream of modern urban design comes. If this is the case, then what alternatives are available for us to consider?

One place to start is by looking at assumptions about science as the foundation for our investigative approach to ourselves and the world around us. Warren Weaver, quoted in Jane Jacobs (1961), argued that science is not just one thing; there are in fact many sciences, and moreover these evolve in history (Weaver 1948). The question is, again according to Jacobs, identifying the right tools for the job, and in her view this is where the mainstream of planning and architecture may have gone adrift. The point with 'orthodox' planners is that they used the right tools for the wrong problem. Cities, she argued, are complex-organized problems, and as such, in order to be understood, need to be approached with a new science, the science of complexity. 'Under the seeming disorder of the old city, wherever the old city is working successfully, is a marvelous order for maintaining the safety of the streets and the freedom of the city. It is a complex order' (Jacobs, J. 1961: 50). That order, Jane Jacobs concluded, is an organic one; it is the order of life, the only one that can contribute to the actual liveability of neighbourhoods and cities, thus the one that should drive us to the sustainable city of the future (Newman and Kenworthy 1999). Unlike the Euclidean geometry, the 'marvellous' complex order of the old city is not visible at a first glance, nor is it imposed by any central agency. Rather it is the result of the fine-grained, gradual contribution of countless agents in time, each following his/her or its own trajectory.

Everyone knows in the network community – an area of scientific research that investigates complex systems through the use of the metaphor of networks and the mathematics of graphs – that a good deal of achievements have been gained in the very recent years since the seminal work of Watts and Strogatz (1998) on the so-called 'small worlds'. The availability of detailed maps of a broad range of self-organized systems – ranging from natural to man-made, from chemical to biological to neural, sexual and even linguistic systems and many others again – as well as an immensely increased computational power have allowed us to understand that all those networks do share some astonishingly similar topological properties (Barabasi 2002; Albert and Barabasi 2002). Among others, recent studies on urban street networks (Porta *et al.* 2006; Crucitti *et al.* 2006) – a form of geographic networks, which are a specific family of complex systems characterized by planarity and metric distance – have shown that the same properties actually apply to those cases as well.

These achievements allow us to acknowledge, under the 'seeming disorder' of self-organized cities, the clues of a hidden order that operates embedded in the most diverse climatic, geographic, economic, social and cultural conditions, an order shared with most non-geographic natural, biological and social systems (Portugali 2000; Salingaros 2003). The 'marvellous complex order' of Jane Jacobs's old city, the 'magic' of Allan Jacobs's 'great streets', now appear a little bit less obscure, as we can clearly see behind the façade the universal sign of nature, the sign of organic complex systems naturally evolved following a rule of preferential attachment and hierarchical topology (Albert and Barabasi 2002; Ravasz and Barabasi 2003). The presence of that kind of order, an order that should now be regarded as a value, a treasure, something like the 'genius of the city' (Whyte 1988), qualifies – Warren Weaver would say – traditional, self-organized, incremental urban fabrics as a 'complex-organized problem': how far is the rich, diverse, organic, vital, deeply ordered structure of self-organized cities from that kind of chaotic mess which, according to the ingenuous eyes of 'The Master' himself, only asses could have designed? The recognition of the hidden order of self-organized cities is a contribution to the actual overcoming of the modernist heritage in city planning and design, as well as to a new set of goals and opportunities for urban designers, academics and professionals in the field.

We would like to continue here by sketching out some ideas relevant to a more integrated concept of human-environment relations which presents a world view different to that characterized by Enlightenment thinking, supports a more holistic view of the human-environment relationship and underpins a way to see urban fabrics as complex-organized entities that tie together more closely human behavioural and psychological functioning with the settings in which it occurs. Elements of this can be traced to counter-Enlightenment movements which emerged as a revolt against material changes in society accompanying the growth of cities and industrial expansion during the eighteenth century. Possibly the most recognizable manifestation of this is the diversity of ideas and cultural expressions that spread across Europe as the Romantic movement. Although relatively short-lived, lasting until the mid-nineteenth century, vestiges of Romantic thought continue today in the modern environmental movement, helping to fuel challenges to the Enlightenment concept of civilization that has gathered pace over the past two decades (Lincoln and Guba 1985). This underpins interest in a more ecological, holistic view of human-environment relations, the general characteristics of which lean towards a more phenomenological philosophy which provides foundations for human experience to be at the heart of the way the concept of place is understood.

Romantic thinkers emphasized organic metaphors and human lived experience to counter the mechanistic world view and primacy of human reason, valuing feelings, emotions, imagination and experience as being equally valid means of access to knowledge. Romantic philosophers raised to prominence the value of the whole of human experience, rather than reason alone, as a route to truth. All aspects of nature, culture and society were analogous with organisms involved in continuous, dynamic and evolutionary change (Taylor 1989). Romantic thought related specifically to the way that human life comes to a sense of self-awareness and fulfilment. Charles Taylor (1975, 1989) has called this 'expressivism', a theory of the human-environment relationship rooted in Isaiah Berlin's interpretation of the German philosopher Herder, and in particular his preoccupation with the inextricable relationship between the human personality and the life it leads in environmental and social contexts. Herder was a thoroughly holistic thinker, and in expressivism connectedness and integration among all things are emphasized over the dualistic separation of the Enlightenment.

Expressivism involves a kind of aesthetic appreciation which stresses the quality of experience evoked over the intrinsic properties of objects. People are assumed to be realizing something about themselves through their expressive actions, and achieve fulfilment by doing so. This is an explicitly phenomenological perspective, elaborated in detail by Merleau-Ponty and others more recently, in which people are defined not in terms of their material bodily presence, but in terms of what they do and where. A key feature of Herder's belief, discussed by Berlin (1965: 95), is the mutually dependent human-environment relationship in which groups and societies both shape and are shaped by their environment. This gives us an entirely different perspective, and ethical position, on how we see ourselves in relation to our surroundings: in a real sense we are defined by where we are and what we do there. The essence of this holistic ontology can be detected today in the way that theories of place have developed. It is particularly evident, for example, in the writings of anthropologist Edward Hall (1966), geographer Yi Fu Tuan (1977) and environmental psychologists Harold Proshansky (1983) and David Canter (1977). Notwithstanding the evident difficulty inherent in bringing a concept of place essentially conceptualized as a synthesis of human behavioural and emotional functioning and its material and spatial context into the environmental design disciplines, the literature includes serious contributions to develop from it design vocabularies and methodologies. We can, for example, include here Gordon Cullen's (1971) seminal description of the components of townscape, Christian Norberg-Schulz's (1971) attempt to tie together human functioning and its spatial context into a schemata for existential space and Christopher Alexander's (1977, 2001) lifelong quest to reveal the structure of environmental form and order through his pattern languages and conceptions of order. More recently attempts have been made to explore this phenomenological conception of people-space relations in landscape architecture and urban design by describing the nature of an experiential landscape and methods for revealing its spatial structure (Thwaites and Simkins 2007).

We would acknowledge here that recourse to aspects of eighteenth-century Romantic thought as part of a philosophical justification for a more humanistic approach to contemporary urban design will not sit comfortably in the minds of many. The idea of environments that are, or can become, expressive media, an intrinsic part of what it is to be fully human, may have, for some, unacceptable metaphysical leanings which are easy to dismiss as irrelevant to modern society and something with which a modern urban design should not be associated. Whatever their respective merits, however, we must not be misinterpreted here as simply making a call for a return to the superficial visual appeal of the pre-modern picturesque, nor an allegiance to the extremes of New Age thinking, criticisms often levelled when counter-Enlightenment ideas are raised in this context. But with due caution we can see that there are intellectual resources here, yet to be sufficiently explored in the environmental design disciplines, that are relevant and perhaps important to the way we see the world around us and may help us understand how to shape it in more satisfying ways. Romantic expressivism, for example, presents us with a conception of human existence that cannot be separated from its environment. Instead it appears to establish humans and environment as two distinguishable components of the same whole, rather like the two sides of a coin. It also shows that the nature of the relationship between human and environment is not one of passivity but is active, characterized as a continuous exchange, a subconscious dialogue through which people develop their full potential in acts of intuitive expression. Here, the environment is not an external container in which people exist, but a means of expression, a voice by which people define themselves and communicate that definition to others.

We want now to move on by looking at how this holistic concept of human-environment relations appears to be evident in aspects of twentieth-century research in the physical sciences. Although at present a contentious area of intellectual enquiry, there are echoes in the findings of modern scientific enquiry that appear to lean in the direction of a much more integrated connection between people and their environments than Enlightenment attitudes allow. Perhaps more significantly, in the context of urban design, this contributes to developing a holistic concept of human-environment relations by introducing an understanding of the nature of order in holistic frameworks. This is important because it shows that order can be understood as active relationships of elements within holistic frameworks, by analogy rather like the concept of urban order as dynamic dance that Jane Jacobs described, and is not merely that which results from the assembly of discrete elements, as in a classical Cartesian sense. It also shows perceptions of order coming from some interpretations of scientific findings as a dynamic and creative tension between the self-assertion of elements to maintain uniqueness and individuality and their tendency towards integration to maintain the supporting whole. Again, Jacobs's dance analogy is apt: as we watch the ballet we can be simultaneously aware of the individuality of each dancer and the contribution they make to shaping a larger collective form of order. Our main purpose here is to highlight that there are some apparent similarities of world view in different intellectual realms, and that they have potential to contribute to the development of new concepts relevant in urban design. Aspects of the so-called new sciences have in fact already crept into the realm of urban planning and design (Batty and Longley 1994; Crompton 2005), architecture (Jencks 1995; Alexander 2001) and landscape architecture (Rosenberg 1986; Motloch 1991; Alvarez and El-Mogazi 1998), raising questions for the interpretation of new science concepts in these areas.

The two principal cornerstones of Newtonian science at question here are that the universe is determinate and reducible to fundamental laws and physical building-blocks; and that these can be discovered by people (given sufficient knowledge, technical apparatus, etc.), who can then study them as independently existing, objective entities. Theoretical and experimental developments, particularly in high-energy particle physics in the twentieth century, present an alternative conception of reality in which, at a fundamental level, the universe appears to consist of a dynamic network of interwoven and interconnected events from which human consciousness cannot be meaningfully detached (Capra 1975; Zukav 1979; Bohm 1980). With this, the solidity of the

Newtonian-Cartesian paradigm in science is undermined and alternative holistic and ecological world views are given, for some, scientific credibility (Capra 1982). Moreover, and more controversially, human consciousness is believed to be an active force in the way some aspects of physical reality become realized in determinate form (Bohm 1980). In his most recent books about the nature of order, Christopher Alexander acknowledges a series of meetings with David Bohm in the late 1980s and how Alexander's concept of wholeness corresponds essentially with Bohm's articulation of an implicate order, a structural characteristic he believes explains scientific observations of sub-atomic systems (Alexander 2001: 108). Here we are not concerned with the technical, mathematical and scientific detail of new science research, but with the way some of this has been and continues to be interpreted, the main philosophical claims made and how they contribute to developing ideas about the nature of order and particularly the role humans are thought to play.

A wide range of scientific developments spanning most of the twentieth century have, since the mid-1970s, been collectively popularized as 'new science' to distinguish it from the mechanistic determinism of the old science associated with Newton. The beginning of modern physics is generally attributed to Einstein's relativity theories and subsequent development of quantum theory, a theory of sub-atomic phenomena in which the hitherto accepted belief that matter consists of assemblages of discrete material particles independent of human observation was to prove unsound. This discovery has its foundations in two principal facets of experimental investigation. The first is related to the apparently paradoxical properties of sub-atomic particles which allow them to behave as either waves (entities spread out in space) or particles (entities confined to small volumes) depending on the way they are investigated. The second facet is the establishment of a precise mathematical form, expanding the conventions of classical science, with which to express this phenomenon: the uncertainty principle of Werner Heisenberg. Fundamentally, the uncertainty principle replaces the determinism previously thought to be a defining characteristic of physical reality with a requirement for indeterminism. Initially formulated in the 1920s, it has brought about a significant shift in the way science thinks about and investigates the nature of reality. With Heisenberg's (1983) uncertainty principle has come the realization that physical reality is undeterministic at its basic level. Scientists working in this area no longer talk of matter existing with certainty at particular points in space and at particular times, but of matter which shows tendencies to exist expressed in the language of probability. Furthermore, the way matter appears in observable form seems inextricably linked to the circumstances of observation, leading some scientists to conclude not only that uncertainty and indeterminism are intrinsic properties of the material world, but that human observation of it, in some sense, influences the way in which the material world appears to us.

Although not directly related to Heisenberg's uncertainty principle, there is research in the architectural and urban design arena that appears to lean towards this relativistic view of the way our world appears to us. Andrew Crompton (2005) explores the fractal characteristics of urban settings. Fractal geometry is a part of the new science genre in that it describes the structural properties of chaotic phenomena. Fractals are patterns with unique yet predictable characteristics arising from dynamic systems on the cusp between order and chaos. In essence they are the visible manifestation of the mathematical expressions of chaos theory which demonstrate that the apparently random and chaotic appearance evident in natural systems actually has an internal complex form of order. This form of order shows that Euclidean geometry, no matter how successful and established, is a very crude approximation when it comes to describing the reality of natural systems, and Crompton's work seeks to explore whether the same could be said about the arrangement of urban environments. In essence Crompton's work appears to confirm that people experience and use urban space in non-Euclidean ways, particularly related to the range of things they can do in or recall about an area or how they navigate their way about it. Crompton shows that perception of distance in urban settings can vary dramatically from its Euclidean dimensions relative to certain kinds of spatial organization. People think they have covered far greater distances than they actually have if the surroundings they moved through bend, twist, change level and variously have incidences that offer choice and engage attention. Similarly, Ramadier and Moser (1998) distinguish between 'propositional' and spatial representations, where the former is a response to the symbolic meanings of physical elements and the latter an 'analogical' representation which develops from such symbolic interpretation. Spatial representations follow symbolic representations, as the 'analogical' application of propositions (ibid.).

New science discoveries have brought profound changes to the way in which the fundamental building-blocks of the material world are perceived in science. The classical concept of sub-atomic particles as minute solid objects which combine in different ways ultimately to create the macro world does not correspond with experimental investigation at sub-atomic levels. Sub-atomic particles have no meaning as isolated objects, but can only be understood in terms of inter-connections between various processes of measurement and observation; processes which appear to include human observers and their experimental apparatus. Nature appears to be 'a complicated tissue of events, in which connections of different kinds alternate or overlap or combine and thereby determine the texture of the whole' (Heisenberg 1963: 139). A picture of reality thus emerges as a unified whole, within which there are distinguishable components in the form of molecules and atoms, etc., but in which, at finer levels of definition, the concept of separate parts does not hold. At the sub-atomic level, particles are not things but interrelationships. This is how modern physics has revealed that the nature of reality is not one of objects, but relationships and networks of patterns. This new world view has been given some experimental verification by John Bell (1987), who was ultimately to develop a theorem which demonstrated not only that sub-atomic events are intrinsically probabilistic and interconnected, but that interconnectedness is sustained over theoretically infinite regions of space. The Cartesian conception of independently existing isolated elements subject only to the effects of local causation does not apply to quantum phenomena, leading some scientists to the conclusion that the universe is either fundamentally lawless or fundamentally inseparable (Stapp 1971).

This holistic model of the human-environment relationship makes it possible to conceive of entities which possess objective properties but which can be defined only partially by those properties. One of the most comprehensive attempts to draw wider social implications from this philosophical position as it is supported by science specifically is probably that of Fritjof Capra in his book *The Turning Point* (1982). His schematic new world view rests mainly on an elaboration of the holism he sees implied by the new science, and the assumption that it holds for macro-systems like human society and necessarily results in cooperative tendencies rather than simply a relativistic tolerance of multiplicity. These are bold assertions and, while they have established Capra's influence on eco-centric environmentalism, are not universally accepted by any means. The principal point of focus here, though, is the contribution Capra's schematic makes to a developing understanding of the structure of holistic conceptions when they are applied to large-scale phenomena like communities.

Capra (1982) emphasizes the concept of systems, drawing particularly from biological and ecological models in his analysis. Organic metaphors are used to illustrate the central point that living organisms, ecosystems, communities and societies are all types of system which share common properties. Broadly, he asserts that these are characterized by distinguishable parts (molecules, cells, organs, people, families, communities, societies, nations, etc.) which collectively are integrated in the form of a stratified order. Each of the parts can be regarded as a whole in the sense that they are, in various ways, integrated systems, but at the same time are also parts of larger wholes of increasing complexity. This analogy is used to illustrate his central point that the whole is reflected in each of the parts. It is a holistic conception in which order is maintained through the dynamic interplay of self-assertion and integration: two complementary, but opposite, tendencies assumed to be possessed by both part and whole. Entities which are conceived as both part and whole together in this sense are given the name 'holons', after Koestler (1978). Each component of a system in Capra's terms, whether biological or social, is assumed to consist of entities which have integrative tendencies to function as part of a larger whole, as well as self-assertive tendencies to preserve their individuality. It is a holistic conception which is self-creative, self-organizing and self-sustaining, relying on the nature and activity of the entities which already exist within it for its future form and progress. The precise character and form in which order will become manifest is indeterminate and emerges from the integrative activity of the whole. In his most recent work, *The Nature of Order*, Christopher Alexander (2001) also argues, as a consequence of his observations of natural and cultural systems and objects, that structure with wholeness, or life, emerges through a succession of structure-preserving transformations that act on the whole. He sees this transformation as an act of differentiation, an increment in the development of a structure, each stage of which should create a barely detectable change to the existing structure. The cumulative effect of a long succession of such transformations would, however, generate a structure very different and more complex than the original: the gradual transformation of an acorn into an oak tree, for example. What is crucial here, if this is to be adopted as a model for developing the built environment – and this is certainly the intention of Alexander – is that pre-existing conditions are to be understood as the seed from which further development of form will take place; and also that change will progress incrementally and gradually, over time, replicating more a process of growth than a process of material intervention.

References

Albert, R. and Barabasi, A. (2002) 'Statistical mechanics of complex networks', *Review of Modern Physics*, 74(1): 47–97.

Alexander, C. (1964) *Notes on the Synthesis of Form*, Harvard University Press, Cambridge, MA.

Alexander, C. (2001) *The Nature of Order: An Essay on the Art of Building and the Nature of the Universe. Book Two: The Process of Creating Life*, Oxford University Press, New York.

Alexander, C., Ishikawa, S., Silverstein, M., Jacobson, M., Fiksdahl-King, I. and Angel, S. (1977) *A Pattern Language*, Oxford University Press, New York.

Alvarez, L. and El-Mogazi, D. (1998) 'The language of fractals: an enhanced design vocabulary', paper presented to Council of Educators in Landscape Architecture (CELA) Conference, 22–27 October, Arlington, Texas.

Barabasi, A. (2002) *Linked: The New Science of Networks*, Perseus, Cambridge, MA.

Batty, M. and Longley, P. (1994) *Fractal Cities: A Geometry of Form and Function*, Academic Press, London.

Bell, J. (1987) *Speakable and Unspeakable in Quantum Mechanics*, Cambridge University Press, Cambridge.

Berlin, I. (1965) 'Herder and the Enlightenment', in Wasserman, E. (ed.) *Aspects of the Eighteenth Century*, The John Hopkins Press, Baltimore.

Bohm, D. (1980) *Wholeness and the Implicate Order*, Routledge, London.

Canter, D. (1977) *The Psychology of Place*, The Architectural Press, London.

Capra, F. (1975) *The Tao of Physics: An Exploration of the Parallels between Modern Physics and Eastern Mysticism*, Wildwood House, London.

Capra, F. (1982) *The Turning Point*, Wildwood House, London.

Corner, J. (1991) 'A discourse on theory II: three tyrannies of contemporary theory and the alternative of hermeneutics', *Landscape Journal*, 10(2): 115–133.

Crompton, A. (2005) 'How big is your city really?', available at: www.cromp.com/work/home.html.

Crucitti, P., Latora, V. and Porta, S. (2006) 'Centrality measures in spatial networks of urban streets', *Physical Review E*, 73: 036125: 1–5.

Cullen, G. (1971) *The Concise Townscape*, Architectural Press, Oxford.

Descartes, R. (1994 [1637]) *Discours de la Methode: Discourse on Method. A Bilingual Edition with an Interpretive Essay*, University of Notre Dame Press, Paris.

Hall, E. (1966) *The Hidden Dimension*, Doubleday, New York.

Heisenberg, W. (1963) *Physics and Philosophy*, Allen and Unwin, London.

Heisenberg, W. (1927) 'Über den anschaulichen Inhalt der quantentheoretischen Kinematik und Mechanik', *Zeitschrift für Physik*, 43: 172–198. English translation: Wheeler, J.A. and Zurek, H. (1983) *Quantum Theory and Measurement*, Princeton University Press, Princeton, NJ, 62–84.

Jacobs, A. (1995), *Great Streets*, The MIT Press, Cambridge, MA.

Jacobs, J. (1989 [1961]), *The Death and Life of Great American Cities*, Random House, New York.

Jencks, C. (1995) *The Architecture of the Jumping Universe*, Academy Editions, London.

Jones, C. (1980) *Design Methods*, John Wiley and Sons, London.

Jones, C. (1984) *Essays in Design*, John Wiley and Sons, London.

Kelsey, J. (1970) 'A design method', *Landscape Architecture*, May: 425–428.

Koestler, A. (1978) *Janus*, Hutchinson, London.

Le Corbusier, C. (1994 [1925]) *Urbanisme*, Flammarion, Paris.

Lincoln, Y. and Guba, E. (1985) *Naturalistic Inquiry*, Sage Publications, California.

Lyle, J. (1985) 'The alternating current of design process', *Landscape Journal*, 4(Spring): 7–13.

Merchant, C. (1980) *The Death of Nature*, Harper and Row, New York.

Motloch, J. (1991) *Introduction to Landscape Design*, Van Nostrand Reinhold, New York.

Newman, P. and Kenworthy, J. (1999) *Sustainability and Cities: Overcoming Automobile Dependence*, Island Press, Washington, D.C.

Norberg-Schulz, C. (1971) *Existence, Space and Architecture*, Praeger, New York.

Parnes, S. (ed.) (1992) *The Source Book of Creative Problem Solving*, Creative Education Foundation Press, London.

Porta, S., Crucitti, P. and Latora, V. (2006) 'The network analysis of urban streets: a primal approach', *Environment and Planning B*, 33(5): 705–725.

Portugali, J. (2000) *Self-organization and the City*, Springer, Berlin.

Proshansky, H., Fabian, A. and Kaminoff, R. (1983) 'Place-identity: physical world socialisation of the self', *Journal of Environmental Psychology*, 3(3): 57–83.

Ramadier, T. and Moser, G. (1998) 'Social legibility, the cognitive map and urban behaviour', *Journal of Environmental Psychology*, 18(3): 307–319.

Ravasz, E. and Barabasi, A. (2003) 'Hierarchical organization in complex networks', *Physical Review Letters*, 67: 026112.

Rosenberg, A. (1986) 'An emerging paradigm for landscape architecture', *Landscape Journal*, 6: 75–82.

Salingaros, N. (2003) 'Connecting the fractal city', keynote speech, Fifth Biennial of Towns and Town Planners in Europe, Barcelona, April, available at: http://www.math.utsa.edu/sphere/salingar/connecting.html.

Stapp, H. (1971) 'S-matrix interpretation of quantum theory', *Physical Review D*, March: 1303–20.

Taylor, C. (1975) *Hegel*, Cambridge University Press, Cambridge.

Taylor, C. (1989) *Sources of the Self: The Making of the Modern Identity*, Cambridge University Press, Cambridge.

Thwaites, K. and Simkins, I. (2007) *Experiential Landscape: An Approach to People, Place and Space*, Routledge, London.

Tuan, Y. (1977) *Space and Place: The Perspective of Experience*, University of Minnesota Press, Minneapolis.

Watts, D. and Strogatz, S. (1998) 'Collective dynamics of small-world networks', *Nature*, 393(6684): 440–442.

Weaver, W. (1948) 'Science and complexity', *American Scientist*, 36: 536–544.

Whyte, W. (1988) *City: Rediscovering the Center*, Doubleday, New York.

Zukav, G. (1979) *The Dancing Wu Li Masters: An Overview of the New Physics*, Rider Hutchinson, London.

4 The beauty of order and complexity

The fact that the idea of complexity in relation to urban forms extends across several layers – functional, economic, social, time and development, visual – makes it, for lack of better words, a complex concept to grasp. In a reality where economic, social and political factors seem to be the most influential in determining the way our environments are shaped, aspects such as the visual *appear* to have a lesser impact on the overall performance of such environments. This chapter seeks to demonstrate that this should not be the case, and that attention to the visual connotation of space is still a fundamental determinant of its success. The concept of aesthetics, as will be described, needs to be reinterpreted to accommodate the value of complexity in relation to the visual appearance of our settings, and what is called 'social aesthetics' needs to become fully embraced in the assessment and transformation of space.

In this sense, the position adopted by the authors of this book is close to that of Peter Bishop (head of the Mayor of London's new architecture and design unit, Design for London), who, at the Kevin Lynch Memorial Lecture 2006, compared cities to well-lived houses full of accretions from the past (including mementoes and junk!).

The importance of visual environmental quality to perceivers

There is nothing so applicable as a good theory
Lewin (1951: 169)

As the first chapters have clearly spelled out, the message of this book is that to build the sustainable cities of the future, the professionals directly charged with their design need help! Not help in the form of a quick-fix answer, but help in recognizing that satisfactory, fulfilling and sustainable urban experience is a complex issue made (also) of interactions and transactions between people and space, which have to be studied and understood. They need help in appreciating this complexity, in appreciating and paying attention to the 'psychology of place'.

The concept of psychology of place should not be mistaken for an irrelevant portion of the problem if compared with broader concepts such as sustainable development: getting things right in a world that is urbanizing at a dramatic rate (it is predicted that by 2050 the urban population will grow to 6 billion people, as compared to 3.2 billion city dwellers today – Jerome Glen, State of the Future Report 2007) is imperative. As much as urban failures have been tolerable and containable in the past – if not from a social point of view, then from a spatially related one – this can obviously no longer be the case. We argue that we have the knowledge (theory and experience) and the tools (assessment, production and normative) to develop our cities in a way which is responsive to and satisfactory for human, ecological and economic needs and pressures.

In relation to urban design, this chapter focuses its attention on those visual aspects that influence environmental experience and the development of a psychology of place. Psychology of place is a fundamental concept and dimension for the authors: we want to concentrate on where people are in their daily lives and on what matters to them; starting, as Jane Jacobs says, from where it is easier, from the immediate and personal dimension of environmental experience.

Environmental experience is the process of perceiving and getting acquainted with one's surroundings, and establishing an emotional and evaluative relationship with space. It is a fundamental concern of urban design because it elicits the formation of a psychology of place. The perceptive process, enabled by concomitant vision, hearing, smell and touch, is a very active one, and happens through four phases: cognitive, affective, interpretative and evaluative (Ittelson 1973), activated by both environmental stimuli and personal experiences and values. The perceived environment is therefore both a biological and a socio-cultural product (Carmona et al. 2003), and will inevitably possess unique properties determined by one's age, lifestyle and other personal characteristics, and shared ones determined by cultural and group learning.

The latter make the environment not neutral, possessing both intrinsic properties and attributed ones, meanings and symbols, which are developed over time through cultural and social processes. The interpretation (decodification) of such symbols and meanings also plays a key role in environmental experience and ultimately in the formation of a psychology of place. Urban design which is socially accountable elicits the expression of cultural-social meanings in a manner which produces, to cite Venturi et al. (1972), neither a world of 'ducks' nor one of 'decorated sheds', but one which is multivalent, not a parody or a pastiche. This urban design is capable of instilling a sense of place, attachment, belonging and identity.

All the contributors to this book come from design or other spatial disciplines. Yet we all share a fundamental belief in the importance that disciplines other than design can have in understanding the process of how people make use of and interact with their surroundings. As mentioned, one of these disciplines is environmental psychology, the study of the relationships between individuals and their physical environment (Gärling 1998), where relationships are molar – that is, comprehensive both of the stimuli and of the perception of them, not purely as a cause-effect set but as a process depending on various factors, which will be explained later in the chapter. Environmental psychology has contributed since the 1960s plentiful material and findings on (urban) space and people. We focus here in the visual aspects of urban design and their impact on environmental experience.

People's response to visual qualities (Lowenthal and Riel 1980; Bourassa 1991), use of space (Kaplan and Kaplan 1974; Russel 1988), interest in and understanding of space (Groat 1988) and attribution of meanings to space (Hershberger 1994) have been proved to be largely affected by the aesthetic response that their environment stimulates in them. Empirical research has studied the effects of the visual quality of the physical environment on human behaviour and well-being, and identified how such effects manifest themselves. Certain attitudes and/or activities depend highly on environmental physical qualities: choice, frequency, modality of use of places (Downs and Stea 1973; Berlyne 1971; Hall, in Broadbent 1988; Coeterier 1994), reactions to places (Kuller, in Hesselgren 1987) and habits (Mikellides 1980; Lang 1994). Psychological and physiological states also depend on them: well-being and fatigue (Maslow and Minz 1956), attachment to places, preferences for places (Groat 1983; Hubbard 1994, 1996; Wilson 1996), self-esteem of users of spaces (Twigger-Ross and Uzzell 1996) and sense of community and crime (Newman 1972; Dias Lay and Tarcisio 1994). Finally, perceptions, attitudes, states and reactions determine the nature of perceivers' image-formation of the places used or observed (Lynch 1960; Francescato and Mebane 1973; Harrison and Howard 1980; Dias Lay and Tarcisio 1994; Ramadier and Moser 1998).

It is important to note, and this might demystify a belief in disciplines such as environmental psychology as providers – to design fields – of definitive pointers on how to design 'a building or space that makes people happy', that these studies only prove that physical surroundings help or hinder environmental experience, but do not determine it. Through our arguments and the tools presented in Part II, we want to show that a time-conscious (hence evolutionary) urban design is one that encourages environmental experiences that are in tune with human requirements of space appropriation, understanding, legibility, attachment, development of values, relationships, etc. In other terms, time-conscious urban design is one that generates well-designed environments where the patterned relationships between things and things, things and people and people and people (Rapoport 1982) are organized on four principles: space, time, communication and meaning (Rapoport 1977, cited in Rapoport 1982). This differs from general environments, where these relationships are organised mainly on spatial terms. Time-conscious urban design is one that is well aware and produces the settings for urban life according to Donald Appleyard and Allan Jacobs (1987): liveability, identity and control, access to opportunities, imagination and joy, authenticity and meaning, community and public life and ultimately self-reliance and justice.

The sense of place derives from the 'collaboration' of three dimensions: the place, the experience of place and the meanings attributed to it. We will go into more detail of some of the physical properties of place. At the foundation of personal experience, is for us, Kelly's (1955) theory of personal constructs. For Kelly, a clinical psychologist and educator, people perceive the world according to the personal constructs that they apply to it: as a consequence, each of us has his/her own way of seeing the world, which influences past, present and future actions.

> Man looks at his world through transparent templates which he creates and then attempts to fit over the realities of which the world is composed. [. . .] Constructs are used for predictions of things to come, and the world keeps on rolling on and revealing these predictions to be either correct or misleading. This fact provides the basis for the revision of constructs and, eventually, of whole construct systems.
>
> Kelly (1955: 8 – 9, 14)

Almost automatically, this belief in one's approach to, in our case, space, gives legitimacy to a whole set of dimensions that a primarily aesthetic and technical approach to design simply rules out: personality, meaning, time and experience, society and culture. These dimensions are about place-making – which is, in fact, about unique and memorable forms and their meaningfulness to those who experience them. Yet it does not deny the associational power and influence that some formal properties of space exercise on how we see, perceive and form an appreciation of them. These will be listed below. It is important, though, not to misunderstand this brief discussion on formal elements as a regression towards Euclidean approaches to space design. We only wish to list some factors that *do* play a part in a more complex problem, and that could somehow be related to more recent theories such as the network theory.

The visual dimension of order and complexity

The interest in the study of the phenomenology of place experience started in the early 1960s, in parallel with the first discoveries of studies and methods in ethnology (i.e. field interaction). Moving from the study of restricted groups in unique environments to the study of life in urban environments, attention was being paid to the influence of the urban environment on social and individual behaviour. Among these investigations, great efforts were devoted to the visual aspects of physical space, as perhaps the most obvious ones to focus upon: the built environment is out there, it can hardly be avoided in people's daily routine. Public space, with its own nature of being public, of belonging to the collectiveness, has even lesser chance of being changed, personalized, adapted to suit one's expectations. It must therefore perform well to start with, but at the same time be able to evolve and adapt, be suited for one and for all at the same time.

At the core of these studies was man *in* space, within a dense network of interactions bouncing back and forth between walls and senses. Initially, several of these theories appeared linking aesthetic appreciation to natural attitudes towards survival and safety. As much as later studies have opened up the scope and understanding of aesthetics (see below), these initial findings are relevant and can help us understand how to value concepts such as order and complexity in relationship to space. This discussion will therefore focus on some visual aspects of the urban environment and in particular on the issue of order. Nasar (1988) lists five properties that determine people's linking of environments: naturalness, upkeep, openness, historical significance and order.

Smith, in Canter *et al.* (1988: 202), suggested that aesthetic appreciation represents an extension of brain programmes relating to adaptation and survival. He argued that attempting to control the environment to survive has led to a form of aesthetic pleasure that comes from the brain's innate capability to extract order from complexity. The perception of order in the world is comforting because there is less chance of being adversely surprised if there is comprehensible order than if there is incomprehensible complexity. For him, the main conditions of success in architecture and urbanism are that wholeness overweighs particularity and that orderliness wins but not too easily (ibid.: 202–203), which means that the urban form has to have enough complexity to make the perception of unity a worthwhile mental achievement. In buildings and urban form, for example, complexity and order should manifest themselves in binary sets – that is, pair identities with logical connection but also a significant level of autonomy. Such binary sets should counterbalance themselves, maintaining differences within a reasonable band of similarity. Binary sets can be of various types, such as balance/equivalence, inside/outside, round/rectangular, sculptured/plain, and can be determined through the conditions of harmony: ambiguity and symbolism (the function of symbolism is to re-establish conceptual order where formal order is missing). The right balance between order and complexity is called the optimum ratio of order and complexity (discrepancy to affinity), and is satisfied if the whole results as more than a fortuitous collision of parts. Both binary sets and the ratio of order and complexity can be found in urban settings, within at least four distinct components, which transcend time and culture (Mikellides 1980: 74).

- *Rhyme* and *pattern*: rhyme is when an object has at the same time familiarity and novelty; it presupposes the simultaneous existence of complexity and pattern with the latter – meaning not repetition but substantial affinity – somewhat predominant. For Humprey (1980), rhyme gives a representation of how the external world looks, how it works and can help predicting characteristics and events, planning behaviour and reducing the thought load. Such representations constitute the framework of the categories that organize the way people analyse and evaluate the built environment. Rhythm, in architecture and urban design, is a property connected to repetition. Smith (1980) cites studies showing how the brain is naturally attracted to and gets pleasure from rhythmic presentations, varying from the simple binary kind to the complex repeated subsystems which are evident in poetry, music and architecture. Pleasure from rhyme is connected to the natural feeling of protection that animals feel in a situation where they can recognize subtle variations of rhythm (in this case 'rhythm' is the perception you get from any situation).
- *Balance* is a form of order that results from a scene where some elements, though different from each other, do not create disturbance by dominating each other. Balance allows the co-presence of different parameters like tone, colour, masses, texture and symbols; it can therefore be perceived on a perceptual and on a cognitive level.
- *Harmony* is the feeling one gets from observing elements coexisting whose difference is evident enough to be recognizable, but not to allow the dominance of one of them.

Any discussion on order and complexity has to refer to the Gestalt theory which suggests that order is a source of aesthetic pleasure: formal aesthetic pleasure derives from our subconscious response to the degree of order, and the mechanism for attaining order, in the geometry of built form (Lang 1994: 322). According to the principles of Gestalt theory, people are naturally sensitive to geometric forms, and to different levels of complexity of such forms. An interesting development of the Gestalt theory is offered by Anne Tyng (Lang 1994: 322), who suggests that an individual is able to integrate greater and greater amounts of the unconscious into his/her conscious life. Suggesting that psychological growth and maturation is accompanied by an empathy for particular geometrical forms – from bilateral, twofold or fourfold symmetry to more complex rotational, helical and spiral forms – Tyng links behavioural control to appropriate architectural symbols and manifestations (Nasar 1988: 25).

The issue of visual appreciation has been addressed with reference to the fields of environmental psychology and visual sciences, and does not necessarily refer just to Euclidean geometry but also, though maybe at a different level, to the compelling properties of more complex configurations such as the fractals and related concepts of scaling and connectivity (Salingaros, 2003). The notion of fractals is mentioned in detail elsewhere in this book. Here we want to focus attention on some properties inherent to fractals which might also be related to some of the characteristics listed above and are said to play a role in aesthetic evaluation: they include substructures at decreasing sizes, related by scaling symmetry, which are coherent and similar and their unique but predictable properties are in a precise balance between order and chaos. Fractals are the structural property of natural, living and communicational organisms, the urban form being one of those; since people's minds have a fractal model imprinted in them, this might be an explanation for their natural attraction to fractals (Salingaros 2003: 4). Fractal theory, translated to the urban form, adds a whole level of interesting complexity and richness to the way we relate to space: the fractals' structural properties relate form and uses through connection, which is the property that determines cities' degrees of life, legitimizing a whole new sets of dimensions as affecting the experience of place – use and choice, and therefore personal as well as societal factors. Once again, it is the topology of spatial systems, rather than their geometry, that contributes to making a place more or less central, with all the externalities that such a property exhibits on a number of relevant urban dynamics like safety, personal orienteering and navigating in cities, retail location, real estate values and so forth.

The notion of complexity, pattern and legibility is interesting when referred to Kelly's (1955) personal construct theory, and to one of the problems of modern (urban) environments. Complex environments, where the amount of information, and therefore the contrast sameness-differences, is high, pose challenges to people's capacity to extract meanings and thus to form and adopt constructs to navigate and appreciate space. This might well be an explanation for the 'rule of preferential attachment and hierarchical topology' described in Chapter 3. If the environment contains more information than one can comprehend at once, such an overload of information can provoke detrimental effects in people, who will find the definition of categories confusing and distracting (Bell *et al.* 1996: 66). In other words, if the level of information provided by an environment is large but not excessive, complex but structured, varied and interesting but not distracting, the mental process we use to create such categories will probably be immediate, instinctive and natural. As a person's relationship with environments is based on interaction, the more the cues are recognizable, the less effort is required from people to set up such interaction.

In the past the built environment was characterized by a limited number of cues, which could be interpreted as meanings from large numbers of people; the related sets of behaviours were then quite easily identifiable. Nowadays, due to globalization – which on one side draws us and space to convergence (sameness through standardization) and on the other to divergence (maintain and reinforce local dimensions, even for economic value) – the numbers of visual cues provided by the built environment tend to increase and their identity to be confused. In fact, whenever clarity decreases, the amount of information provided by the environment should naturally increase, to support the needed amount of references. This phenomenon is called redundancy, and consists of the provision of further inputs to 'adjust' an environmental deficiency; it happens when the environment is not culture-specific, when it loses its peculiarities and tends to be uniform to others. The immediate effect of this lack of specificity is called the *disease of our age*, and concerns individuals forced to act without clear referents (Rapoport 1982: 151). Time-conscious urban design does the opposite: it tries to offer a recognizable and manageable set of clues, built upon developed and shared values, favouring the emergence of spaces that possess qualities – such as liveable streets and neighbourhoods, an appropriate residential density, an integration of activities, defined public spaces, distinctive buildings of different age and scope (Appleyard and Jacobs, 1982). Time-conscious urban design wants to produce spaces that matter, that people can belong to, that generate pride and attachment: urban design of our places, not of our time, to paraphrase a famous quote by Andres Duany, the well-known Cuban-American (new) urbanist. Despite the new technological capability to traverse the world at high speeds and in a short time – which threatens to reduce places to no more than particular geographical locations, just a matter of specific experiences – places cannot be simply considered as points of geographical interest. They do reveal something about human ways of being in the world (Hough 1990). There is interestingly an economic argument to support this: Dovey (1999) highlights the benefit for space to maintain a local dimension because recognizable urban difference is attractive to global marketing strategies; a proof of this might be considered the extreme phenomenon of 'invented places', which are exaggerated distortions of a sum of recognizable realties (Carmona *et al.* 2003: 102) and show the human need for familiar (spatial) references.

The field of research in environment-behaviour studies has acknowledged that environmental evaluation is based on many more factors beyond the formal ones already mentioned: these are in fact intertwined with symbolic, cultural and personal factors. Those in charge of designing space need some form of clarity and guidance about the effects of such factors and the role of space in eliciting them, certainly not to prescribe rationally what good environments are, but to make our intuition accountable, and understand what are the right tools for the right job, in the words of Jacobs (1961). This information is in large part already available – perhaps in a format which is not yet clear and accessible (and there is currently much debate on how this should be amended), but it is there and should be at the base of designers' theory and practice. Organizations such as EDRA (the Environmental Design Research Association) and IAPS (the International Association for People-Environment Studies), to name but two, have been pioneering research and championing the need to create bridges with more traditional design-oriented professions since their foundation.

Clitheroe (1998) sums up quite clearly the current state of debate on this complex network of factors, studying the interactions of individual or group behaviour with the socio-physical-temporal settings in which it occurs, and identifies as a result four major groups of factors affecting a response by an individual or a group: personal factors, formal social factors, informal social factors and physical factors. For him, personal factors include personality traits, interpersonal dynamics, attitudes and communication processes. Formal social factors include the relatively stable relationships between individuals or groups, a group's standard approach to problem-solving and a hierarchical authority structure. Social factors include relationships between individuals or groups; finally, physical factors include aspects of the natural settings, man-made structures, objects, surfaces and ambient conditions. On top of these, there are human needs which play a major role in the whole perceptual, cognitive and evaluative process, affecting the amount and type of environmental stimuli perceivers can absorb, how they process them and to what purpose – Maslow (1954), Max-Neef (1991) and Coeterier (1994) are perhaps the most revealing studies on needs and urban perception. Interestingly, needs and their satisfaction are also associated with the notion of order and therefore aesthetic experience in the work of Coeterier (in Neary 1994), who works on Max-Neef's definition of needs and Berlyne's aesthetic theory (Romice 2000).

For Berlyne (1971), people's preferences for environmental stimuli depend on a balance between the needs for arousal and uncertainty: they are always striving for the fulfilment of these two opposite feelings, one reducing and the other enhancing the need (Berlyne calls this a 'conflict'). The relationship between these two opposites and their relative equilibrium, repeated for several needs (that manifest simultaneously as for Max-Neef, not in sequence as for Maslow), constitutes the complementary interrelationship of people to the environment.

The relationships between people and their environment take place, for Coeterier (1994), as causes, effects and external conditions. Needs are causes, some of them related to the external environment. Effects are the fulfilment – or dissatisfaction – that derives from addressing a need. The environment, with its properties, constitutes the external conditions in which causes and effects act and and therefore affects them. Needs and external conditions mutually affect each other: a need can be exasperated or facilitated by external conditions; in turn, environmental responsiveness to needs can affect the feeling of attachment or alienation about those environmental settings.

In a study conducted in the Netherlands, aimed at identifying the environmental attributes with a potential effect on people's experience of the urban scene, Coeterier studied the main reasons attracting people to the town centres of Amersfoot and Utrecht, and found these to be the purpose of gathering information; recreation; the need to belong to a greater whole; and the need to take part in a richer variety of possibilities for action (Coeterier 1994: 304). In particular, such behavioural attitudes – determined by human needs – were found to be enhanced or reduced by several environmental factors, which Coeterier classified as existential, functional and visual conditions (Coeterier 1994: 301). We are interested in this discussion in the visual ones.

Existential conditions are linked to the provision of feelings of security, stability and safety within physical settings. Functional conditions are related to the role of the environment, or part of it, as a supporter of people's daily activities, as well as to its flexibility in leaving choice to users – that is, its capacity of not programming too many of such activities. Visual conditions are related to the capacity of the environment to offer visual *variety* and stimulate the *users' curiosity* without overwhelming them – once again, a new interpretation of order and complexity.

Coeterier analysed in detail these three groups of conditions and focused in particular on the notion of diversity. It is interesting to present his findings in this book, because they are comprehensive in defining a notion of diversity which is very appropriate to the discourse on time-conscious urban design. In particular, he identified sets of environmental factors that can influence needs' satisfaction and hence environmental perception and evaluation. Moreover, or once again, diversity has a specific characteristic: it determines preferences *only when* it reaches a certain level – not too much to be confusing, not too little to be boring. These environmental factors are as follows.

- *Diversity of people* – which happens through organized happenings and by maintaining residential functions in the city centre – influences people's perception of liveliness and their need for self-expression and socialization.
- A good *diversity of functions* enhances the choices available and responds to needs for leisure, creativity, identity and freedom. In particular, Coeterier found diversity to be enhanced by the variety of shops and specialized activities in the town centre, and a good choice of routes each with a multi-functional lay-out. More specific activities, such as coffee shops and little restaurants, street life, public services, exercising of trades, culture and recreation and protection of economically weak functions, also play a major role in the satisfaction of such needs.
- What Coeterier calls *diversity of urban detail* in buildings and public spaces (ibid.: 305) is greenery, historical buildings and places, spatial differentiation and proportionality both in blocks and streets, decoration (street furniture, decorative pavements) and an information structure of mobile and/or temporary objects, posters, advertisement boards.
- *Social and physical accessibility* encompasses parking facilities, access to public transport systems, traffic regulation and access to shop in certain areas, and can have a major effect

on needs satisfaction and therefore on environmental experience. A shopping area where the prices and facilities offered are too group-specific, becoming socio-economically exclusive, risks discouraging other clients, with major repercussions for their potential sense of belonging to that place, their curiosity, enthusiasm, self-esteem, tranquillity, spontaneity and maybe even their security.

- The *management and regulation of spaces* – including maintenance, safety and surveillance, the availability of squares for pedestrians and not only for parking cars – as well as the freedom for private citizens to organize things, can affect feelings of safety and also satisfy people's need for creativity and self-expression.

Despite the illusive attractiveness that Euclidean geometry still exercises for our professions, we have reached a point where, confronted with evidence from different disciplines in different fields (we have mentioned environmental psychology, sociology and lately physics), quite clearly we have to come to terms with the fact that Euclidean geometry is no longer appropriate to interpret and take into account this range of factors, nor to grasp the notion of *development* which is inherently imbedded in all these factors and the extent to which they manifest themselves in generating the 'psychology of place'. What is also clear, and has been well demonstrated, is that the aesthetic evaluations of space – which are important to people in their relationship with space – differ among groups (Groat 1983, 1988; Hubbard 1994, 1996; Wilson 1996), and that therefore evaluation by the so-called experts cannot be considered representative of a wider group of users and should not, therefore, be used solely as a design determinant.

The notion of urban aesthetics has thus changed, developing from a formal to a socio-cultural basis, as described in the next section.

Urban aesthetics

> *I am the space where I am.*
> Bachelard (1958) in Stefanovic (1998: 47)

As soon as we mention the idea of individual experience as being significant in the overall establishment of urban quality, concepts such as aesthetics become critical. Aesthetics is a common ground upon which to understand, if not measure, how well our cities perform. What aesthetics of urban form has value, then, when we search for liveable environments?

Traditionally, the concept of aesthetics has been linked to élitist meanings, to the point that talking of aesthetics in relation to the city seemed to be more a form of perpetuation of control rather than an attempt to guarantee good design (Alcock 1993). Alcock identifies three forms of urban aesthetics in the history of city form; the first he calls the subjective approach or 'aesthetics of proportions', and is based on the idea that viewers respond appropriately to visual stimuli of high aesthetic quality. This implies that people's aesthetic values are similar, but it also recognizes that there are differences in 'taste', distinguishing between good and bad among groups of observers. The second form of urban aesthetics he calls 'aesthetics of the plan' (ibid.: 43); it is based on the objective value of geometrical arrangements of forms, and supports classical ordering rules as well as geometrical hierarchies. Its limits consist in the universality of the values it proposes; the question is who guarantees they are understood, accepted and most of all responsive to needs and culture. The third form of urban aesthetics is 'artistic aesthetics', an élitist and abstract expression of ideas through urban design; for Alcock this is the clearer form of designers' domination, with social effects and repercussion.

Alcock suggests therefore a fourth form of urban aesthetics, which he calls 'social aesthetics', based on the importance of subjective experience of space, and aiming at taking care – in meaningful and constructive ways – of such experiences. This is the idea of aesthetics that we can apply in our environments characterized by diversity, complexity and development, disentangling them from the risk of dehumanization and retreat to formalism, and enriching them with properties such as place memory, the human ability to connect natural and built environment to cultural landscapes and the orientation to change (Hayden 1995).

The social role of organized complexity

We have so far run through ideas and principles on urban design, and through criticism and arguments, hopefully persuading the reader that time-conscious urban design, one that acknowledges existing structures – be they physical, societal, economic – and develops them through a process which is at peace with human development, can contribute to sustainable development.

The problems with urban space performance come today from several fronts. On the one side they are caused by the inescapable pressure exercised by mass society, with its increasing number of people involved within a space that 'has lost its power to gather them together, to relate and separate them at the same time' (Arendt 1987). On the other hand they are caused by the pressure exercised by the urban failures that keep on accumulating and exacerbate the situation. Finally, they are caused by economic and political pressures (see Chapter 7), and ecological pressures.

Space has to be reinvested with the capacity to relate and separate people, offering, at least in the urban setting upon which this book focuses, proximity and concentration, permeability, variety, legibility and a democratic pattern that allows at the same time coexistence, privacy, enhancement and justice. Economics and politics must act as responsive and responsible drivers in the process of physical change, and environmental performance at every level – from personal to global space – must guide this change.

Kevin Lynch's quest for a theory of good form for our cities, for a normative theory and in particular for 'performance dimensions' to create vitality, sense, fit, access, control and ultimately justice and efficiency is more than ever valid today and by no means completed. The characteristics he identified in 1981 to assess the relative goodness of a place were a starting point whose value, as he admitted, 'remains to be seen' (Lynch 1981).

At what stage are we now, more than 20 years on? So many of us have looked before at the work of Jane Jacobs, Lynch, Cullen, Allan Jacobs, Appleyard, Alexander and many more. We surely no longer need yet another panegyric of their work. We have reached Sherry Arnstein's (1969) famous comparison between the goodness of participation and the goodness of eating spinach ('everybody knows it is good for you but nobody likes it really') could easily apply to their work, with a twist in the plot: 'Everybody knows it but nobody does anything about it!'.

Perhaps what we need is a clear, definitive statement which confronts urban design to be firm on pinpointing values for good urban performance which, yes, derive from the work listed above. We all think we know these works so well, but the values must be able to encompass *all* the messages they had at their core, *including* that time counts, the lack of which has lead urban design astray up to now. The areas which need such values for good urban performance are those which support the qualities of urban life listed previously, including Lynch's meta-dimensions of efficiency and justice. We need a real cultural shift in the theory and practice of urban design which allows us to consider time as *the* requirement for successful development and a final commitment in making urban design a (partially) normative theory. Perhaps this final commitment should come from our governments in recognizing urban design as a legitimate driving profession for development.

Does this message sound trite? Well, then there is nothing bad with it. Technology changes and progresses, but people are still the same, with social, personal and interactional needs of self-expression and communication. Yet we have shown that mistakes are still being made, therefore it is worth repeating the values of each of the relevant theories quoted, and using them once and for all with the fundamental addition of time.

Time-conscious urban design 'normative theory' should then bring together the seminal works cited (and more), with their core messages spelled out and understood in *all* its parts, summarize these within ranges or target values, then apply each of these innovative tools to assess, quantify and guide development for specific settings and problems. The framework should not change, but the tools attached to each part of the framework do change, to take into account a cultural shift towards innovative technological progress and scientific advancement.

Part II presents a number of exemplar tools that are attached to some aspects of this ideal theoretical framework; they can for the moment be illustrated through liveability, identity and control, access to opportunities, imagination and joy, authenticity and meaning, community and public life, self-reliance and justice. For example, there are tools to help the assessment and delivery of identity and control over settings (Chapters 18 and 19), tools of access to opportunities (Chapters 9 and 10), tools supporting community and public life (Chapters 15 and 16), social justice (Chapter 10), self-reliance (Chapter 12), centrality and liveability (Chapter 11), environmental performance, liveability and self-reliance (Chapter 14). These tools offer ideas on how to study interaction and use it in urban design, how to act upon the knowledge gathered, but they are not intended an exhaustive list on how to design urban settings. It is up to readers to feel inspired by them.

References

Alcock, A. (1993) 'Aesthetics and urban design', in Hayward, R. and McGlynn, S. (eds.) *Making Places: Urban Design Now,* Butterworth Architecture, Oxford.

Appleyard, D. and Jacobs, A. (1987) 'Towards an urban design manifesto', in Larice, M. and Macdonald, E. (eds.) *The Urban Design Reader*, Routledge, London.

Arendt, H. (1987) 'The public realm: the commons', in Glazer, N. and Lilla, M. (eds.) *The Public Face of Architecture: Civic Culture and Public Spaces*, The Free Press, New York.

Arnstein, S. (1969) 'A ladder of citizen participation', *Journal of the American Planning Association*, 35(4): 216–224.

Bachelard, G. (1958) *The Poetics of Space*, Beacon Press, Boston, MA.

Bell, P., Greene, T., Fisher, J. and Baum, A. (1996) *Environmental Psychology,* Harcourt Brace College Publishers, New York.

Berlyne, D. (1971) *Aesthetics and Psychobiology,* Meredith, New York.

Bourassa, S. (1991) *The Aesthetic of Landscape,* Belhaven Press, London & New York.

Broadbent, G. (1988) *Design in Architecture: Architecture and the Human Sciences*, David Fulton Publishers, London.

Canter, D., Krampen, M. and Stead, D. (eds.) (1988) *Environmental Perspectives*, Gower Publisher, Aldershot.

Carmona, M., Oc, T., Tiesdell, S. and Heath, T. (2003) *Public Places – Urban Spaces: A Guide to Urban Design*, Butterworth Heinemann, Oxford.

Clitheroe, H.C. (1998) 'Conceptualizing the context of environment and behavior', *Journal of Environmental Psychology*, 18(1): 103–112.

Coeterier, J. (1994) 'Liveliness in town centers', in Neary, S.J., Symes, M.S. and Brown, F.E. (eds.) *The Urban Experience. A People-Environment Perspective*, St Esmondsbury Press, Suffolk.

Dias Lay, M. and Tarcisio Da Luz Reis, A. (1994) 'The impact of housing quality on the urban image', in Neary, S.J., Symes, M.S. and Brown, F.E. (eds.) *The Urban Experience. A People-Environment Perspective*, St Esmondsbury Press, Suffolk.

Dovey, K. (1999) *Urban Transformations. Power, People and Urban Design*, Routledge, London.

Downs, R. and Stea, D. (eds.) (1973) *Image and Environment*, Arnold, London.

Francescato, D. and Mebane, W. (1973) 'How citizens view two great cities: Milan and Rome', in Downs, R. and Stea, D. (eds.) *Image and Environment*, Arnold, London.

Gärling, T. (1998) 'Conceptualizations of human environments', *Journal of Environmental Psychology*, 18(1): 69–73.

Glen, J.C. and Gordon, T.J. (2007) *State of the Future*, Millennium Projects.

Groat, L. (1983) 'Measuring the fit of new to old', *The AIA Journal*, Nov: 58–61.

Groat, L. (1988) 'Contextual compatibility in architecture', in Canter, D., Krampen, M. and Stead, D. (eds.) *Environmental Perspectives*, Gower Publisher, Aldershot.

Harrison, D. and Howard, W. (1980) 'The role of meaning in the urban image', in Broadbent, G., Bunt, R. and Lorens, T. (eds.) *Meaning and Behavior in the Built Environment,* John Wiley & Sons, Chester.

Hayden, D. (1995) *The Power of Place: Urban Landscapes as Public History*, The MIT Press, Cambridge, MA.

Hershberger, R. (1994) 'Predicting meanings in architecture', in Lang, J. (ed.) *Urban Design: The American Experience*, Van Nostrand Reinhold, New York.

Hesselgren, S. (1987) *On Architecture. An Architectural Theory Based on Psychological Research*, S.H. and Student literature, Lund.

Hough, M. (1990) 'Restoring identity to the regional landscape', in Larice, M. and Macdonald, E. (eds.) *The Urban Design Reader*, Routledge, London.

Hubbard, P. (1994) 'Diverging evaluations of the built environment: planners versus the public', in Neary, S.J., Symes, M.S. and Brown, F.E. (eds.) *The Urban Experience. A People-Environment Perspective,* St Esmondsbury Press, Suffolk.

Hubbard, P. (1996) 'Conflicting interpretations of architecture', *Journal of Environmental Psychology*, 16: 75–92.

Humphrey, N. (1980) 'Natural aesthetics', in Mikellides, B. (ed.) *Architecture for People: Explorations in a New Humane Environment*, Studio Vista, London.

Ittelson, W.H. (1973) *Environment and Cognition*, Seminar Press, New York.

Kaplan, R. and Kaplan, S. (1974) 'Predictors of environmental preferences: designers and "clients"', in Prieser, W. (ed.) *Environmental Research Vol 1. Selected papers EDRA 4*, Dowden, Hutchinson & Ross, PA.

Kelly, G. (1955) *The Psychology of Personal Constructs*, Norton & Co., New York.

Lang, J. (1994) *Urban Design: The American Experience*, Van Nostrand Reinhold, New York.

Lewin, K. (1951) *Field Theory in Social Science,* Harper and Row, New York.

Lowenthal, D. and Riel, M. (1980) 'The nature of perceived and imagined environments', in Broadbent, G., Bunt, R. and Lorens, T. (eds.) *Meaning and Behavior in the Built Environment,* John Wiley & Sons, Chester.

Lynch, K. (1960) *The Image of the City*, The MIT Press, Cambridge, MA.

Lynch, K. (1981) *A Theory of Good City Form*, The MIT Press, Cambridge, MA.

Maslow, A. (1954) *Motivation and Personality*, Harper & Row, New York and London.

Maslow, A. and Minz, N. (1956) 'Effects of aesthetic surrounding: initial effects of three aesthetic conditions upon perceiving 'energy' and 'well-being' in faces', *Journal of Psychology*, 41: 247–254.

Max-Neef, M. (1991) *Human Needs and Human-scale Development*, The Apex Press, New York.

Mikellides, B. (ed.) (1980) *Architecture for People: Explorations in a New Humane Environment*, Studio Vista, London.

Nasar, J. (1988) *Environmental Aesthetics: Theory, Research and Applications*, Cambridge University Press, Cambridge, MA.

Neary, S.J., Symes, M.S. and Brown, F.E. (1994) *The Urban Experience. A People-Environment Perspective*, St. Edmondsbury Press, Suffolk.

Newman, O. (1972) *Defensible Space: People and Design in the Violent City*, Macmillan, New York.

Ramadier, T. and Moser, G. (1998) 'Social legibility, the cognitive map and urban behaviour', *Journal of Environmental Psychology*, 18(3): 307–319.

Rapoport, A. (1977) *Human Aspects of Urban Form: Towards a Man-Environment Approach to Urban Form and Design*, Pergamon Press, New York.

Rapoport, A. (1982) *The Meaning of the Built Environment: A Non Verbal Communication Approach*, Sage Publications, Beverly Hills, CA.

Romice, O. (2000) *Visual literacy and environmental evaluation. A programme for the participation of community groups in design*, PhD Thesis, University of Strathclyde, Glasgow.

Russel, J. (1988) 'Affective appraisals of environments', in Nasar, J. *Environmental Aesthetics. Theory, Research & Applications*, Cambridge University Press, Cambridge, MA.

Salingaros, N. (2003) 'Connecting the fractal city', keynote speech, Fifth Biennial of Towns and Town Planners in Europe, Barcelona, April. Available at: www.math.utsa.edu/sphere/salingar/connecting.html.

Smith, P. (1980) 'Urban aesthetics', in Mikellides, B. (ed.) *Architecture for People: Explorations in a New Humane Environment*, Studio Vista, London.

Stefanovic, I. (1998) 'Phenomenological encounters with place: Cavtak to Square One', *Journal of Environmental Psychology*, 18(1): 31–44.

Twigger-Ross, C. and Uzzell, D. (1996) 'Place and identity processes', *Journal of Environmental Psychology*, 16: 205–220.

Venturi, R., Scott Brown, D. and Izenour, S. (1972) *Learning from Las Vegas*, The MIT Press, Cambridge, MA.

Wilson, M. (1996) 'The socialization of architectural preference', *Journal of Environmental Psychology*, 16: 33–34.

5 The building of order and complexity

What we are dealing with here is a universal notion of isolation that extends over all scales. Anti-urbanist interventions cut human connections. High-tech architectural fantasies cut people off physically and emotionally from surfaces, and from the built environment in general. We cannot solve the present crisis until we acknowledge that the architecture and urbanism of the twentieth century had as its principal goal the isolation of people, from buildings and from each other. That admission necessitates the even more difficult acknowledgment that the idols of modernism were false gods, and that several generations of planners and politicians were deceived into destroying our cities by applying inappropriate urban principles

Salingaros (2004)

Is it true that city planning has had one of the worst post-modernisms ever? This is difficult to say, but certainly our discipline began to challenge the tenets of modernism far later than many other art and scientific fields, and much later than epistemology and philosophy in general. Almost two centuries have passed since topology began to question the foundations of Euclidean geometry and eighty years have elapsed since cubism challenged the pictorial device of perspective that enabled us to reduce three-dimensional space to a plan. The solidity of matter and certainty of determinism have long been revealed as approximations by developments in quantum theory, and relativity theory has at the very least demonstrated that the Newtonian conception of the universe has its limits. Like André Corboz (1993) and Charles Jencks (1995) did almost 15 years ago, perhaps still today we may ask if it might be the time now for architects and city planners to acknowledge that Newton has died and absolute space is good for nothing any more?

Moreover, in this case the delay did not come alone: it is even a matter of discussion if a real post-modernism in architecture and city planning did actually happen at all. In fact, there is compelling evidence that what many authors since the early 1960s have been reporting – or promoting – as 'revolutionary' movements against the modernist gospel were actually just different ways of playing the same music. If one refers to some of the most popular branches of mainstream post-modernism, like neo-rationalism, neo-pop historicism and 'new spirit' (Thomas 1995), the authors would agree with Nan Ellin in arguing that

Ultimately, despite its efforts to counter the negative aspects of modern urbanism, post-modern urbanism falls into many of the same traps. Despite its eagerness to counter the human insensitivity of modern urbanism, post-modern urbanism's preoccupation with surfaces and irony makes it equally guilty of neglecting the human component. By denying transformations that have taken place, post-modern urbanism may even be accentuating the most criticized elements of modern urbanism such as the emphasis on formal considerations and elitism.

Ellin (1996: 162)

The authors would then conclude, again with Thomas:

> Could it be that today's theory, which speaks first and foremost only to its own circle, is delivered from the same avant-garde perch as has been the case for the past hundred years? [. . .] Today avant-garde falls into the same trap as did its predecessors, believing that it rests atop the pinnacle of history, poised as none before have ever been poised to leap into the future. Such a view was the principal cause of large blind spots scattered throughout the often brilliant histories and theories of Giedeon, Pevsner, and Le Corbusier, as well as the work of lesser purveyors of the Modernist gospel. It is a belief that can seduce otherwise rational and prescient scholars and builders into assuming that they are, in the words of the historian Herbert Butterfield, 'co-operators with progress itself'.
>
> Thomas (1995: 490)

In short, what is then the chain that links together conventional modernism with its pretended post-modernist alternatives in a single chorus? Using the same phrase as Thomas, it is that sort of *heroic attitude* that transforms the designer into a messiah who stands just between the god of arts (or that of knowledge) and the rest of human beings, yesterday stating the virtues of Euclidean order, identical iteration and rational hierarchies, today those of fragmentation, atopisms and iconism? According to such heroism the work of an architect or an urban designer ceases to be a social service and climbs the stairway to heaven by means of exclusive jargons and connotative languages. It puts emphasis on solutions as absolute findings and provides no real explanation of the subjective conditions at the heart of the real-life problems with which architects and urban designers deal. It is hard to imagine, for example, anything less functional than 'functionalistic' modern architecture and urbanism which amounted to little more than a tireless intellectual debate on the *aesthetics* of function. Doctrines like formalism dominate the scene, and the post-modern formalistic mainstream has mostly brought neo-contextualist or neo-historicist developments that appear to have landed like aliens, undermining and at worst destroying existing historical contexts and fabrics as never before. Either that or we have symbolic celebrations of technology without connection to anything but the celebration of technology itself. People and life in modernism were at least present, albeit in a thoroughly reductive and mechanistic conception; in the later, post-modern era, they appear sometimes to have been jettisoned altogether as an aesthetic intrusion.

Is that all? The reader who searches for actual alternatives to the formalistic mainstream of modern, as well as post-modern, urbanism may easily get frustrated in understanding that this is the case. Heterogeneous contributions are here and there acknowledged, of course, but mostly as side-effects of that general opposition to modernism that was mainly represented by formalistic post-modernism. The 'townscape' movement, for instance, is generally accounted for as a romantic reaction against modernist positivism or as a prelude to the successive contextualism and then again to the formalistic happy end. Characters like Oscar Newman, Jane Jacobs or even Kevin Lynch are almost removed from the scene or cited in niche contexts like that of the social fights against urban renewal in the late 1960s. On the contrary, it is important to understand that although the formalistic answers to the (equally formalistic) achievements of modernist architecture and city planning have actually constituted a mainstream in the discipline, as they mostly do still in our days, we can clearly see in the early 1960s the beginning of a real, deeply different approach. A long story is being told that has built the foundations of what we call today sustainable city planning and urban design, the dawn of a real anti-heroic counter-revolution.[1]

Chapter 2 proposed a list of key oppositions between the modern and the sustainable approaches in terms of actual programmes for the construction of the city. Those oppositions actually come from more fundamental differences which belong to the basic attitude of the designer towards her or his role in relation to that of other actors and to the outer reality as a whole (Table 5.1). Moreover, the modernistic attitude of a heroic approach to city planning and design paves the way for mostly formalistic results which offer no acknowledgement to what has gone before.

Table 5.1 The opposition between the heroic/formalistic mainstream and the anti-heroic foundations of the sustainable counter-revolution

	Language		Implementation	Approach to reality	Concept of the city	Attitude to pre-existence	Process
	Text	Figure					
Heroic formalism	Technical Jargon	Specialist Formal Maths/ statistics Cybernetic	Project planning	Structuralist Visionary	Model	Cancellation Isolation and monumental-ization	Top-down Artistic
Anti-heroic sustainable urbanism	Plain Ordinary	Pictorial Pop Figurative Mixed	Urban husbandry	Observative Descriptive	Social construction	Preservation Valorization Inclusion and reuse	Bottom-up Participatory

So here one can see the contemporary cultural brake that counters the sustainability agenda and actually makes it so hard to put in practice real time-conscious processes and solutions. Essentially, in our attempts to respond to the problems that we perceive to emanate from the dominance of modernism, we have developed the counter-culture of the post-modern. Yet in many crucial ways the new formalistic 'post-modernist' mainstream, in socially responsive terms at least, has more or less the same shortcomings as its modernist predecessors. Falling somewhere between these, rapidly growing against the foundations of the modernist culture in city planning and design, is the confrontation that began to emerge in the early 1960s, pioneered by Lynch, Jacobs, Newman and their like. It is possible that, in the context of the rise of the so-called post-modern solution, there has been a misunderstanding, or even a marginalization, of some of their messages that has helped deviate the course of sustainable urban design towards a gradual absorption into a 'new' version of the old formalistic mainstream. More recently, though, this has turned into a more structured and visible juxtaposition as the anti-heroic, participative movement merging with and animating the sustainability agenda for the urban case. This is not a recall to orthodoxy: it is a recall to tools and concepts, techniques and values, that constitute the identity of our disciplinary personality; in short, a recall to our difference.

Note

1   Among the many contributions one would highlight Oscar Newman, Clare Cooper Marcus and professionals like Project for Public Space; Jane Jacobs, Allan Jacobs, Henry Sanoff and Robert Sommer; Amos Rapoport, Christopher Alexander and John Peponis; Dolores Hayden and Ann Moudon; Jan Gehl and Lars Gemzøe, Donald Appleyard and Peter Bosselmann; Kevin Lynch, Jack Nasar and professionals like Anton Nelessen; Gordon Cullen, Francis Tibbalds and Ian Bentley; Peter Newman, Hildebrand Frey, the Urban Task Force and other professional practitioners like Llewelyn-Davies-Yeang and academic/professionals like Space Syntax and Intelligent Space.

References

Corboz, A. (1993) 'Avete detto spazio?', Casabella, 597–598.

Ellin, N. (1996) Postmodern Urbanism, Blackwell, Oxford.

Jencks, C. (1995) The Architecture of the Jumping Universe, Academy Editions, London.

Salingaros, N. (2004) City of Chaos – Part1, 'Greekworks.com', available at: www.greekworks.com/content/index.php/weblog/extended/city_of_chaos1/.

Thomas, B. (1995) 'Hesitation and heroics: the New Spirit (again) in urban design', Proceedings of the 83rd Annual Meeting of the Association of the Collegiate Schools of Architecture, Seattle, WA, March 18–21.

Section Three

TIME-CONSCIOUS URBAN DESIGN – CLUES TO A STARTING POINT

6 Cultural biases and disciplinary contradictions against time-conscious urban design

The great suburban build-out is over. It was wonderful for business in the short term, and a disaster for our civilisation when the short term expired. We shall have to live with these consequences for a long time. The chief consequence is that the living arrangements most Americans think of as "normal" is bankrupting us both personally and at every level of government. This is the true meaning of the word deficit, which has resounded so hollowly the past ten years as to have lost its power to distress us. Now that we have built the sprawling system of far-flung houses, offices, and discount marts connected by freeways, we can't afford to live in it. We also failed to anticipate the costs of the social problems we created in letting our towns and cities go to hell.

A further consequence is that two generations have grown up and matured in America without experiencing what it is like to live in a human habitat of quality. We have lost so much culture in the sense of how to build things well. Bodies of knowledge and sets of skills that took centuries to develop were tossed in the garbage, and we will not get them back easily. The culture of architecture was lost to Modernism and its dogmas. The culture of town planning was handed over to lawyers and bureaucrats, with pockets of resistance mopped up by the automobile, highway, and real estate interests.

The average citizen – who went to school in a building modelled on a shoe factory, who works in a suburban office park, who lives in a raised ranch house, who vacations in Las Vegas – would not recognise a building of quality if a tornado dropped it in his yard. But the professional architects, who ought to know better, have lost almost as much ability to discern the good from the bad, the human from the antihuman. The consequence of losing our planning skills is the monotony and soullessness of single use-zoning, which banished the variety that was the essence of our best communities. Most important, we have lost our knowledge of how physically to connect things in our everyday world, except by car and telephone.

Kunstler (1993: 245 – 246)

In seems apparent that a planner working in the public sector in a large metropolitan city would most likely have the feeling that the economic drivers of development can still result in the delivery of socially responsive, and even culturally and environmentally considerate, development. This optimism, perhaps idealistic, should be based intrinsically on an enthusiasm for an interesting and perhaps even beautiful urban environment, one that is rich and complex, vital and viable, and motivational. The planner must maintain this enthusiasm in the face of innumerable obstacles and widely held beliefs that the profession has lost its way, credibility and perhaps even value to society based on its débâcles in the later half of the twentieth century (and through to today).

The world, and in particular the urban form, character and life of European cities, towns and villages, has provided inspiration for planners and architects for generations. The goal should be to leave a positive legacy of their work, which inherently requires an appreciation of how places work and the difference between good and bad places and good and bad design. Copenhagen, Bruges, Edinburgh, Urbino in Italy, Dinan in France and Dunkeld in Scotland – places of timeless qualities that due to the planning profession's devotion to policies and procedures are now largely unattainable – nonetheless continue to provide the standards for the planner concerned with evolutionary urban design. Planning in the United Kingdom today is largely about the procedure of creating places and has lost, or gifted, the actual visioning of the elusive urban renaissance to other professionals, largely the architects. However, as urban design is still not recognized as being the sole province of any individual professional discipline, the planning profession should be compelled to reclaim a stake in urban design, especially as planning has traditionally been more socially responsive than architecture or civil engineering.

The message about the importance of urban design as a legitimate concern and profession has been gaining momentum of late, but do professional planners adhere to the concept of 'evolutionary urban design'? This concept, based on the principle that urbanism and community are built over time, taking into consideration and best utilizing what is there already, is nominally entrenched in the planning policy. However, planning professionals are probably less concerned with what you call it – that is for the academics to analyse and theorize about – and should be more concerned with whether it ultimately delivers 'places' that function and are lively and liveable; and whether it is principled, clearly understandable and accessible enough to give further momentum to the importance of matters such as human scale, compatible mixed uses, quality public spaces, etc. Fundamentally, the severe and spartan design simplicity of the modernist era of planning failed to create the enduring places people want and need. Perhaps if planners did not keep repeating so many of the mistakes of the past one could argue that the notion of 'evolutionary design' is trite. However, the planning profession must meet some challenges before this argument can be justly made. To begin with, as a perhaps temporarily misguided but fundamental contributor to urban design, it has to rediscover confidence in its ability to look beyond policies and procedures and deliver places, places of merit and character, that people are proud of and want to live in. It must also accept these as the norm rather than the exception. Until the planning profession actually gets this and, more to the point, demonstrates consistently that it has, then it must take not only cognizance of urban design theories but embrace them with a degree of enthusiasm.

So are the planners listening to any of this theory of urban design? Good question, but our guess is that, judging by the profession's propensity for repeating the mistakes of the past, one would say not very well, perhaps bits and pieces. Glasgow as a city was decimated in the 1960s, its urban landscape blighted and ruined by the imposition of motorways and high-rise residential towers. These developments were undertaken with the best of intentions by planners and architects with a vision, albeit a misguided one, and one that has ensured a hefty and consistent workload for the planning profession ever since. In one sense the planners of the 1960s spoiled the fun for later generations of planners: not only did they really get it wrong on the ground, but they have left us with negative perceptions and a certain lack of confidence in the profession. The failure of the modernist movement led to city planners focusing on an empiricist approach to planning, one that emphasized social construction over the art of urban planning and has ultimately hamstrung the profession in a procedural and policy-ridden quagmire. Planning and planners have become slaves to open-space standards, density requirements, window-to-window distances and rigid parking requirements. Such matters are included in development plans and are adhered to strictly, even to the point where deviations within individual masterplans are issues of considerable contentiousness. The result is that the three-dimensional qualities of the city and the abstract virtues of place-making have been neglected, with planners concentrating more on social and economic concerns and the 'process of planning' and less on actual place-making, or evolutionary urban design.

There is therefore a sense of urgency required for planners to rediscover the form and function of planning in delivering quality urban environments as we continue not only to explore but actually to build schemes of dubious architectural merit, let alone sensitive urban design, many similar to the infamous ones of the 1960s. The city of Glasgow continues to look at 'orbitals' or motorways as solutions to access and transport issues. Mono-functional, single-tenure housing estates continue to get built all over the city. Glasgow Harbour, a much-lauded example of urban regeneration along the Clyde River, contains proposals very reminiscent of the high-rise towers that are being pulled down all over the city.

To its credit, there have been success stories in Glasgow, such as the New Gorbals and the Oatlands, where former street patterns have been or are being reinstated along with traditional tenemental scales of development within new mixed-use areas. However, the New Gorbals is still evolving and its neighbour the Oatlands is only in the earliest stages of detailed design and development. But even the area in Glasgow most likely to be trumpeted for its successful regeneration and as an exemplar of evolutionary urban design – the Merchant City, as described earlier – is not an urban utopia.

It does, however, raise the issue of what we do consider a 'success' in terms of regeneration. Perhaps the Merchant City can be considered a success. Maybe we should just set our standards a little lower and call it an urban quarter – especially considering the myriad of problems faced by planners, both of their own making and circumstances that are inherent in the development field. As planning has lost its confidence and vision, its faith in the design profession to provide these have compounded the difficulties in achieving evolutionary urban design. Without, or unable to provide, a vision the planners have largely ceded this aspect of urban design to the architects and civil engineers. But at what cost? Do architects have the skills or even the desire to deliver evolutionary urban design? Planners seem to think so; such is our apparent faith in them to deliver urban design frameworks and masterplans. Architects often win commissions for large-scale urban design frameworks based on planners extrapolating some work the architects have done on a single street – hey, if they can get it right in a small scale we can be convinced that the same approach will work on a large area. But it often does not, as the skills to convert a historic building and throw in some modern touches to make it kind of shiny do not necessarily transfer to making spaces between buildings work, especially over a large area. Often what you end up with is an urban design framework that is largely an architectural response, and is all about providing settings for landmark buildings. Can you really blame them, though? Are they not just doing what comes naturally? Traditionally it was the role of the planner to provide a response, at the heart of which was that places matter more than individual components and that it is the spaces between the buildings that should be prioritized.

Why do we acquiesce so often with the architects? Even on the individual sites that should be the architect's urban regeneration bread and butter we are still too trusting or perhaps timid, believing the hype that 'iconic architecture' is a legitimate regeneration delivery vehicle. Can regeneration be as simple as throwing up one or two buildings? Does iconic architecture convey a bold statement of intentions to put a city back on the map or instil investor confidence, or is it mere concessions to the indulgences of architects more concerned with creating a striking built form? What and where are the convictions of the planner in this? Rarely do these buildings adhere to the cherished urban design principles of active street-level frontages and enclosed public spaces. Peer pressure often means we, the planners, give in; who wants to risk being branded as intellectually dull by failing to see the genius in the design?

A recent case highlighted the plight of a development in Porthcawl in Wales, in which a 42-unit apartment block with some ground-floor retailing was given a design award by the Royal Society of Architects in Wales. The building includes a cacophony of bright green panels, porthole openings and a weird bulging façade (among other 'embellishments') completely at odds with its (conservation area) surroundings. Architectural judges praised its mix of 'humour, charm, intelligence, populism and solid architectural pragmatism'. Alternatively, one local resident referred to shortly and sharply as an 'abortion'. Who is right? And what was the role of the planner, who should have been asking if it would have improved the public space in Porthcawl town centre?

This is just one example: a weekly read of *Building Design* provides enough material on the latest attention-seeking architectural indulgence to question the urban design ethos or competence of those involved. There is no doubt that the sketches for all these buildings draw oohs and aahs from all involved at the planning stages, but do they really work when considered within a enduring and successful urban context? Can they really provide a legitimate basis for a long-term sustainable built environment? And why do planners continue to give in? Are the architects or the planners to blame for a seeming inability to deliver simple, well-executed buildings that fit seamlessly into an enduring urban fabric?

It could be that overriding economic or political concerns are involved. It is often said that quality development cannot by itself solve social and economic problems, but neither can economic vitality, social well-being and environmental health be sustained without a coherent and supportive physical structure. But what happens in the towns and cities that are desperate for investment and where any development is welcomed regardless of what it looks like or how it fits into the community? It tends to be a short-sighted approach, but for these places urban design, let alone evolutionary urban design, often takes a back seat to getting developers and investment into the town, under the guise that any development is 'regeneration'. What of the Kilmarnocks (Scotland) of the world, places that are suffering from poor employment prospects, an already degraded environment and a wealth of social problems, where investment of any form is welcomed? These towns often have large underutilized and neglected areas, many adjacent to established town centres. In planning policy terms it is often difficult to argue against the proposed development, but how much leverage does the planner have in design matters in these degraded areas – they do not want to put the developers off too much by asking for even so much as a pedestrian-friendly street frontage, for fear of losing the deal. But what of the place that is being created? Is it regeneration if a 120,000 sq ft superstore locates adjacent to a town centre or even in a town centre, as numerous have sought to do recently. The issue of impacts on numerous smaller independent traders, the ones that contribute significantly to giving the town character and a distinct identity, has been gaining momentum lately, but the public and politicians can be easily seduced under the guise of 'regeneration'.

In city and town centres across the UK, it is large-scale retailers that are often calling the shots. Are the local authority, planners or politicians going to protest too much if the developer insists that a retail shed (the same as those provided in Sheffield, Plymouth or Livingstone) with a sea of parking in front of it (even though the development site is in the town centre) is the only viable option and that any one-off design which sensitively incorporates car-parking provision is not workable? Evolutionary urban design becomes a luxury. The reality is that planning operates in the realms of politics and economics, that developers are only too aware of this and that they are going to remain equally aware until a major cultural shift takes place in the political, economic, social and professional arenas, changing the conditions that currently make it hard even to think about time-conscious, evolutionary city-building. While planning policies may say one thing, who wants to be on the hook for allowing a substantial investment to slip away to a neighbouring town/city that will not be so strict on design matters? In the end councils get bullied.

Even if the planner could persuasively convince the retailer/developer to provide an appropriate response in architectural/urban design terms, would he know how to do it? Since planning has become formulaic and procedural, can the planners really be trusted to deliver proper and sensitive urban design? This highlights another area where cultural biases leave planning with a lot of ground to make up. Most planners, during their education, receive little or no training in design appreciation, let alone the technical aspects of design. At university planners get hammered in the social elements of the profession, with only slightly less emphasis on economics, but no idea of how to deal with these issues in spatial terms. Although planners are but one player dealing with these issues, the proportion of educational training is weighted almost exclusively towards dealing with them not from a spatial or design perspective, the theories of how urban form might impact on social interaction, but purely from a sociological perspective. Urban design is merely given a token nod. Planning professionals often have to educate themselves in matters of design. Planners and planning education have lost sight of what it actually does, the real nuts and bolts of town planning – providing both the vision and the direction to deliver sustainable development and communities.

As a matter of urgency and from a professional perspective, it is still about getting the often unobtainable basics right. And this requires revisiting the key themes and principles: compatible mixed uses, human scale, coherent and attractive public spaces, agreeable and adaptable urban grain, safe and welcoming places, planning for change, etc. Planning, incorporating urban design – call it evolutionary, sensitive, holistic, etc. – that still appreciates the creation of actual places, under whatever name or in whatever context you use to appraise it, still matters; and planning needs to regain the skills, confidence and vision to deliver its message. After all, planning must still deliver places for people, places that can successfully evolve, and to do this an awareness of and commitment to the principles of time-conscious urban design are paramount.

References

Kunstler, H. (1993) *The Geography of Nowhere: The Rise and Decline of America's Man-Made Landscape*, Touchstone, New York.

7 Notices of time-conscious urban design: practices and projects

In this section we will first try to summarize some key principles of time-conscious urban design, and then consider ways in which this might appear in our urban surroundings through built examples from the last half-century that exhibit some or all of these principles. Generally speaking, projects of time-conscious urban design are those that are sensitive to, or in some sense arise from, the human and environmental circumstances prevailing there at the time. Such circumstances may be cultural, physical, social, ecological or experiential, for example: they might be rooted in the physicality of a place where its appearance has evolved gradually over time, through changing usage, developing needs and economic circumstances; or they might be a consequence of the experiential development of particular communities, social networks, etc. where the uniqueness of place resides in, and emanates from, the routine habits and life patterns of inhabitants. Whatever the foundation, though, time-conscious urban design is that which takes as its starting point what is there already, the essence of the place, and acts on that essence so as to protect it, nurture it, improve it and gradually bring forth a change that is inclusive of different perspectives and possible configurations, harmonious and in tune with that essence, even though eventually the final form of the project might have an entirely different appearance and an ever-changing face.

This is a form of urban order quite at odds with the aspirations of Descartes and his subsequent adherents who wished to see urban form sweep away life's untidiness, cleansing it with the cold, straight discipline of Enlightenment rationality. But time-conscious urban design does not, must not, mean a naïve return to historicism. Beautiful though the Italian hill town of Siena undoubtedly is, for example, the underlying syntheses of social, political, cultural and economic forces that have woven through time its appearance today are not those prevailing everywhere and every time. Siena, like many old towns, is a physical expression of its particular and unique time and place, and we should not aim at mere reproduction just because we now see this as beautiful or desirable. Time-conscious urban design requires sensitivity to the underlying forces that are particular to the situation in which we are at work at the time, and our response must therefore be entirely context dependent. This kind of approach to an evolutionary development of urban order is similar in principle to what Christopher Alexander (2002) describes as a process of structure preserving transformations. Here, the purpose of design is not about immediate, arresting, eye-catching interventions, it is more about the gradual development of complex order by transforming some aspect of an existing situation incrementally (Figure 7.1).

This is, for Alexander, an attempt to argue for an approach to design driven by an explicitly biological metaphor, suggesting that better architectural and urban design solutions, in his view those with 'life', come from processes that allow a complex form to grow from pre-existent states – the way an acorn gradually changes into an oak tree, or an embryo into an adult human being,

7.1 Evolutionary growth of a settlement
for Christopher Alexander

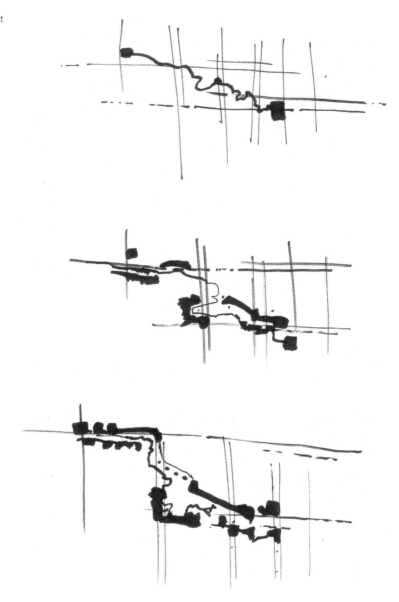

for example. This has not endeared him to the mainstream of the architectural community: order as a kind of life force applied to inanimate objects like buildings and towns, somehow thought of as coded in the circumstances of their location in space and time, is simply a step too far for many. 'What of architects' imaginations?' they might say. Descartes would probably have been just as sceptical. But if we return momentarily to The Calls and Riverside development in Leeds mentioned in Chapter 1, we can highlight features of this real-world example that may help develop our theme of time-conscious urban design.

Figures 7.2 and 7.3 show different phases of The Calls and Riverside development. The photographs in Figure 7.2 are the earlier, taken on the north bank of the River Aire. They show an urban setting with a design language derived from the vernacular of Victorian warehouses that once defined this area of Leeds city as a thriving industrial heart: a gateway and repository for goods and materials to service the commercial life of Victorian Leeds. This purpose is now long

7.2 Sensitive response to historical essence

gone, and after decades of dereliction and neglect a period of regeneration has brought new purpose to the north bank of the Aire with a mix of residential accommodation, hotels and restaurants and small businesses of various kinds. A walk along The Calls road reveals a city quarter unmistakably modern in appearance, with new street surfacing and signage, parking provision, new buildings and contemporary adornments to the refurbishment of existing buildings. It looks new and up to date, it has an appealing domesticated feel in places and it is reassuringly flawed in other places: good quality is hardly ever found to be perfect! Much of it does feel real, comfortable, settled and lived in: this pushes through, and in many ways is enhanced by elements of contemporary styling and the ensemble continues to speak of its proud industrial and commercial past, the reason for its existence in the first place. Its new form and purpose have grown from a pre-existent state still evident in its appearance through sensitive urban design decisions begun over 20 years ago and still underway today. Sensitivity to, but not reproduction of, its historical

essence, coupled with a gradual regeneration over time, seems to have contributed to making a place with a largely settled feel, a distinctive city quarter, special for its own sake yet completely rooted in its previous life and purpose. In Alexander's terms, either by accident or design the regeneration of much of the north bank of the River Aire has evolved by means of a series of structure-preserving transformations at different levels of scale, guided by the light touch of the original masterplan.

If much of the regeneration on the north bank remains faithful to its pre-existent essence, its sense of place, quite a different design language is spoken to the south of the river (Figure 7.3). What has happened here is impressive in the sense that large tracts of disused land have been quickly restructured with an arrangement of public spaces and smart buildings, accommodating residential, commercial and leisure purposes. But here the design language cannot be understood as derived from any kind of pre-existent circumstance, nor can the development be said to have evolved, adapted and settled over time. Well over £100 million has, in little more than five years, given much of this area of Leeds the anonymity and sterility of international 'anywhere'. It is an example of the now prevailing approach to urban regeneration that seems to have no time to discover, consider and accommodate the essence of the place, choosing instead the rapidity and often vacuity of the latest trends and styles: an interventionist rather than evolutionary approach to urban design. Admittedly, much of the south bank did not have the same tightly knit spatial infrastructure given by the rows of Victorian warehouses and ancillary buildings on the north side, but this seems insufficient justification for the approach adopted here, particularly when there are pockets of fine industrial architecture and streets, earlier redeveloped, that could have inspired solutions more in tune with the essence of this locality (Figure 7.4). The bulk of the development south of the Aire began at least 15 years after the north-side development, and if this is meant to represent progress in urban design then surely we must now be asking if we are heading in the right direction?

How, then, are designers to cope with the problem of planning or designing the spontaneous evolution of settlements or neighbourhoods? Central to this is the matter of design. Lord Rogers of Riverside firmly established in 1999 an important role for design in *Towards an Urban Renaissance* (DETR, 1999). The very first key proposal of Rogers' Task Force Report for creating the sustainable city is to 'Create a national urban design framework, disseminating key design principles through land use planning and public funding guidance' (ibid.: 11). Rogers goes on to say that design in this context must be understood as both a process and a product: not only should it determine the quality of the built environment, but it should also deliver many of the instruments for implementation of the urban renaissance. This gives designers of the built environment huge responsibilities and challenges, because it means that they should not simply be concerned with what the output of their effort looks like and how it functions, etc., but they should also be concerned with how these outputs are brought into being. Rogers is quite clear that this involves close attention to social and ecological dimensions of urban life as well as the physicality of built form. This is very important because it means that, for Rogers and his colleagues at least, urban design is a means by which cities, society and nature are brought together in harmony. This transforms what urban design means at a stroke because, although urban physicality in the form of buildings and open spaces can be conceived and imposed in increasingly short time frames,

7.4 Sense of place overlooked by later development phases south of the Aire river

society and nature cannot. Communities, neighbourhoods and societies grow, change and develop from one form to the next over time according to the prevailing circumstances, which themselves are in a state of continuous flux and indeterminism. The same is true for ecological systems. Ecology and society are concepts that require time: to embed, to develop, to grow, to settle, to change, to thrive and become sustainable. Quick-fix alien solutions instantly imposed, like those on much of the south bank of the Aire in Leeds, have few of these attributes. Solutions spread out over longer time frames where even longer stretches of time can be read in their form, like those on the north bank, may instead offer a sense of reassurance and permanence, rootedness and robustness, potentially more capable of weathering the inevitable evolution of social and environmental change.

Developing from this, we would like to propose some principles that define time-conscious approaches to urban design, and then highlight examples which have design content of different kinds to exemplify some or all of them.

In Chapter 2 it was stated that time-conscious urban design includes and merges together at least three functions, namely *architectural heritage preservation*, *ordinary old buildings' preservation* and *incremental multi-actorial change*. It was also stated that each of these functions implies a different level of change from current practices and cultural beliefs: in particular, incremental multi-actorial change appeared as the most challenging, though probably the most critical, among such functions. This is partly because it deeply impacts on well-rooted, and often taken for granted, organizational, cultural and disciplinary assets as well as established hierarchies of power and profession, to the point that only a deep cultural shift can set the conditions for such an horizontal change to happen. If we look to some current practices in order to envision the future, however, we can shed some light on how a time-conscious urban design 'project' can be developed and achieved. With this in mind, and with special reference to the incremental multi-actorial function, we can distinguish three different approaches to the building of a time-conscious application.

The first way is *making the application itself an outcome of an evolutionary process*, where the creativity of the designer is more oriented to the process than to the appearance of the designed product in its final form. Participative or consensual multi-actorial strategies are the engine of this perspective, as the product of the process is not a unitary design but rather a set of incentives, norms and prescriptions aimed at the definition of a space-temporal area where a 'spontaneous' fragmented development is not just allowed, but expected and accurately instructed. More than three decades ago Lucien Kroll experimented in Rwanda with a cutting-edge proposal for the construction of a new settlement around the Kigali urban region, which led the incremental multi-actorial approach to an interesting definition (Figure 7.5). The idea was that the planner (and the public authority) should just define the highest level of road connections, and put on the ground only some activities that were supposed to act like a catalyst, activating a spontaneous process of urban construction which was to be 'assisted' by technically trained officials with no power of final decision. Kroll's work in Rwanda inaugurated other efforts in the same direction, but such a 'radical' way to an incremental multi-actorial approach has as yet failed in penetrating the social, political and economic environment of developed countries in the age of massive urbanization. That, of course, should not be any surprise: the implementation of a real incremental and multi-actorial approach implies a significant impact on the real estate side and the balance between the land property and the public sector which holds a power of control, legitimation and orientation of decisions. No part of this could be achieved without a deep cultural shift.

The second way involves *close identification of and building upon the circumstances that have led to the way in which the 'project' situation has evolved and matured over time to how it appears in the present day*. Examples are historical characteristics, stratification of cultural heritage, urban diffused environmental and architectural values, collective memories and experience, etc. This should not simply be taken to mean the preservation of buildings and open spaces strictly for their historical or other significance. What we mean here is more of a respect for and responsiveness to the diversity of factors that have led to present situations, and these are equally likely to involve non-material and spatial issues, including for instance collective memories, social habits and the human local cultures in general, as well as the social capital of mutual trust, the political capital of relationships and agreements among key players and the economical capital of the local network of small-medium enterprises. Moreover, another extension of the word 'preservation' which is worth considering is the positive attitude to *transformation* that can make evolutionary resources like those mentioned above newly available and meaningful, or available in new shapes and meanings, for our contemporary sensibility and expectations. In this sense, preservation has nothing to do with the reduction of reality to a museum, nor with the plain imitation of past shapes, but instead tends to the respectful reinvention of patterns and resources in order to give them new life: preservation is nothing without imagination.

The third way is risky but still worth trying, with some cautions and certain conditions: it is the *production of a 'project' which is intended to incorporate and interpret some inner rules of incremental change as they appear to the eyes of the designer alone*. The risk is evident: since the rules are set by the designer (or by any other central agency of decision), then the design elevates itself over complexity and evolution, which will make the product, no matter how good the intentions or bravery, neither *authentically* incremental nor complex. The risk is the Rossi effect, as we can call it, drawing from Aldo Rossi's work in Schutzenstrasse, Berlin (Figure 7.6): in short, fakery. More interesting, in the context of this book, it is that this fakery brings to an extreme consequence the same attitude that, under more subtle arguments and with more appealing results, also touches experiments of 'evolutionary' project-for-change designs or 'generative' approaches like those discussed in Chapter 8 under the notion of a 'sophistication trap'. But if Rossi fell into the artistic interpretation of complexity, a temperate version of this approach may well work, provided that some 'temperating factors' are put at work in the process.

The first of such factors is that the focus is in any case maintained on the users' needs, not on the designer's. Since in this case it is the designer's task to portray the identity of the users and the nature of their needs, the success of this approach relies heavily on her or his personal commitment to and capability of making the project a social product rather than an individual realization of the self. A crucial role in this perspective is played by implementing an 'observative' rather than 'visionary' approach to both analysis and design (Porta 2002). Admittedly, however, we have many examples where a designer's deep personal commitment towards an open and socially sensible product has fostered good results, habitats that proved to be open to change and external interventions, and finally good environments for human life, especially when the process took place in an arena which was not too complex or where the interplay between stakeholders was not too conflictive.

7.5 The evolutionary growth of a settlement for Lucien Kroll

7.6 The sophistication trap at work: when the designs are believed to possess the generative key of evolutionary diversity, the risk is fakery, as in this Aldo Rossi's work in Schutzenstrasse, Berlin

Another temperating factor is that attention is paid to avoiding unfamiliar shapes and environmental assets, which is often the case when a solipsistic interpretation of generative rules or biological metaphors brings evidently a-contextual results. In such cases what we see at the end is just another iconic architectural 'masterpiece', and generative or evolutionary arguments do not change the reality of things on the ground. Of course, iconic architecture has its own contribution to offer to our cities, which often need landmark objects to express highly symbolic and visually catching values, but it is important to distinguish what is the real need of the city and the community: when it comes to building good urban environments for city living and exchanging, iconic architecture can sometimes be effectively the exception but never the rule.

A third temperating factor is preservation itself. Too often 'evolutionary' projects are proposed on the basis of a full clearance of all that pre-existed on the ground, no matter if spatial, social or cultural. That approach is clearly built on a cultural bias against the pre-existent urban fabric and community which, like all biases, in most cases is revealed to be largely unjustified on deeper inspection, and is even more unacceptable because hidden behind smoke-screens of socially sensible rhetorics.

Based on the irrefutable evidence provided by the overwhelming majority of what gets built in the United Kingdom and elsewhere, the principles of time-conscious urban design are far from universally understood and accepted. However, there is undoubted confirmation, in terms of both policy, future planned communities and development on the ground, that many of the tenets embodied in time-conscious urban design are nonetheless gaining in momentum and acceptance. Policy guidance in England and Wales is becoming more sensitive to these requirements – if not explicitly, then in essence (PPS1 and the *Manual for Streets*). Developments are being planned and designed (Western Harbour, Tornagrain) and alliances made to ensure that future developments by many of the biggest housebuilders in Britain incorporate many of the key themes of time-conscious urban design. In short, ideas that have been widely promoted in academia, research and rather limited urban design discussion groups have filtered through to become not just models of best practice but financially viable products.

If recent policy guidance documents are to be believed and more importantly adhered to, then we will be seeing more and more time-sensitive urban regeneration to come. The recently published Planning Policy Statement 1 (PPS1), which sets out the government's overarching planning policies on the delivery of sustainable development through the planning system, signals a shift towards better design. It is far from a perfect template for time-sensitive design-led regeneration and development revolution, but it does at least indicate a progression in policy emphasis from a negative 'no acceptance of poor design' to a more positively toned 'only accept good design'. It also makes it a requirement to refuse mediocre designs that do not positively improve a place or its character, empowering local planning authorities, which in the past have often been perceived as reticent to determine a planning application on design terms at the risk of a potentially costly planning appeals process, to give adequate weighting to design matters. This document also provides a more overt requirement for good design and acts as a foundation for more detailed guidance to follow in documents such as the forthcoming *Manual for Streets*.

The *Manual for Streets*, a joint project by the UK's Department for Transport and the Department for Communities and Local Government, is intended to bring about a fundamental shift in the way that engineers, urban designers and other stakeholders think about the design of local streets. Streets are recognized for the complex roles they perform – as a focus for social interaction, and having potential to improve visual qualities and local distinctiveness, in addition to the movement of traffic. The place function of streets may equal or even outweigh the movement function. The concept of sustainable and mixed communities is at the heart of the document, which proposes to show how street design considerations can help to improve the local environmental quality and contribute to creating sustainable communities. The document accepts earlier failures and warns against the dangers of repeating the mistakes and dysfunctional forms of the modernist era, in which traditional streets were rejected in favour of car-oriented and zoned development patterns. Instead there is an emphasis on the need to recognize that street patterns which support walkable mixed-use neighbourhoods are a vitally important determinant of successful urban development, and should be based on urban structures and places that have stood the test of time and evolved successfully.

Many of the ideas within the *Manual for Streets* have been influenced by the success of Poundbury, an urban extension of Dorchester, England, originally masterplanned by Leon Krier for the Duchy of Cornwall, an estate vested in the Prince of Wales. Poundbury is based on many of the evolutionary design principles that have enabled places not only to endure but successfully to evolve and thrive over time. The development gives priority to the pedestrian experience over cars; it is primarily residential (both private and high-quality social rented), but sprinkled with commercial buildings and retail and leisure facilities to create a walkable community (Figure 7.7). The critics who have dismissed Poundbury as hopelessly old-fashioned and dangerously romantic based on architectural stylings miss the point: a problem not helped by the fact that it is usually referred to as Prince Charles's model village everytime it appears in the media. Poundbury may not be perfect, but its spatial organization is far better than many new settlement schemes built or under construction today, and it provides a worthwhile physical template because of the faithfulness to urban design principles that emphasize local character, harmony, walkability, income mix, workplaces, services, communal facilities and housing, all combined and built to evolve. It is set out to work in a long-term, sustainable way, and excessive criticism at such an early stage in its evolution runs the risk of generating a widespread lack of confidence in an approach that may well bring considerable benefit to sustainable settlement design.

If Poundbury is yet to win over some in the design community, it continues to gain acceptance from private sector developers and housebuilders as a model that makes business sense and is now almost a 'brand'. There are now a number of Poundbury look-alikes across England, and an alliance between the Prince Charles-sponsored Prince's Foundation for the Built Environment and the Home Builders Federation, whose members build 80 per cent of all homes in England and Wales every year, was recently announced. Under the scheme the housebuilders were invited to submit three recently completed projects with the goal of having their developments officially 'recognized' by

7.7 Poundbury, Dorset

the foundation. So long as this does not degenerate into a shallow, repetitive 'pattern-book' approach fuelled by an interest in exploiting the commercial potential of picturesque pastiche, then, as a precedent and exemplar for a worthwhile way forward, there is reason for optimism.

In Scotland two substantial projects that give further hope for time-conscious urban design are in their formative stages: Western Harbour in Leith, Edinburgh, and Tornagrain, near Inverness in the Highlands. Western Harbour, an urban extension to Edinburgh masterplanned by Robert Adam Architects, is meant to house approximately 13,000 people on reclaimed and former industrial land, and is founded on the principles of improving connections, efficient use of space and the creation of desirable *places*. The urban structure is based on proper streets, crescents, squares and parks as a foundation to deliver a rich and complex scheme with different activities compressed together in a street or neighbourhood full of vibrant shops, offices, cafés and other leisure facilities. Design codes are used to ensure adherence to density, mix of uses, widths of streets, heights of buildings and so on. A certain degree of distinctiveness is ensured through the coding requirement that all buildings are constructed in local materials and designed with reference to the local building character, avoiding the development looking and feeling as though it could be anywhere. The goal is to provide an environment that encourages people to think they are living and working within a proper city, not some randomly produced architects' and developers' sprawl, and ultimately to present an urban form that is designed to adapt over the long term.

A masterplan that shares many of the same urban design philosophies, including the use of design codes, is the recently unveiled plans for a new town in the Scottish Highlands near the rapidly expanding town of Inverness. Tornagrain is a proposed new town which when complete will house approximately 10,000 people; it will include schools, shops, pubs and restaurants and incorporate a large element of commercial office space, and has been designed by architect/town planner Andres Duany of Duany Plater-Zyberk & Company. The masterplan was produced during the UK's first design 'charrette', held in Inverness in September 2006 to engage public opinion and inform design proposals. Further background work included thorough research into what makes successful places, with the focus on the nature, layout and urban form of these places as well as looking at local economic and social conditions. Ultimately a masterplan was produced for a long-term sustainable community built (literally) on the principles of time-conscious urban design.

Western Harbour and Tornagrain are by no means the only communities currently being masterplanned to adhere to concepts of evolutionary urban design, but they have been highlighted as two fairly high-profile examples. The success of Poundbury and the developments at Western Harbour and Tornagrain (among other potential examples) throw up an important question, in that they provide or at least hope to provide evidence that something which usually grows organically over hundreds of years *can* be created in a single 'temperate' generation. And with an increasingly compliant or even encouraging policy framework and recognition among developers and housebuilders of the merits of time-conscious urban design, maybe we are finally getting it, maybe there is cause for optimism. We will move on from this cautious note of optimism to look at four very contrasting examples of development that, with very different visual outcomes, also exhibit aspects of time-conscious urban design.

Chapel Allerton, North Leeds, UK

Chapel Allerton is a district of Leeds, United Kingdom, that lies approximately five kilometres to the north of the city centre. It is a well-established, thriving and lively residential community with a diversity of housing type and style, from substantial early Victorian townhouses, terraces and semi-detached family homes to recently constructed apartments and low-cost public housing. The residential provision is woven together with shops and other small businesses, churches, community buildings and public open spaces to create an eclectic and thriving neighbourhood character. Chapel Allerton's appeal as a desirable residential environment has grown significantly over the last decade, and this has been reflected in increasing property values and levels of rent. Its increasing residential popularity appears to have led to a significant growth in the area's attraction as an evening leisure and recreation centre. Many of its resident population, and indeed others from neighbouring communities, prefer to socialize in the growing number of bars and restaurants that continue to emerge in the area of the main street rather than travel into the city centre. It is evident that there is a strong sense of community cohesion in the Chapel Allerton area which draws together its resident and business inhabitants. One of the most visible manifestations of this is the annual summer Chapel Allerton Festival that extends over three days of street entertainment, staged music, food and craft stalls. All of this gives Chapel Allerton the air of an urban village, a clearly distinguishable region of the city characterized by a wide range of interwoven leisure, commercial and residential activities.

In many ways Chapel Allerton exhibits evidence of all three of our time-conscious urban design characteristics, and we will try to describe it in more detail by reference to them. The first thing to note is that, as a distinguishable settlement on the outskirts of Leeds, Chapel Allerton today is not really a product of design at all but very much a product of incremental social processes. It is a rarity: a village that has been smothered by a city and has not only survived but prospered. Evidence has it that there has been a settlement at this location for more than a thousand years, predating the construction of the first chapel by Cistercian monks around c1240. Although there are no buildings still existing from this period, the social and commercial epicentre of Chapel Allerton today has grown adjacent to this location: social activity, of worship, trade and leisure, has sustained at this site for well over 850 years. This retains Chapel Allerton's clear sense of a core, and even though the main Harrogate Road, an arterial route from Leeds to the prosperous areas of Moortown and Alwoodley beyond, bisects it and significantly undermines comfortable pedestrian movement from east to west, this location and its accessibility from all points north, east, south and west are clearly a key factor in its popularity beyond the resident population.

Even though Chapel Allerton is now seamlessly connected to the north Leeds suburban expansion, it retains a distinctive village-like quality much treasured by its inhabitants. The origins of this owe much to the fact that woollen manufacture, responsible for the growth of industrial Leeds during the Victorian period, was never established in the area, sparing this part of Leeds the mills that appeared elsewhere. Even with a subsequent growth in development of terrace houses and shops on the main road, without the imposing scale of industrial mills Chapel Allerton managed to retain its air of intimate human scale. As pollution began to make living conditions in Leeds city unpleasant, those who could afford it gradually moved out to the developing suburbs, contributing to a swelling of Chapel Allerton's population by almost 600 per cent to over 5,800 in the century from 1800. More people brought increased demand for local leisure facilities, including several public houses, a new church and park. By the dawn of the Second World War Chapel Allerton had, with the exception of a few later additions, grown to the form that can be seen today. More recent changes have been stimulated in part by changes in patterns of housing stock ownership. Properties once owned by housing associations and rented out to families and pensioners were sold off, attracting more affluent young professionals, and the last decade or so has seen an increase in the business population and a huge increase in bar and restaurant culture.

Perhaps the principal significance of Chapel Allerton in respect of time-conscious urban design principles is that continuous evolution in social composition and patterns of use have brought about and are expressed in its form today. As a whole, Chapel Allerton is a product of an evolutionary system, and a failure to recognize this in local authority planning policy, inappropriate scale and type of commercial development, or indeed public apathy, for example, could easily have threatened or destroyed its village-like integrity. The essence of Chapel Allerton is sensitive to change, but not in a precious, excessively preservationist sense. Chapel Allerton's essence has proven itself robust for centuries: indeed, it seems to depend on change to sustain and enrich it, for its form has never been an entirely static one and is not to this day. This is why in evolutionary urban design we have to be able to identify and understand the essence, the fundamental identity, the kernel, of a place as something fluid and often, like Chapel Allerton, dependent on change, and not as a static, finite absolute always to be revered and preserved as if in aspic. The search for a finite and absolute form of order is, from a time-conscious urban design perspective, pointless.

For Chapel Allerton has changed, and indeed at the present time it seems to going through a period of accelerated change. But we can see many of these changes in terms similar to the structure-preserving changes that Christopher Alexander describes. Development work is presently taking place more or less all the time, but to all but the very familiar much of this is hardly noticeable against the integrity of the wider whole. Examples can be found at a grassroots community level where inhabitants have cooperated in extending garden space into rear alleys, a legacy of Victorian residential layout now redundant, hard to maintain and perceived by many as a potential security threat. More conventional development projects established at the heart of the Chapel Allerton community include a sheltered housing complex in a prominent location overlooking the park, and a nearby low-cost housing project. Both of these consist of low-key and thoroughly unremarkable buildings in themselves, but they have been woven into the existing street and open-space network with such skill that, despite being visibly different, they have somehow become so thoroughly embedded into the locality that it is hard to imagine Chapel Allerton without their contribution to its increasingly eclectic mixture of built forms. More recently, the local police have relocated to a new headquarters close by, vacating a corner building with a very iconic presence on the main road. This is now a trendy bar with apartments and parking to the rear, and forms a flagship part of a growth in the provision of bars and restaurants at the core of the community. This kind of development now characterizes Chapel Allerton as the place to be seen in north Leeds, and is itself encouraging more confident and individualistic expressions of architectural and interior styling that increasingly spill out on to the wide streets, giving a cosmopolitan air that would have been unthinkable there 30 years ago.

Such design and development initiatives can thus be said to be embedded in the existing evolutionary system: they consciously or unconsciously seem to be in tune with the natural way that Chapel Allerton grows, by small piecemeal additions and changes, simultaneously catalysts for and responses to social developments, and for the most part in harmony with its natural grain and pattern. There is increasing evidence of designers' imaginations, but these are finding their expression within the robust and sustainable framework of evolutionary properties that have held Chapel Allerton's essence together through centuries of change (Figure 7.8).

The Phoenix Project, Coventry, UK

Chapel Allerton is an example of an evolving form subtly enriched with understated design interventions responsive to its long and continuous social evolution and adding to a gradually developing appearance and sense of place. The interventions and contribution of design are evident but for the most part a light touch, illuminating the background of a place with an essence that has remained firmly intact for centuries. Chapel Allerton continues to grow slowly and gradually in form and social integrity. Coventry's Phoenix project is, by comparison, a bold and ambitious masterplan-driven urban design intervention: the product of architects MacCormac Jamieson Prichard, landscape architects Rummey Design Associates, a group of seven artists and a poet. It is a project that exhibits characteristics of time-conscious urban design in the way that the design team have tapped into the heart and soul of Coventry and sought to bring this back into prominence as a high-visibility expression of the city's identity and sense of self. Through an awareness of Coventry as a larger developing system, the design team has sought to heal a wound in its evolutionary process, the physical and social consequences of which have blighted the reputation and self-respect of the city for decades. It is worth summarizing the nature of this wound before looking at the response of the Phoenix Initiative.

7.8 The faces of Chapel Allerton

Despite its modern appearance Coventry is an old city. Remnants of the city walls and other forms of archeological evidence, particularly of its ecclesiastical heritage, remain visible. Various industrial activities have brought periodic prosperity, most recently through car manufacturing. But Coventry has perhaps become best known for the consequences of post-war redevelopment that sought to regenerate the city's physical infrastructure after savage bombing laid waste huge swathes of the old city centre. The success of Basil Spence's cathedral has gone hand in hand with less successful aspects of post-war reconstruction that saw Coventry become an icon of modernist urban planning. Despite well-meaning concerns for pedestrian spaces and local amenity, adoption of the modernist ideology prevalent in the 1940s and 1950s brought a deterministic approach to the creation of a new city that all but swept away the historic urban grain and street patterns, introducing a segregated city fabric with a pedestrianized shopping precinct at the core. Segregation continued to dominate future planning initiatives, and over a short period of time the city centre became dominated by monolithic buildings in single-use blocks for shopping, commerce, education and to service an increasing need for car parking. Against this background the decline in local motor manufacture that had revitalized Coventry's economy after the war contributed to physical neglect and social problems that would eventually characterize Coventry as the archetypal concrete jungle where no one saw need or desire to venture unless to service the narrow range of functions the city centre now accommodated. Especially at night, anti-social behaviour began to dominate the central area, further contributing to a lack of hope and opportunity.

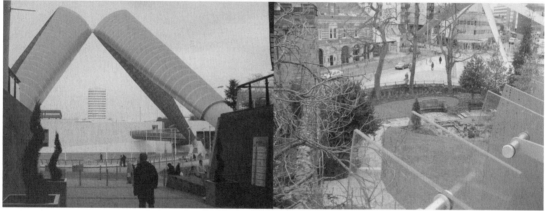

7.9 The Phoenix Initiative

This attempt to raise the phoenix of Coventry from the ashes of wartime devastation by imposing a form of order alien to the city's past may have temporarily treated the wound but it failed to make it heal, contributing instead to a gradual deterioration in social health and civic pride. The Phoenix Initiative, begun in 1997, adopted an entirely different, more incremental approach that would respect and respond to site-specific evidence of Coventry's heritage while producing a strikingly contemporary visual impact through a series of interwoven public spaces and a blend of bold public art installations and archaeology (Figure 7.9). The whole delivers a sequence of varying spatial experiences that link together in seamless continuity the cathedral, the city's Transport Museum and a new garden space made by combining the regenerated Edwardian Lady Herbert's Garden with the new Garden of International Friendship. One of the most interesting aspects of the Phoenix Initiative is that it conceptually seeks to convey through its sequence of spaces from cathedral to gardens, not only a journey through physical space but also a journey through time. A new evolutionary narrative is thus returned to Coventry in the symbolic and physical connection of the 1,000-year history of the Benedictine Priory, excavated to form Priory Garden, through the present-day civic activities staged in Millennium Place to the future hope represented by the Garden of International Friendship. Coventry's Phoenix Initiative is an example of time-conscious urban design principles that celebrates the vision and creativity of its designers through the way they recover connection with properties of Coventry as a larger incremental urban and social system. By this means a new urban quarter has been developed that is embedded in Coventry's cultural heritage and its collective memories and experiences but also paves the way for new growth in urban form, economic regeneration and social activity, giving the project a distinct sense of an optimistic future as well as a respectful past.

Mexicali

We have tried to construct a housing process in which human feeling and human dignity come first; in which the housing process is re-established as the fundamental human process in which people integrate their values and themselves, in which they form social bonds, in which they become anchored in the earth, in which the houses which are made have, above all, human worth, in the simple, old-fashioned sense that people feel proud and happy to be living in them and would not give them up for anything, because they are their houses, because they are the product of their lives, because the house is everything to them, the concrete expression of their place in the world, the concrete expression of themselves.

Alexander *et al.* (1985: 16)

Mexicali lies just south of the Californian border with Mexico, and the project Christopher Alexander talks about here is a small housing development there that he and some Berkeley University architecture students worked on in the 1970s. One of the aims of the project was to engage as closely as possible with the people who would ultimately occupy the settlement in the process of planning and building the houses. What Alexander says here clearly establishes that the architectural processes adopted were not about making houses as mere receptacles for living in. These houses were to be nothing less than the physical embodiment of the souls who would help make and then occupy them. Earlier, in Chapter 3, we talked about the ideas of expressivism: that human activity does not simply result in objective products of that activity, independent of their maker, but is rather the expression of some aspect of the self through that action, and that this is important to quality of life. Expressivism ties intimately together the development and communication of the human self with the outputs of its expressive action, because such outputs are seen to be projections of the self into the world at large and they are what binds us together with the environments we inhabit. Alexander's approach to design and building in Mexicali provides an example of how the essence of expressivist thought can be applied in an architectural context. It speaks of a participatory approach with profound implications for how architects are defined and the roles they adopt. It is an approach reminiscent in Lucien Kroll's work in the development of a settlement in Rwanda, refered to earlier and described in the next section.

One of the most significant aspects of Alexander's statement, and one that hints at the consequences for architects, is that he does not say they are going to construct houses: they are intent instead on constructing a process that will allow human feeling and dignity to predominate. This is explicitly a form of architecture intent, first and foremost, on delivering fulfilled lives, and this is not usually, at least not explicitly, what architects get paid for. Alexander's approach here was motivated by earlier building projects which had used the principles of his pattern language but where he felt something essential was lacking in the results. He thought this might be because the pattern language had been used primarily as a design generator, and that something of the spirit of its human purpose had become sterilized by the construction of the designs using conventional contracting processes. These observations and experiences drew Alexander's practice into contracting activity expressly to make sure that the humanistic principles embodied in the pattern language theory could continue to evolve throughout the construction phases and into the subsequent occupation. The pattern language was used in Mexicali in a more explicitly social way, as a common means for groups of families to cooperate in the shaping and making of their own environments directly. The focus is placed on what Alexander calls 'fine-grain' (Alexander *et al.* 1985: 36) control, instead of centralized interventions. The end product should not be predetermined, only guided.

In the Mexicali project, this kind of hands-on, evolutionary process of creativity led Alexander to a system of eight basic principles which he thought were necessary to its wider application for housebuilding generally (see Box 7.1). These are significant because they describe acts of design and build as integrated processes involving social, design and making attributes, each of which intentionally evolves over time as the process gradually unfolds. Design is focused on the reality of space as it is directly experienced, and is mostly carried out on site involving actual builders and users supported by models which are produced in parallel.

A concern with social forces and human impulse in design is not, of course, unique. These factors are regularly included in surveys and, sometimes, in the design processes adopted in the approaches of the modern architecture he criticizes. What sets Alexander apart is that he sees social forces not simply as a facet of survey information or even as a component of a design process, but as an actual generator of form in the environment: good environmental form is simply a physical manifestation of social forces in Alexander's view.

The Mexicali project exemplifies Alexander's determination to ensure that the integration of human purpose with the act of making places extends throughout every stage of the process and is not simply confined to the design stages. This does not necessarily mean that people have to be involved physically with acts of construction, but they must have the freedom to influence the outcome, in its finest detail, as the building process actually unfolds on the ground. A significant freedom, according to Alexander, is removed from people when they are remote from, or only indirectly involved with, the making of places which they will use, and as a consequence there will be a lack of correspondence between user and place. This is highly resonant in Kroll's experiences in Rwanda where the continuous evolution and adaptation of the dwelling in response to the changing nature of family structure is so central to the culture that the end of change to the house is associated with the end of the occupant's life. The concept of the architect-builder has got Alexander into trouble with the architectural mainstream because it is sometimes seen to imply a mission for architecture without architects. On the contrary, though, the Mexicali project demonstrates the benefits that can accrue from a different kind of professional involvement in projects. He envisages this being fulfilled by locally based professionals who have responsibilities which are broader in scope than those of a conventional architect, but smaller in scale and more concerned with the management of a participatory process which evolves and changes throughout the life of the project and where everyone involved is able to experience a level of creative engagement and ownership.

A post-occupancy study carried out at the Mexicali site several years after completion shows that relationships among the occupying families had become less cohesive than at the outset, and gradually a series of adaptations to the development had taken place which emphasize greater levels of privacy against the maintenance of communal spaces (Fromm and Bosselmann 1984). This could be taken to indicate that the ideals Mexicali was supposed to embody, of a close-knit community living around shared spaces, have not sustained through the realities of daily life. More positively, perhaps, is that the families' familiarity with the processes of design and construction on which they were so intimately involved has empowered them to initiate and make changes, incrementally, to their physical surroundings reflecting changes in their social relations and individual needs. This illustrates the gradual evolution of form in direct response to the evolution of human functioning through processes of self-determination and direct action. Although on a small scale, as just one phase of houses in a more ambitious settlement plan were ultimately constructed, it shows a particular approach to environmental design that can facilitate social expression through an evolving environmental form.

Box 7.1 The Mexicali eight rules after Christopher Alexander

The architect-builder. This is an integration of the functions of architect and contractor, and in concept it shares some commonality with the traditional master-builder. This allows even relatively significant factors, like the final dimensions of walls, the positioning of windows and doors, etc., to be fine-tuned actually on site instead of having them predetermined on drawings prepared beforehand.

The builder's yard. The central idea here is that a builder's yard, closely associated with each building site, would perform a social function as well as being a repository of materials and equipment. In Alexander's scheme, the builder's yard is a critical feature of what is, in effect, a dramatic attempt at decentralizing the building and construction industry, to bring it more under local control and accountability.

Collective design of common land. All of the five families included in the project were involved in determining the extent and configuration of common land first. Determining a rough shape for each dwelling allowed them to visualize and modify the fit between the private and communal spaces. The purpose of this is to try to achieve a sense of collective ownership over the whole, so that the common areas are 'a collective expression of their will' (Alexander *et al.* 1985: 119).

Operational steps. This principle establishes the sequence of key operations involved in the process: a simple description of what should be done, to dig a foundation trench, erect a post, fit a window, etc. rather than a specialized technical specification and drawing. At this level, the operations are couched in terms which attempt to integrate, rather than simply accommodate, user participation.

Layout of individual houses. Alexander acknowledges that it may not always be possible for individuals actually to be involved physically with construction processes. Nevertheless, he considers that it is essential for the user to be involved as directly as possible, and at the very least the layout of the house should be driven by the users themselves. Ultimately, a level of coordination in the development is achieved through the collective decision-making about common areas, materials and construction methods, but within that there is uniqueness in each dwelling which reflects the uniqueness of each user.

Step-by-step construction. This is a significant innovation which moves the emphasis in construction away from components to be assembled to systems of operations. 'In this case we define the building system in terms of the actions that are needed to produce the building, not in terms of the physical components' (Alexander *et al.* 1985: 222). The operations are supposed to generate the building, rather than 'fill in' the reality of a previous design. This was undertaken in the interests of facilitating participation and keeping creative opportunities fluid. It assumes a kind of craft orientation in which acts of human expression are empowered by operational guidelines, but not constrained by prescriptive documentation.

Cost control. For Alexander, this system of building not only produces better houses, in the sense of their connectedness to the people who live in them, but it also produces them at low cost. Central to this achievement is a more decentralized system of cost control and spending.

The human rhythm of the process. In this principle, Alexander is attempting to articulate that there is a qualitative difference, in terms of both the built result and the human experience of achieving it, between the conventional idea of working for pay and working for the purpose of creativity. His argument is that merely working for pay is creatively demotivating because the focus of the activity (the pay cheque) is disconnected from the creativity of the task being performed for it.

Kimihurura

Echoes of Alexander's Mexicali experience can be heard in Kroll's approach to the development of a new urban community at Kimihurura in the Kigali urban region, Rwanda. It is evident from Kroll's account of the project that he was extremely sensitive about the potentially detrimental impact of Western interventions in this sensitive African context. 'And if in our countries our intelligences and our modern fanatic methods had become unbearable, what could happen in that fragile civilisation' (Kroll 2006: 94). Like Alexander, Kroll's starting point is an appreciation of the unique and integrated quality of the place, an essence of location which he poetically sees in the seamless grace of a landscape made from a harmonization of 'people, paths, fields, trees, dances, hugs. . .' (Kroll 2006: 94). What kind of urban form is appropriate here and how can anyone ever design here without brutalizing were questions central to the purpose. Just as Alexander believed that the right kind of form and order was always intimately related to the prevailing social forces, Kroll also saw the solution in the uniqueness of the Rwandan social and family structures and how this related to the spatial organization of their communities. Rational and technical procedures that aim to conceive definitive solutions would be rejected in favour of a process-oriented approach that would allow Rwandan cultural values expression in an evolving development, reflecting in particular that domestic and communal spaces and communication corridors achieve their form through patterns of use and not by predetermined planning.

Indeed, Kroll's approach in Kimihurura reads more like a process of watching and waiting than of design. 'Ideally we should wait that pedestrians mark their paths spontaneously, as they have been doing for millennia, and only after that we should make them official along with facilities' (Kroll 2006: 97). This essentially piecemeal approach characterizes every part of the development project, so that the impact of small-scale interventions can be witnessed and they are allowed to grow and develop naturally. It is as though each thing done acts as a catalyst for subsequent activity and behavioural evolution so that its effect can become embedded into the gradually growing form. This way the arrangement of dwellings develops in harmony with adjacent streets, which themselves take on either primary or secondary significance, gradually developing into a complex network each part of which takes on its own character and identity as an expression of its use.

Like Mexicali, the process is also an intrinsically participative one in which the professionals have an essentially facilitating role, stripped of the power of determination. 'The strategy here is to encourage inhabitants to present their own project, their handiwork, their neighbourhood setting, with the presence of the builder-assistant, deprived of any power, as well as that of the cooperative administrator with no creative role' (Kroll 2006: 97). This aspect also seems to be a necessary response to the unique cultural circumstances, in the sense that building a house is seen as a continuously evolving process that ends only at death. Dwellings are not fixed and static, but evolve continuously in response to changing family life and circumstances: the house is truly an expression of the life of its occupants at that particular time and place, and tradition has it that one should put off laying the final stone for as long as possible because stopping the evolution of the house means nothing other than the stopping of life. In these circumstances the active participation of people in the building process is an essential component of the quality of life for individuals because, as Kroll points out, 'If you put some families into lines of identical houses then something in those families will die, especially if they are poor. The human being will become depressed and weak as their houses and their imagination will cease' (Kroll 2006: 97). Kroll, too, sees this form of evolutionary development requiring a different kind of architecture professional: one who possesses special skills to assist participant communities to realize their own aspirations rather than to impose his or her own rationalized solutions.

References

Alexander, C. (2002) *The Nature of Order. Book 2, The Process of Creating Life*, Center for Environmental Structure, Berkeley, CA.

Alexander, C., Davis, H., Martinez, J. and Corner, D. (1985) *The Production of Houses*, Oxford University Press, New York.

Department of Transport (2007) *Manual for Streets*, Thomas Telford, Trowbridge.

DETR (1999) *Towards an Urban Renaissance: Final Report of The Urban Task Force*, Urban Task Force, London.

Fromm, D. and Bosselmann, P. (1984) 'Mexicali revisited: seven years later', *Places*, 1(4): 78–89.

Kroll, L. (2006) 'Urban de-colonization in Kimihurura, Rwanda, 1966', in Porta, S. (ed.) (2006) *Il Recupero dei Quartieri di Edilizia Sociale: Una Questione Ancke Disiplinare*, Libreria Clup, Milano.

Porta, S. (2002) *Dancing Streets: Scena Pubblica e Vita Sociale*, Unicopli, Milano.

PART II
ANALYSIS FOR THE SUSTAINABLE CITY

Design professionals today are often part of the problem. In too many cases we design for places and people we do not know and grant them very little power or acknowledgement. Too many professionals are more part of a universal professional culture than part of the local cultures for whom we produce their plans and products. We carry our "bags of tricks" around the world and bring them out wherever we land.

There is too little inquiry, too much proposing. Quick surveys, instant solutions, and the rest of the time spent persuading the clients. Limits of time and budgets drive us on, but so does lack of understanding and placeless culture.

Jacobs and Appleyard, in Larice and Macdonald (1987: 102)

8 Analytical techniques for a sustainable city

We are dedicating a considerable part of this book to the presentation of 'tools' for the analysis of urban areas because we think that analysis matters. This statement is much less obvious than it might appear at a first sight: after having spent, at least since the end of the Second World War, a good three or four decades under the hypnosis of hyper-scientism and cyber-modelling, city planning has more recently faced the sudden awareness that its foundations have fallen into a deep crisis and rationality is not welcome anymore. The academic debate opened to different 'paradigms' especially focusing the specificity of public policy in conditions of uncertainty and the 'discursive' nature of planning practice: planning, in short, let alone the real stuff of building cities, should be regarded as the outcome of self-organized processes of mutual adjustment that 'stakeholders' would reach throughout processes of 'consensus-building'. The emergence of that area of research and practice has moved the focus of planning as a whole towards the management of interests, social actors and organizations, finding in the *relational* environment among them the most appropriate arena for delivering decisions in a complex democratic world. The idea is that no one has the key, and therefore all stances are, in fact, just stances, and decisions are the outcome of the interplay between arguments. But there are other interesting ideas under this approach: first, the empowerment of non-competent knowledge and, as a consequence, of non-competent knowledge-holders like citizens and organizations belonging to the social and political context in which the issue is handled; second, that in the absence of anything like a shared truth – or a shared idea of what the common good should be for the community as a whole (the same idea of community has been severely put in question) – what really counts is basically to push the process ahead. The effective decision is the one that minimizes the risk of raising conflicts which, in advanced and fragmented democracies, have the power to block the process of decision-making.

Clearly, all that does not favour space, nor technical analysis. In fact space and analysis are largely absent in this area, which means that they are almost absent in recent city planning in general. Urban design, however, has witnessed a growing fortune in the last 15 years, especially – as one of the many ironies of our story – because *designing* future scenarios make them pretty easily understandable; that is, for the intrinsic discursive and communicative properties of the means. But how can we practise the design of spaces at large scales without falling in the same modernist top-down traps that we are escaping from? How can we practise analysis and competent knowledge in a form that fits a multi-actorial participatory interpretation of city building? Trying this does not mean practising an oxymoron? Well, yes, it does.

Practising an oxymoron: life-world, technical knowledge and the need for episteme diversity

The oxymoron is about participation and competent knowledge: should we dismiss the 'toolbox' of concepts, language and technicality that constitutes our disciplinary tradition in favour of a more democratic and experiential kind of knowledge? The answer we are giving here is: yes, *to some extent*. Or better: we should not *dismiss* the technical core of our disciplines, we should *work on it* in order to demolish barriers, target new programmes and goals and experiment with it in new arenas.

In a sense, keeping the problem in a pragmatic dimension, there are two things we can do in working on the question. On the one hand, we can place the technically informed arguments, the competent knowledge, in an uncomfortable, difficult, even hostile arena: an arena that pretends to understand, that does not trust jargon results and obscure lexicon, that, in a word, *challenges* the discipline from outside. Sustainability is therefore an ideal framework for urban studies: the sustainability agenda in fact only accepts open and multidisciplinary processes that include social action as well as the technical contribution. There are few doubts that a sustainability programme sets up different tables where arguments are translated into plain language, disciplinary jargons are considered unreceivable, the extraordinary information embedded in inhabitants' life-worlds are given relevance and obstructions due to the fragmentation of the traditional channels of political representation are at least partially overcome. These are favourable environments. Complex arenas, but vital. On the other hand, in order for this argument to be debatable in such arena, it must be well produced and – this is the point – it cannot be produced other than within its discipline. So the best thing we can do is to stay enrooted in our disciplines while being involved in the general game of systems in evolution.

Despite some counterarguments, disciplines have not disappeared. Perhaps it would be a good thing if they had done so, but they have not. Disciplines are always there; actually, it seems they have never been in better shape. The novelty is our awareness that our opinion, our representation, is just one of the many that are possible and legitimate, which means *the withdrawal from domination over knowledges*. This is what should drive us, first of all within our 'disciplinary home'. Stating that the disciplines have disappeared is just another way to let them stay where they are, untouched, firmly set to establish the argument's legitimacy about everything that moves around in the real world. While we jump towards the flowered gardens of the trans-disciplinary or the hyper-realistic tautology (the decision is right just because it was taken), disciplines are still in every office, in every seminar, in every handbook, proudly affirming their own tradition. The withdrawal from domination over knowledges is worth applying firstly where knowledges have been codified in teams and legions, set to face the traditional lethal enemy: relativism. There, *within* the disciplines, it is possible to question habits and organizations: to open them to contamination, simplify the jargon, adapt to plain confrontation, welcome the different and the unknown, with the consciousness that disciplinary honesty is the only handle available to give representations a certain solidity – representations that one day will be on the table when decisions are being framed, remanded, dealt with, taken, rejected, where other representations are intervening along the way. Sustainability sets the stage for entirely new arenas at the local level which constitute by themselves challenging and stimulating environments for our disciplinary endeavours.

Moreover, urban sustainability implies new visions that cannot leave technical analysis as it has always been: setting new goals for city planning and design, sustainability requires different analysis, because analysis is never objective but is rather, at least in part, the product of the same visions for which it sets the stage. But sustainability also requires the deep interaction between points of view coming from diverse fields and disciplines, as well as non-disciplinary areas and modes of understanding and experiencing the real world. If you do not know which place you belong to, you will never really be a voyager. If you do not know where your home is, you will never really experience the sense of homelessness that makes the voyage what it is. Building competent knowledge for multi-actorial arenas does mean 'certificating' it within the discipline, rewording the discipline, re-orienteering the discipline, overcoming the discipline.

What are the obstacles in front of this innovation? One obstacle is thinking that we can deal with fragmentation, uncertainty, the crisis of foundations, by means of a *particularly advanced* technical representation or initiative – thinking to find in *a sophistication of the tool* the means to control uncertainty, and that because the machine which produces arguments does it unsatisfactorily (implicit: unsatisfactorily relative to our desire of absoluteness), then we need another machine. Faster, or more flexible, or more coloured. This is a risk that threatens the so-called 'science of complexity' and its pretence to elaborate models which actually embed uncertainty, like statistical sciences' embedded models that deal with many variables, summarizing them in a description of the system as a whole: to elaborate, describe, quantify, model even the uncertain by means of a next-generation machine. In urban design history, an approach of this kind can easily be identified in the stream of 'evolutionary' urban design that emerged in the early 1960s, took the front stage with the PREVI competition in Lima, Peru, in 1969 and is still alive under the skin of the discipline – as the recent Quinta Monroy estate in Iquique and the subsequent 'Elemental competition for social housing estates' in Chile demonstrate. In this stream of research the project not only decides what is the proposed time-zero configuration of spaces, buildings and streets, but also decides what changes are admitted into being for the future time-one, time-two, time-three steps and so forth. An even more intriguing approach of the same kind tries to control complexity by nothing less than synthesizing the DNA, the inner code of change, with the aid of advanced computational resources (Frazer 1995, 2001; Soddu 1994; Soddu and Colabella 2005; Tsui 1999). Inspiring as such lines of action can be for all of us, nothing there is about incremental multi-actorial urban design; instead, it should be considered a power elevation of the project planning attitude, which expands to embrace and constrict the future by devitalizing the dimension of uncertainty (Figure 8.1). This *sophistication trap* is an obstacle of which scientists and urban designers should be aware; the *control* of complexity should not be considered a goal for scientific or whatever competent applications in sustainable arenas: the *activation* and, at best, the *interpretation* of complexity should be.

But there is an obstacle also for the strategies of social inclusion in decision-making: thinking of being able to manage complexity by governing the decisional processes, the 'negotiative', 'interactive', 'participatory' and, in any case, 'consensual' aspects of the process. Because at the end there is always 'consensus', but consensual approaches exhibit problems as well: problems of *democracy* (who establishes the criteria for the legitimation of a decision, though consensual? And what if that night, while the 'forum' decided, one was at the theatre? Or on vacation? Or in hospital? Or just felt too tired to go out? Do people not have the right to feel too tired?); problems of *demagogy* (who establishes the threshold beyond which the facilitator produces invasive behaviours? When, in short, the referee whistles always 'in one direction', affecting the final score?); problems of *rightness* (who guarantees that the shared decision is also the right one?). To state that does not imply denying to the political-technical-cultural élites the possibility of playing a socially useful role of avant-garde. Is it not exactly that – to put it brutally – such élites are paid for by society as a whole? Is it not true, following Lyotard (1986), that to some extent consensus brutalizes the heterogeneity of linguistic games? Moreover, too often the competition of arguments in a discursive arena is not really free: actors do not start from the same point and with the same (cultural, linguistic, experiential) resources, and after all the arguments that win are just the *stronger* (in the given situation), which does not necessarily mean the *better* for the community. This is an obstacle of which advocates of, and participants in, processes of consensus-building should be aware: the control of complexity should not be considered a goal for participatory decision-makers in sustainable arenas either.

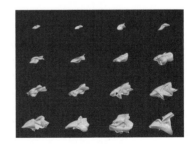

8.1 The sophistication trap at work in John Frazer's – otherwise attractive – 'generative design' application

Therefore, taking the stance that either competent or life-world knowledge is best does not seem to help in any way. Actually, complex arenas and problems badly need both. For instance, thinking that any competent interpretation is in itself a superstructure, a coverage, a mystification of some 'authentic' and 'hidden' reality, can lead scientists to a sort of self-slavery where their point of view is simply omitted. City planners or anthropologists take off their clothes in order to stand naked in front of their statements, limiting themselves to stating them. But is not this 'minimalist' attitude just another form of abrasion? Are not the points of view of city planners, anthropologists and scientists of all kinds just another manifestation of reality's diversity, which in turn constitutes and enriches reality, often in surprising ways, often very brilliantly? For each renouncement of interpretation we have a world which is poorer and more stupid, not truer nor necessarily fairer. If biodiversity is a value for naturalists, should we not consider, even just for fun, 'episteme diversity' being a value for knowledge?

The tools

What is needed is not a precisely mathematical procedure that treats the environments we live in like some great machine that we do not quite understand, but an approach to the design of the lived-world of both everyday and exceptional experiences – an approach that is wholly self-conscious yet does not seek to create wholly designed environments into which people must be fitted, an approach that is responsive to local structures of meaning and experience, to particular situations and to the variety of levels of meaning of place; an approach that takes its inspiration from the existential significance of place, the need that many people have found for a profound attachment to places, and the ontological principles of dwelling and sparing identified by Heidegger (Vycinas, 1961). Such an approach cannot provide precise solutions to clearly defined problems, but, proceeding from an appreciation of the significance of place and the particular activities and local situations, it would perhaps provide a way of outlining some of the main directions and possibilities, thus allowing scope for individual and groups to make their own places, and to give those places authenticity and significance by modifying them and by dwelling in them.

Edward in Larice and Macdonald (1976: 123)

The subsequent chapters in this book illustrate tools, fairly immediately usable instruments – be they computer programs, methodologies of work or handbooks – to inform and guide design towards the main goals of vitality, density, imageability, reachability and efficiency.

All these tools were generated to respond to an increasing demand for spatial analysis to be available in a format which is informative, understandable and practical for those involved in the decision-making and design process as well as for those directly interested by change. Also, they were produced thanks to the development of more advanced and comprehensive knowledge systems for inclusive design, such as GIS (which is shifting towards a strong human geography focus) and multi-modal assessment techniques which are able to take into account different modalities of environmental experience and can therefore supply more precise and comprehensive information about it. All the authors who contributed a chapter, that is a tool, are heavily involved in the environment analysis field, and their work is considered by the editors of this book to be of some significance to the debate on time-conscious urban design.

In particular, the chapters include the following contributions.

Chapter 9

This work on travel time budgets relates the density of local neighbourhood and metropolitan centres to sustainable transport, to help urban designers target and plan the activity intensity of development in conjunction to better infrastructure, and allow to car ownership without succumbing to its dependency.

Chapter 10

This work on mixed development stems from a lack of clarity on prime concepts such as mixed use, and sustainable mix in both legislation and design guidance. The tool blends data analysis and GIS synthesis of aspects that constitute the compact city, to which it is then possible to apply other sets of data for an assessment of the quality of life.

Chapter 11

The multiple central assessment offers an evidence-based approach to the understanding and mapping of centrality in cities. Centrality turns out to be both a key factor in the incremental evolution of complex systems, not limited to urban or spatial systems, and a driving force in shaping the potential that any space in a city offers to the life of the community as a whole in many fundamental and interrelated ways.

Chapter 12

This investigation of the performance of transport precincts helps select between alternatives, considering multidimensional factors and leaving leverage to local and regional communities to identify better responsive solutions to specific circumstances.

Chapter 13

The chapter outlines street audit and mapping of accessibility to transport nodes for vulnerable groups to assist both design and planning.

Chapter 14

This work is on the assessment of environmental qualities – in particular energy efficiency and human comfort in relation to morphological characteristics of the built space.

Chapters 15 and 16

These chapters propose methods for user engagement in design visioning at different urban scales which progressively builds environmental awareness.

Chapter 17

This chapter presents a tool which combines behavioural maps and GIS to study place performance for evaluation, implementation and management.

Chapter 18

This multi-modal tool helps uncover experiential characteristics of places, adding a human dimension to more conventional analytical techniques and to how physical settings are developed.

Chapters 19 and 20

These deal with the experience of place by usually neglected mainstream groups, people with learning disabilities and children, to add layers of fundamental relevance to design and performance of place.

The tools can be organized according to a number of principles, but two are more evident and perhaps interesting: *spatially*, in relation to the territory they refer to and can comment upon; and *functionally*, in relation to what they can contribute to, be this design or normative.

In the first instance, the area of influence of Chapters 9, 11 and 12 is the regional and urban scale; that of Chapters 10, 13, 15 and 16 is the neighbourhood scale; and that of Chapters 14, 17, 18 and 19 is 'places'. Still, the edges of this spatial classification are very fuzzy, each example bordering between different scales, and they all acknowledge that local episodes or characteristics have an impact at greater scales and vice versa.

Functionally, some of the contributions can directly guide decision-making and are therefore more normative (Chapters 9, 10, 12, 13, 15 and 16), while others are more related to design and its implementation, such as Chapters 14, 17, 18 and 19.

Since the 'key concept' of this book is what we called evolutionary urban design, it is important to mention how the tools address the issue of time and evolution in the work they refer to. They do so directly and indirectly. Those chapters that focus on the perceptual dimension of space (Chapters 15, 17, 18 and 19) to ascertain the value it holds for individuals make an intrinsic reference to the notion of personal time and development. Time counts because they study personal responses; the perceived quality of space depends on age, emotional development, use and goals.

For the other chapters the concept of time is extruded into the future, clearly bringing concepts of accessibility, density and development of the built form to the sustainable planning agenda, and thankfully clarifying its mystic nature. This is quite refreshing on two fronts. First of all, our frequent references to time-sensitive urban design should not be misunderstood as nostalgia for the past or even worse as a rejection of anything new on a scale greater than the building and the occasional space in between: while urban designers should not lose sight of the goal of social accountability and environmental sustainability, they can achieve these in stages (see Chapter 9 in particular). A clear reference to this are some of the cited examples: The Calls in Leeds and the Merchant City in Glasgow. On the second count, these chapters offer methodologies and thresholds to work with, to test development, to assess existing qualities and plan change, contributing a great deal towards making the ineffable concept of sustainability a bit clearer.

There is hopefully a lasting lesson arising from our collection of ideas: that sustainable, socially responsible development can happen and we are getting there. We hope that some of the examples we present will persuade the reader this is the case, and help him or her to contribute their bit.

References

Edward, R. (1976) 'Prospects for places', in Larice, M. and Macdonald, E. (2006) *The Urban Designer Reader*, Routledge, London.

Frazer, J. (1995) *An Evolutionary Architecture*, Architecture Association Publications, London.

Jacobs, A. and Appleyard, D. (1987) 'Toward an urban design manifesto', *Journal of the American Planning Association*, 53(1): 112–120.

Lyotard, J. (1986) *Le Postmoderne Expliqué aux Enfanys*, Edition Galilée, Paris.

Soddu, C. (1994) 'The design of morphogenesis: an experimental research about the logical procedures in design processes', *Demetra Magazine*. Available at: http://soddu2.dst.polimi.it.

Soddu, C. and Colabella, E. (2005) 'Argenia, a mother tongue in infinite variations', DCC conference workshop, MIT Boston.

Tsui, E. (1999) *Evolutionary Architecture: Nature as a Basis for Design*, John Wiley, New York.

Vycinas, V. (1961) *Earth and Gods: An Introduction to the Philosophy of Martin Heidegger*, Martinus Nijhoff, The Hague.

9 Travel time budgets as a tool for sustainable urban design

Peter Newman

Introduction

Cities are shaped by transport and hence sustainable transport – good transit, walkability and cycling facilities – should help shape sustainable cities. This chapter tries to show how this can be facilitated by urban designers through knowing how dense to make centres. This is analysed through a theoretical approach based on travel time budgets (TTBs).

In order to provide policy options to reduce traffic, more sustainable transport options must be provided that can be competitive with the car in terms of time. Cities need to have corridors where a faster public transport option is provided than the general flow of traffic, and centres need to enable walking and cycling to have priority over cars (Newman and Kenworthy 2007). Urban designers play a critical role in this, as there must be sufficient density and mix to enable sustainable transport options to be viable. The question is: how much development is needed to make sustainable transport work?

Transport and city form: why the TTB was created

Transport behaviour is limited by the Marchetti travel time budget of around one hour's average travel time per day. Cities are structured around this, as it appears to be a basic fact of human nature that we need to fit around this time constraint. Studies in the UK show that the one-hour travel time budget has held for at least the last 600 years of urban living (SACTRA 1994).

Our global cities database shows that most cities keep within this, and where they go over this the politics of transport means that either land use changes or infrastructure is changed to adapt (Newman and Kenworthy 1999).

Historically this has meant that:

- Walking cities were (and are) dense, mixed-use areas no more than five kilometres across, as this is how far you can walk in one hour (or an average journey of half an hour there and half an hour back). These cities were the major urban form for 8,000 years, and remain important as the core functional centres of all cities.
- Transit cities from 1850 to 1950 were based on trams and trains, which meant they could spread 20 – 30 kilometres with dense clusters of corridors following the rail lines and stations. The centres remained as walking cities, but strung along the rail lines.
- Automobile cities from the 1950s onwards could spread 50 kilometres in all directions, and at low density.

Most cities have some part of each of these city types. Many cities are reaching the limits of their urban form based on automobile systems, and are looking for a way out for the future. Local and global sustainability issues at the metropolitan and neighbourhood levels are now framing urban policy, and hence planners are looking for tools to rebuild more sustainably. Most cities, certainly all Australian cities, are trying to reassert the role of transit along corridors for the metropolitan system and the importance of centres to provide a local solution for more sustainable transport (Newman and Kenworthy 2007).

Travel time will still drive these new plans, as people will not live for long in a situation where they go over this constraint. The biological basis of the Marchetti constant seems to be a need for a more reflective or restorative period between home and work, but it cannot go on for too long before people become very frustrated due to the need to be more occupied rather than just 'wasting' time between activities. This can be used to help frame what urban designers need to do in helping make cities more sustainable.

What kind of centres are needed?

The link between urban intensity and automobile dependence has been repeatedly confirmed by numerous authors and studies (Newman and

Kenworthy 1989, 1999; Kenworthy and Laube 1999; Cervero 1995, 1998; Holtzclaw 1990, 1994; Naess, 1993a, 1993b). Our international comparative data on cities show that when measures of urban density (population per urban hectare or jobs per urban hectare or both together – called activity intensity) are correlated with either car use or passenger transport energy use per capita, extremely strong relationships are found, with r-square values between 0.77 and 0.82.

Figure 9.1 shows the relationship between per capita car travel and activity intensity in 58 higher-income metropolitan areas around the world, revealing an extremely tight relationship where some 82 per cent of the variance in car use internationally can be explained by variations in activity intensity (Kenworthy and Laube 2001).

When activity intensity is used on the horizontal axis, the point on the graph where rapid acceleration in car dependence appears to occur seems to be around 35 people and

ACTIVITY INTENSITY VERSUS PRIVATE CAR TRAVEL IN 58 HIGHER-INCOME CITIES

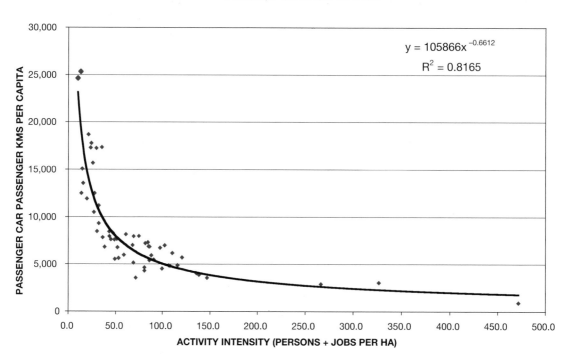

$$y = 105866x^{-0.6612}$$
$$R^2 = 0.8165$$

9.1 Activity intensity versus passenger car use in 58 higher-income cities, 1995

jobs per hectare; the error band is around 30–40 per hectare.[1]

The same shaped relationships can be found within cities. Transport energy studies by the authors on Sydney and Melbourne local government areas (LEAs) over a 22-year period show a sharp reduction in per capita transport energy use (and by implication car use) as density reaches certain cut-off levels. Studies from 1980 for Melbourne and 1981 for Sydney reveal r-square values of 0.64 in each case when activity intensity is correlated with per capita passenger transport energy use. The data have been recently collected again for 2002 for these two cities, and show an even stronger relationship between transport energy use per capita and land-use intensity, with an r-square value of 0.74 for Melbourne (Figure 9.2) and 0.70 for Sydney. The same clear influence of urban land-use intensity thus emerges, despite the fact that in this 20-year period the inner, higher-density local areas have become significantly wealthier than the outer areas. Wealth seems to be much less of an issue in determining transport activity than urban design.

The interesting threshold point at around 35 people and jobs per hectare is not something that has been unnoticed by others who have collected urban data. Calthorpe (1993) came to a similar figure based on his impressions of what makes a viable centre. Holtzclaw et al. (2002) have more recently compiled detailed data on San Francisco, Los Angeles and Chicago, with the same pattern of sharp increases in car use below this kind of density. Data have been examined for cities as different as Paris (INRETS 1995), New York (Newman and Kenworthy 1989) and San Francisco (Holtzclaw 1990). Data for the latter two are shown in Table 9.1. Naess (1993a, 1993b) developed similar data for Scandinavian cities. Jeffrey Zupan, quoted in Owen (2004), states the following about the idea of a critical threshold density:

> The basic point is that you need density to support public transit. In all cities, not just in New York, once you get above a certain density two things happen. First, you get less travel by mechanical means, which is another way of saying you get more people walking and biking; and second, you get a decrease in trips by auto and an increase in trips by transit. That threshold tends to be around seven dwellings per acre. Once you cross that line, a bus company can put buses out there, because they know they're going to have enough passengers to support a reasonable frequency of service.

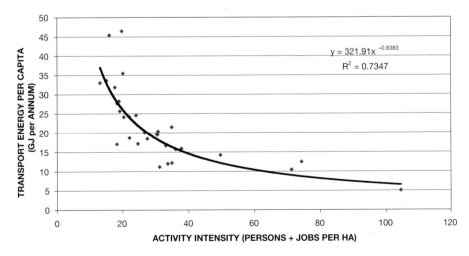

TRANSPORT ENERGY USE VERSUS ACTIVITY INTENSITY IN MELBOURNE, 2002

$y = 321.91x^{-0.8383}$

$R^2 = 0.7347$

9.2 Per capita passenger transport energy use versus activity intensity in Melbourne LGAs, 2002

Table 9.1 Urban density versus gasoline use for the San Francisco and New York regions

City and area	Gasoline use (MJ per capita)	Urban density (persons per ha)
San Francisco(1990)		
Central San Francisco	17,449	128
Inner city (City of San Francisco)	33,337	57
Middle suburb with strong sub-centre (Rockridge/Berkeley)	45,548	25
Middle suburb with no sub-centre (Walnut Creek)	49,641	10
Outer suburb (Danville-San Ramon)	67,090	5
New York (1980)		
Central City (New York County, including Manhattan)	11,860	251
Inner city (City of New York)	20,120	107
Whole city (Tri-State Metropolitan Region)	44,033	20
Outer suburbs	59,590	13

Seven dwellings per acre at a reasonable dwelling occupancy is equivalent to around 35 – 40 persons per hectare. In Grenoble a similar study found that bicycling became very significant at around that density and transit started growing significantly, but most of all it took off at about 50 persons hectare. Walking became highly significant at 100 people per hectare, and this has also been found in other studies.

The question therefore arises as to what may be behind this.[2] Questions of wealth do not appear to be driving this phenomenon, as there is an inverse relationship between urban intensity and household income in Australian cities and a variety of wealth patterns across all the cities quoted above. As the data on Melbourne (Table 9.2) indicate, it is the poorer households who are driving more, using public transport less and walking less.

There are obviously other factors beyond the intensity of activity affecting transport, otherwise there would be an even stronger relationship within cities between activity intensity and transport patterns; such factors include the network of services provided, income, prices, cultural factors, etc. but all of these can also be linked back to the intensity of activity in various ways. Thus although many discussions have tried to explain transport in non-land-use terms (e.g. Brindle 1996; Mindali *et al.* 2004), the data suggest that the physical layout of a city does have a fundamental impact on movement patterns. The role of this chapter is to take the next step and explain how the relationship between transport and activity intensity works.

How does TTB work?

Some policy-relevant physical design parameters can be calculated by using the activity intensity data suggested above as the threshold or critical value for creating less car-dependent urban centres – both local neighbourhood centres and metropolitan centres.

Table 9.2 Differences in wealth and travel patterns from the urban core to the fringe in Melbourne

	Core	Inner	Middle	Fringe
Percentage of households earning >$70,000 p.a.	12	11	10	6
Car use (trips/day/cap)	2.12	2.52	2.86	3.92
Public transport (trips/day/cap)	0.66	0.46	0.29	0.21
Walk/bike (trips/day/cap)	2.62	1.61	1.08	0.81

Source: Kenworthy and Newman (2001)

Local neighbourhood centre

A pedestrian catchment area or 'ped-shed', based on a ten-minute walk, creates an area of approximately 220 – 550 hectares for walking speeds of 5 – 8 km/h. Thus for an area of around 300 hectares developed at 35 people and jobs per hectare, there is a threshold requirement of approximately *10,000 residents and jobs within this ten-minute walking area or around 1 km radius from the centre*. The range would be from about 8,000 – 19,000 based on the 5 – 8 km/h speeds. Some centres will have a lot more jobs than others, but the important physical planning guideline is to have a combined minimum activity intensity of residents and jobs necessary for a reasonable local centre and a public transport service to support it. Other authors support these kinds of numbers for viable local centres and public transport services (Pushkarev and Zupan 1997; Ewing 1996; Frank and Pivo 1994; Cervero *et al.* 2004). The number of residents or jobs can be increased to the full 10,000 in any combination, as residents and jobs are similar in terms of transport demand. Either way, the number suggests a threshold below which services become non-competitive without relying primarily on car access to extend the catchment area.

Many new car-dependent suburbs have densities more like 12 persons per hectare and hence have only one-third of the population and jobs required for a viable centre. When a centre is built for such suburbs it tends to have just shops, with job densities little higher than the surrounding population densities. Hence the ped-shed never reaches the kind of intensity which enables a walkable environment to be created. Large areas of car parking are needed to make the centre functional in terms of viable numbers within the Marchetti travel time budget. Many New Urbanist developments are primarily emphasizing changes to improve the legibility and permeability of street networks, with less attention to the density of activity. As important as such changes are to the physical layout of streets, we should not be surprised when the resulting centres are not able to attract viable commercial arrangements and have only weak public transport. Although it may have the designation of a 'walkable centre' due to street layout, a centre will never work as such while its density remains below this threshold. However, centres can be built in stages, with much lower numbers to begin with, provided the goal is to reach a density of at least 35 per hectare through enabling infill at higher intensities.

Metropolitan centres

The 100 people and jobs per hectare point where walking becomes dominant is consistent with our experience of the world's old city centres that were built around walking. New centres like Vancouver that have developed housing for 100,000 new residents in the past decade are also strongly walking oriented, with reports of substantial reductions in car use (40,000 trips per day) and increases in walking/cycling (over 100,000 per day) (see City of Vancouver 1997). In these metropolitan centres everything is within half an hour by walking, and most things indeed are within a ten-minute walk, or a total of half an hour including transit using metros, buses, light rail or a short car trip (often taxi).

If a ten-minute ped-shed is created at these densities then you end up with around *100,000 people and jobs that are required for such metropolitan centres within a 1 km radius*. If a 30-minute ped-shed is created, then the area of the catchment extends to between 2,000 and 5,000 hectares or a 3 km radius. Thus 35 people and jobs per hectare would provide the same 100,000 residents and jobs within this 30-minute walking area (based on 3,000 hectares) or about a 3 km radius. The range again is from around 70,000 to 175,000 people and jobs.

Thus this number of 100,000 residents and jobs could provide for a viable metropolitan centre, based on either walking predominantly if it is in the ten-minute ped-shed (1 km radius) or transit and walking within the half-hour ped-shed (3 km radius). Fewer numbers than this mean services in a metropolitan centre are non-viable and it becomes necessary to increase the centre's catchment through widespread dependence on driving from much farther afield. This also means that the human design qualities of the centre are compromised because of the need for excessive amounts of parking. Of course, many driving trips within a walking ped-shed still occur. However, if sufficient amenities and services are provided then only short car trips are needed, which is still part of making the centre less car-dependent.

If a centre is already at these densities then it is entirely feasible to try and remove the impact of cars on the centre; this will be successful, as the densities are sufficient to allow viability based on the other modes. Thus the viability of Copenhagen was continued during its 30-year process of removing 2 per cent of its car parking each year and facilitating biking and walking (Gehl et al. 2006).

'Footloose jobs', particularly those related to the global economy, can theoretically go anywhere in a city and can make the difference between a viable centre or not. However, there is considerable evidence that such jobs are locating in dense centres of activity due to the need for networking and quick 'face-to-face' meetings between professionals. High-amenity, walking-scale environments are better able to attract such jobs because they offer the kind of environmental quality, liveability and diversity that these professionals are seeking. Thus cities attempting to create such work opportunities will need to see that they do not come easily below these threshold densities.

Politics of sustainable transport and urban design

The growth of cities globally will continue. Wealth is likely to increase across all cities, and in the past this has meant greater mobility based on greater car use. Just as has occurred with electricity growth being decoupled from wealth, it is entirely possible to imagine mobility being decoupled from wealth. Trends suggest this is already beginning to occur (Newman and Kenworthy 1999, 2007; Newman 2003; Kenworthy and Laube 2005). The key to this move towards sustainability is better provision of access to transit that is faster than cars along corridors, and better provision for walking and cycling in local areas. However, urban designers must be supportive in land-use structure of intensive centres with minimum land-use activity

intensity in local centres of 35 people and jobs per hectare (and preferably closer to 50) if transit is to work, and 100 people and jobs per hectare if it is to be predominantly a walking-based metropolitan centre. This is due to a fundamental need to ensure travel time is still within a budget of one hour a day.

Conclusions

Sustainability is a powerful and relevant concept for managing the cities of the world as we move rapidly to an urbanized global economy. Sustainable transport is not just a case of developing better technology. We must also develop ways of overcoming car dependence. This has been explained in terms of the Marchetti constant on travel time budgets and the average speed of modes in cities. With few options for sustainable transport modes if travel time budgets are to be maintained, the main planning agenda for cities in the twenty-first century is to build reduced automobile dependence through better infrastructure and urban design. Other economic and social programmes will help, but if the infrastructure to enable people to travel by sustainable transport modes within the Marchetti budget limits is not provided, then it will be very hard to make much change happen. Sustainable transport will require ways of accommodating car ownership but not car dependence. It will require that viable, convenient and speed-competitive sustainable transport modes are provided in such a way that people will choose them for most trip purposes. Urban designers can ensure that this happens by building local neighbourhood centres that are at least 35 people and jobs per hecatre and metropolitan centres that are at least 100 people and jobs per hectare.

Notes

1   Note that the density figures referred to here are genuine 'urban density', in that they use total urbanized land as the denominator (residential, commercial, industrial land, local parks and open spaces, plus roads and any other urban land uses). The denominator excludes large areas of undeveloped land such urban zoned yet-to-be-developed land, regional-scale open spaces, agriculture and forestry land, etc. The relationships shown in this chapter will not work with other

measures of density, such as residential density, because these are irrelevant to transport issues.

2   Brindle (1994) suggested that our attempts to link transport and density were flawed by a statistical problem involving per capita relationships on both axes. Evill (1995) explained how the graphical relationship was quite correct. If the per capita factor is removed from both then you just relate transport for the whole city to the area of the city. This is no difference when it comes to policy on how to reduce transport energy (reduce the area for the city, i.e. increase its density), but it is harder to follow. The emphasis on the ecological footprint of cities today perhaps makes it easier to see by just presenting transport energy and the area of the city, but in terms of planning for people and jobs it is more policy relevant to see the threshold density figure of 35 per hectare and how cities or parts of cities become much more or less auto-dependent as density varies.

References and bibliography

Brindle, R. E. (1994) 'Lies, damned lies and "automobile dependence" – some hyperbolic reflections', *Australian Transport Research Forum*, 94: 117–131.

Brindle, R. E. (1996) 'Transport and urban form: the not so vital link', *Transport and Liveable Cities*, District 8/ITE Australia Section Inaugural Regional Conference, Melbourne.

Calthorpe, P. (1993) *The Next American Metropolis: Ecology, Community and the American Dream*, Harvard University Press, Boston.

Cervero, R. (1995) 'Sustainable new towns: Stockholm's rail served satellites', *Cities*, 12(1): 41–51.

Cervero, R. (1998) *The Transit Metropolis*, Island Press, Washington, D.C.

Cervero, R. *et al.* (2004) *Transit Oriented Development in America: Experiences, Challenges and Prospects*, Transportation Research Board, National Research Council, Washington, D.C.

City of Vancouver (1997) *Transportation Plan*, May, City of Vancouver.

Evill, B. (1995) 'Population, urban density, and fuel use: eliminating spurious correlation', *Urban Policy and Research*, 13(1): 29–36.

Ewing, R. (1996) *Transit Oriented Development in the Sun Belt, Transportation Research Record 1552*, Transportation Research Board, National Research Council, Washington, D.C.

Frank, L. and Pivo, G. (1994) *Relationships Between Land Use and Travel Behaviour in the Puget Sound Region*, WA-RD 351.1, Washington State, Department of Transportation.

Gehl, J., Gemzoe, L., Kirknaes, S. and Ekland, B. (2006) *New City Life*, The Danish Architectural Press, Copenhagen.

Holtzclaw, J. (1990) *Explaining Urban Density and Transit Impacts on Auto Use*, Natural Resources Defense Council and The Sierra Club, San Francisco.

Holtzclaw, J. (1994) *Using Residential Patterns and Transit to Decrease Auto Dependence and Costs*, Natural Resources Defense Council, San Francisco.

Holtzclaw, J., Clear, R., Dittmar, H., Goldstein, D. and Haas, P. (2002) 'Location efficiency: neighbourhood and socio-economic characteristics determine auto ownership and use – studies in Chicago, Los Angeles and San Francisco', *Transportation Planning and Technology*, 25(1): 1–27.

INRETS (1995) *Budgets Energie Environnement des Déplacements (BEED) en Ile-de-France – Analyse de la Dépense Energétique et des Emissions Polluantes Liées à la Mobilité des Franciliens. Rapport de Convention ADEME-INRETS n°690–9306-RB*, Institut National de Recherche sur les Transports et leur Sécurité, Arceuil, Paris.

Kenworthy, J. (2002) 'Traffic 2042 – a more global perspective', *Transport Policy*, 9(1): 11–15.

Kenworthy, J.R. and Laube, F.B. (1996) 'Automobile dependence in cities: an international comparison of urban transport and land use patterns with implications for sustainability', *Environmental Impact Assessment Review*, Special Issue: Managing Urban Sustainability, 16(4–6): 279–308.

Kenworthy, J.R. and Laube, F.B. (1999) 'Patterns of automobile dependence in cities: an international overview of key physical and economic dimensions with some implications for urban policy', *Transportation Research A*, 33: 691–723.

Kenworthy, J, and Laube, F. (2001) 'The Millennium Cities Database for Sustainable Transport', *Brussels and Perth: International Union of Public Transport (UITP), and Institute for Sustainability and Technology Policy (ISTP)*, CD ROM database.

Kenworthy, J. and Laube, F. (2005) 'An international comparative perspective on sustainable transport in European Cities', *European Spatial Research and Policy*, 12(1): 11–50.

Kenworthy J., Laube, F., Raad, T., Poboon, C. and Guia, B. (1999) *An International Sourcebook of Automobile Dependence in Cities, 1960–1990*, University Press of Colorado, Boulder.

Kenworthy, J. and Newman, P. (2001) 'Melbourne in an international comparison of urban transport systems', *A Report to the Department of Infrastructure, Melbourne as part of the Melbourne Strategy*, Institute for Sustainability and Technology Policy, Perth.

Marchetti, C. (1994) 'Anthropological invariants in travel behaviour', *Technical Forecasting and Social Change*, 47(1): 75–78.

Mercat, N. (2006) 'Evaluating exposure to the risk of accident in the Grenoble conurbation', *European Transport Conference*, 2006, Strasbourg.

Mindali, O., Raveh, A. and Salomon, I. (2004) 'Urban density and energy consumption: a new look at old statistics', *Transportation Research, Part A*, 38: 143–162.

Naess, P. (1993a) *Energy Use for Transport in 22 Nordic Towns*, NIBR Report No. 2, Norwegian Institute for Urban and Regional Research, Oslo.

Naess, P. (1993b) 'Transportation energy in Swedish towns and regions', *Scandinavian Housing and Planning Research*, 10(4): 187–206.

Newman, P.W.G. and Kenworthy, J.R. (1989) *Cities and Automobile Dependence: An International Sourcebook*, Gower, Aldershot.

Newman, P.W.G. and Kenworthy, J.R. (1999) *Sustainability and Cities: Overcoming Automobile Dependence*, Island Press, Washington, D.C.

Newman, P. (2001) 'Railways and reurbanisation in Perth', in Williams, J. and Stimson, R. (eds.) *Case Studies in Planning Success*, Elsevier, New York.

Newman, P.W.G. (2003) 'Global cities, transport, energy and the future: will ecosocialisation reverse the historic trends?', in Low, N. and Gleeson, B. (eds.) *Making Urban Transport Sustainable*, Palgrave-Macmillan, Basingstoke.

Newman, P. and Kenworthy, J. (2007) 'Greening urban transportation', *State of the World 07*, Worldwatch Institute, Norton, Washington, D.C.

Owen, D. (2004) 'Green Manhattan: why New York is the greenest city in the US', *The New Yorker*, 18 October.

Pushkarev, B. and Zupan, J. (1997) *Public Transportation and Land Use Policy*, Indiana Press, Bloomington and London.

SACTRA (1994) *Trunk Roads and the Generation of Traffic*, Department of Transport, London.

Tolley, R. (ed.) (2003) *Sustainable Transport: Planning for Walking and Cycling in Urban Environments*, Woodhead Publishing, Cambridge.

10 The generation of diversity: mixed use and urban sustainability

Graeme Evans and Jo Foord

Introduction

This chapter presents the development of a GIS-based analysis and planning tool arising from a study of mixed-use inner-city areas. The study forms part of a major research project, 'VivaCity-2020: Urban Sustainability for the 24-hour City', supported under the UK Engineering and Physical Sciences Research Council's Sustainable Urban Environment programme. The meta-theme of sustainable development, as defined in Brundtland (1987), has been operationalized in the UK in terms of the performance and progress of a set of quality of life indicators (DETR 2000), applied at national, regional and local 'quality of life counts' levels. It is at the local level that quality of life is both experienced and expressed, and where local governance, environmental management and liveability are most manifest.

VivaCity has taken an ambitious approach to interrogating urban sustainability and developing practical solutions and a knowledge base by which urban design, planning and development can be better integrated and understood (see www.vivacity2020.org). Uniquely, this has entailed empirical research into the social, economic, environmental and related design and planning processes that contribute to urban quality of life. This includes environmental quality such as air and noise pollution, crime, housing layout and amenities such as public toilets. The notion of the compact city, which is the subject of this particular toolkit, encompasses:

1 social mix – income, housing tenure, demography, visitors, lifestyles;

2 economic mix – activity, industry, scales (micro to large), consumption and production;

3 physical land-use mix – planning use class, vertical and horizontal, amenity/open space;

4 temporal mix (of items 1 – 3) – 24-hour economy, shared use of premises/space, e.g. street markets, entertainment, live work.

These urban environmental elements that combine to determine the quality of life in higher-density, mixed-use locations can be triangulated in terms of the key features shown in Figure 10.1. These elements have traditionally been treated as separate factors in urban policy and practice, but their dynamic interaction and conflicts are fundamental to understanding urban carrying capacity and the impacts of development and land-use change.

Why was this tool created: mixed use or mixed messages?

The imperatives driving the promotion of mixed-use and high-density residential and employment land use – 'densification' – derive from core aspects of the urban sustainability agenda. These include the demand for additional housing arising from increased population, inward migration and social change (e.g. single/childless couples, ageing population) and limits to supply

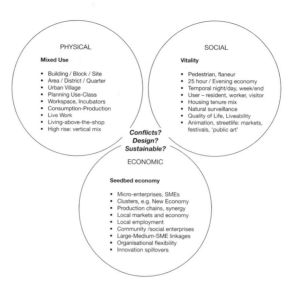

10.1 Mixed-use elements

due to current density levels and land use and development control on green-belt land. Another factor is the need to reduce car and other vehicular use in order to reduce carbon emissions and pollution. Solutions include the increased use of brownfield sites (previously developed land) as well as the reuse of non-residential buildings (e.g. industrial premises) for housing and services employment and facilities, and the development of higher-density, mixed-use buildings for housing, retail, commercial/office and amenities (e.g. health, leisure) – thus encouraging local employment and consequent reduced travel to work and routine activities (Evans 2005). The advantages of greater mixed-use development are summarized in Table 10.1.

While mixed-use, higher-density development and compact city hierarchies now underpin sustainable communities and housing growth plans, these basic concepts are reflected neither in legislation nor in guidance which can inform the design, location and impact assessment of mixed-use. For example, there is no planning use class for mixed use, nor an institutional property investment category (separate residential, retail and commercial sectors), and thus no detailed standards on what constitutes a sustainable mix, at what scale or in what combination of activity (Evans, 2005). Conversely, building regulations can restrict and limit the flexible use of space. In short, this is a policy panacea without a sound evidence base.

Table 10.1 The advantages of greater mixed-use development

Concentration and diversity of activities		
Vitality	Less need to travel	Local economy and clusters
A more secure environment	Less reliance on car	Production chain Innovation spillovers
More attractive and better-quality town centres	More use of and opportunity for public transport	More local employment and services

Economic, social and environmental benefits
Source: Adapted from DoE (1995)

Plate 1 Land use by floor (ground, first,
above-first floor). © Crown Copyright.
Ordnance Survey. All rights reserved.

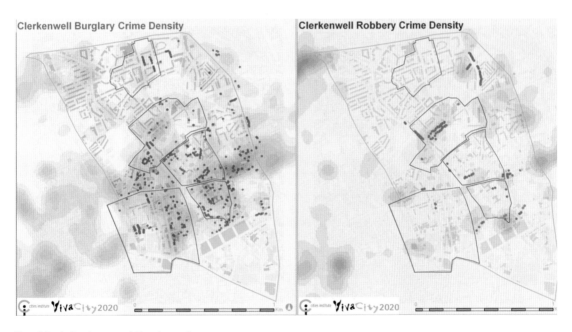

Plate 2 Proximity of commercial burglary and
offices, and 'street' crime and evening economy
(bars, clubs, restaurants). © Crown Copyright.
Ordnance Survey. All rights reserved.

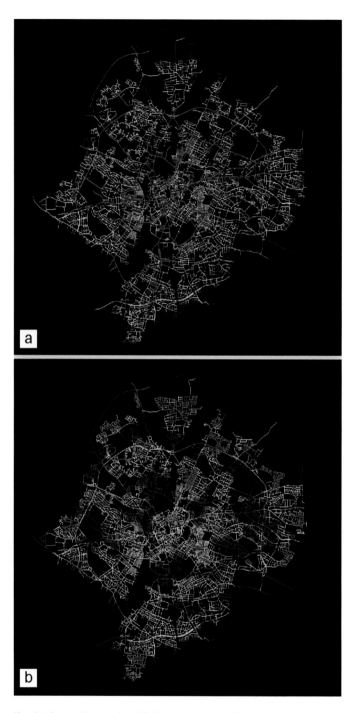

Plate 3 Leicester, UK: mapping global betweenness (a) and local (d=1.600mt) closeness (b). The two indices capture two of the many different hidden hierarchies that are inherent properties of the urban structure always at work together in shaping the cognitive and geographic dimension of our relationship with urban spaces. Application developed within the City Form research framework.

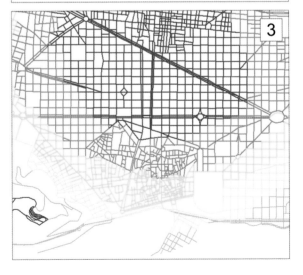

Plate 4 Barcelona, Spain: MCA shows closeness centrality investigated locally (1. d=1.200mt; 2. d=2.400mt) and globally (3). The centrality of contemporary places retains clues of the process of the city's historical evolution: here the Rambla, which lies on the footprint of the ancient city walls, emerges as a 'canyon' of low centrality at the neighbourhood (1) scale, not as a peak as could be expected. It is a peak, actually, at the district (2) and, to a lesser extent, at the global (3) levels. Application developed in partnership with the Agencia de Ecologia Urbana of Barcelona.

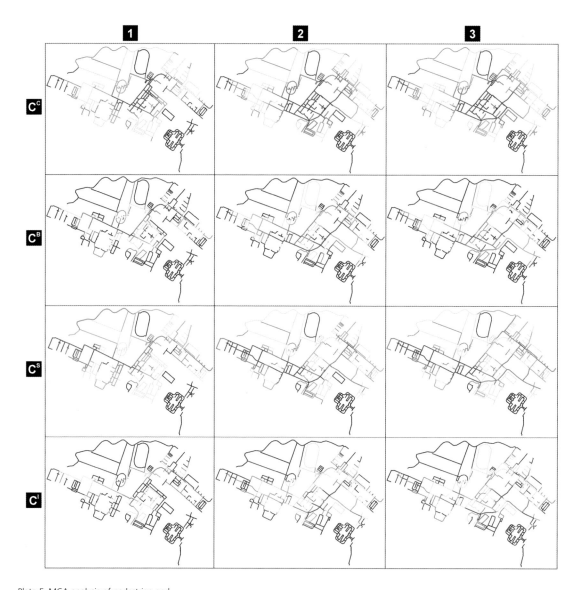

Plate 5 MCA analysis of pedestrian and cycle paths in the university campus of Parma, northern Italy: existing situation (col. 1), first alternative proposal 'the spine' (col. 2) and second alternative proposal 'the ring' (col. 3); centrality: closeness (C^C), betweenness (C^B), straightness (C^S) and information (C^I). The spine solution result was more consistent and was adopted as the basis for the final urban design plan. Application developed in partnership with Rivi Engineering, Italy.

Plate 6 Fruitvale Transit Village. Located in Oakland, California, the Fruitvale Transit Village combines affordable housing, retail, employment and community services such as seniors', daycare and healthcare centres, and a library in a pedestrian- and bicycle-friendly, transit-oriented urban environment. This photograph was taken from the BART train station platform.

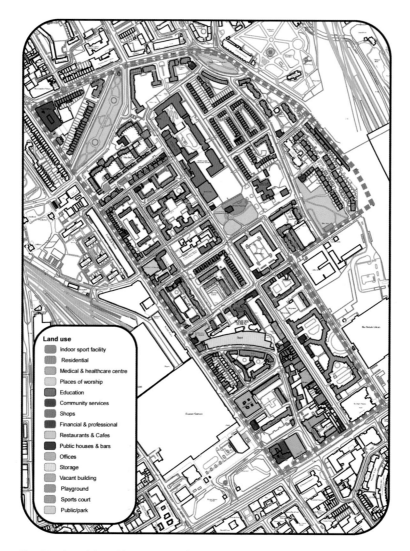

Land use
- Indoor sport facility
- Residential
- Medical & healthcare centre
- Places of worship
- Education
- Community services
- Shops
- Financial & professional
- Restaurants & Cafes
- Public houses & bars
- Offices
- Storage
- Vacant building
- Playground
- Sports court
- Public/park

Plate 7 Land use (adapted from NDUL classification). © Crown Copyright. Ordnance Survey.
All rights reserved.

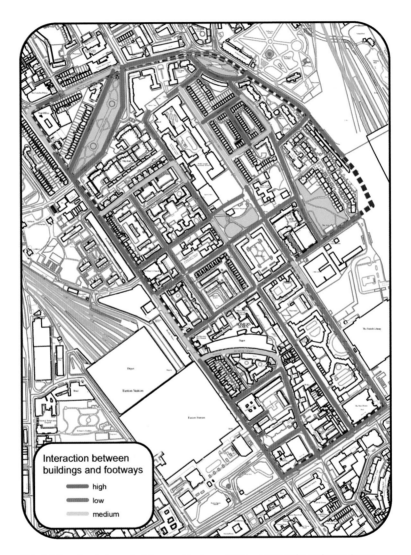

Plate 8 Interaction between buildings and footways. © Crown Copyright. Ordnance Survey.
All rights reserved.

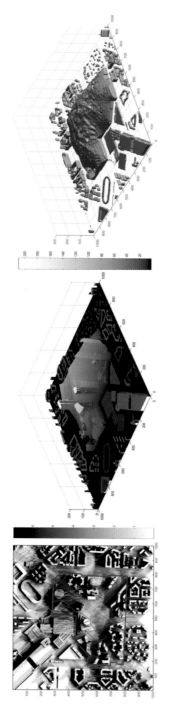

Plate 9 Sunscapes: Different analyses on the solar accessibility on the urban texture. From left: the shadows generated by buildings on the neighbourhood on 21 December; the buildable volumes determined by the 'solar envelope' calculated on 21 December and based on the rhythm of the sun as form-giver; the 'iso solar rights surface', calculated on the real solar energy received on the city.

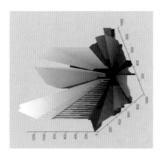

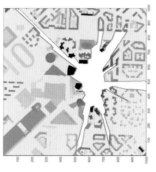

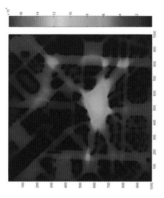

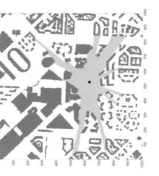

Plate 10 Visual perception: Different visibility analyses for describing the visual experience in the urban texture: the isovistfield of an open public space describing the openness of the vistas for each point; the 3D isovist represented on a plan and its negative in 3D.

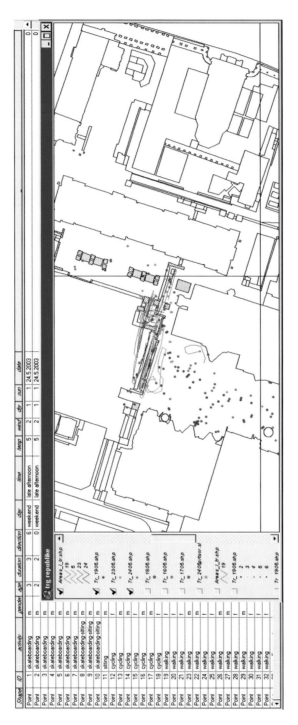

Plate 11 A table showing some records of daily observation in Trg Republike, Ljubljana and the subsequent map consisting of layers of daily records for four different days.

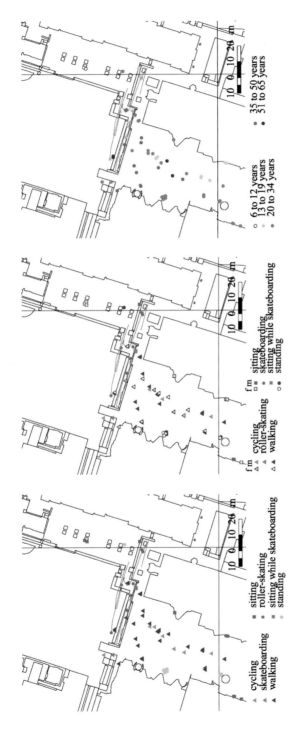

Plate 12 GIS behavioural maps, showing different aspects of usage-spatial relationship in Trg Republike, Ljubljana.

Plate 13 On the left is the experiential landscape map generated from one of the resident participant interviews; on the right is the composite of all resident participants showing a build-up of strong incremental sensations along the western road (Leeming Lane) and the concentration of experiential intensity at the village core.

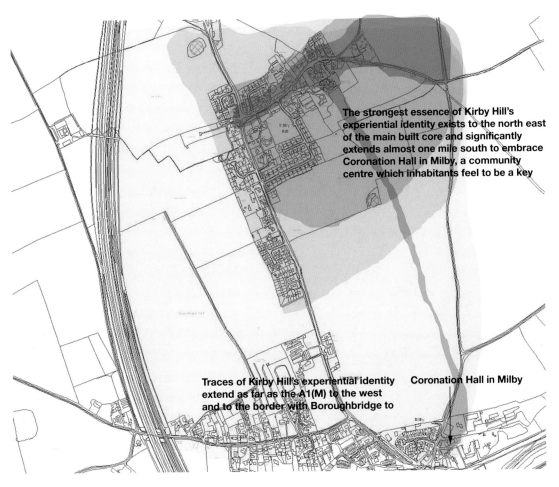

The strongest essence of Kirby Hill's experiential identity exists to the north east of the main built core and significantly extends almost one mile south to embrace Coronation Hall in Milby, a community centre which inhabitants feel to be a key

Traces of Kirby Hill's experiential identity extend as far as the A1(M) to the west and to the border with Boroughbridge to

Coronation Hall in Milby

Plate 14 The essence of Kirby Hill's experiential identity is not contained within static and determinate boundaries, but rather extends into the surrounding environment with varying degrees of intensity related to how places become embedded in the consciousness of inhabitants.

Plate 15 Warren: 'I was trying to get like, get, all the water out!'.

Plate 16 Warren's canvas in the local arts centre exhibition.

Plate 17 Neighbourhoods being constructed by Paul and Julie.

Common requests from those we have consulted have thus included the proportional mix of uses in building design (architects); models of urban carrying capacity, e.g. retail, evening economy and transport (town planning and licensing officers); and housing mix in terms of tenure, amenities and densities (housing associations and developers).

Scale and distinctions

The scale at which 'mixed use' operates and has evolved – until recently 'organically', rather than plan or design-led – ranges from the micro to meso level, and at larger and smaller physical scales. Rowley (1996) identifies a number of key variables in mixed use, suggesting that the practice is not homogeneous and local/specific conditions need to be taken into account.

- *Location types, uses and activities* – Nature of users, occupiers, comings and goings, mix and balance of primary and other uses, compatibility, synergy.
- *Intensity/density, grain of development, permeability* – street layout, ease of movement, footfall along routes.
- *Character of surrounding development* – age of area and buildings; capacity to respond to and accommodate change; range of design considerations within and between buildings/public spaces, vertically and horizontally, size of units, visibility and legibility of uses.
- *Market* – local/regional property and development economics; organizational flexibility.
- *Social-cultural mix* – history, settlement; lifestyle trends/demands, tenure.
- *Planning and urban policy* – regeneration, design guidance, licensing.

The generation of diversity therefore seeks to assess how the physical (including design), the economic (production, consumption, location) and the social interrelate in sustainable urban environments and at differing scales. This includes where synergies and advantages are realized (Table 10.1), but also where conflicts of use arise.

Tool development

A response to the conceptual and qualitative question surrounding mixed use in its various guises has been, firstly, the development of a comprehensive data architecture to capture and interrogate the social, economic, land-use and related aspects that make up the compact city in practice. This entailed drawing on and analysing data, policy and indicators which previously had not been considered or viewed together, let alone synthesized. A typology of geodata included:

- socio-economic – Census (community, demography, travel to work);
- Index of Multiple Deprivation (IMD) – areas ranked by factors of need/risk;
- economic activity and 'health' – industry activity (Standard Industrial Classification) and descriptors, employment (scale), start-ups/closures, benefit payments (e.g. unemployment);
- crime – recorded crime data (e.g. burglary, street, vehicle);
- land use – UDAL (Urban Design Alliance) classifications, floor space and valuation (non-domestic premises);
- pollution – noise complaints, air quality and commercial traffic flow;
- points of interest – commercial, retail, visitor attractions, amenities and transport.

National administrative data, supplemented with locally generated data (e.g. crime), exist at various levels of local geography representing output areas (OAs – lower, middle, upper) below the level of ward (electoral area), as well as point and postcode data, e.g. businesses, recorded crime. Premises data, key to modelling mixed use, are divided between non-domestic and housing, however, while the vertical mix and activity classifications needed to understand economic and social interrelationships and flows required a more detailed analysis, which was undertaken in this case through local area surveys. This entailed land-use surveys based on observation and the creation of a classification database which expanded normal land-use categories, recording aspects such as opening and closing times and street-level (ground-floor) activity during day and night times. Pedestrian activity was also monitored though timed counts at key nodes.

Tool pilot

A test-bed area in which to pilot the methodology and toolkit was selected: Clerkenwell – based on a historic and contemporary mixed-use 'urban village' (Aldous, 1992) with established and growing residential ('loft living'), office, evening entertainment and 'new economy' activity situated on the fringe of the City of London and straddling three local authorities. The demonstration pilot used here was followed by test-beds in city centres of Sheffield and Manchester.

A key issue in the mixed-use, high-density debate is 'quality of life': is it sustainable and what mix does or does not work and at what scale – building, block, street, neighbourhood? The compact city model also suggests that vibrant local economies can be supported without significant inward travel (commuting), and that business location choices and markets reflect this. In order to test out this aspect, questionnaire-based interviews were conducted with residents and businesses, as well as semi-structured interviews with policy and development industry representatives, to gauge their respective views and approach to mixed use in practice. A more detailed analysis of the survey findings and spatial analysis is available in Aiesha and Perdokliani (2005); Aiesha and Evans (2007). There is a comprehensive VivaCity explication in Cooper *et al.* (2008).

A sample of the set of results from the mapping and visualization of primary and secondary data is shown below. Correlating land use and economic activity with social and other environmental factors has for the first time enabled concepts and questions of mixed-use scale and impacts to be assessed objectively, supported by empirical and experiential evidence drawn from local stakeholders.

The first set (Plate 1) shows the results of the vertical land-use analysis by floor, and in terms of land-use types (colour coded). Five zones within the area were selected for detailed observation, based on analysis of building types/morphology, road/pedestrian networks (space

syntax) and land-use mix. This clearly shows the north-south separation between residential and more commercial/mixed-use zones, but also the residential use above first floor, as the purple (darker) shaded blocks expand upwards with high-rise dwellings and encroach into the more mixed land-use area.

The second set (Plate 2) overlays recorded crime densities ('hotspots') firstly for commercial burglary, mapped against office/services premises. This indicates the concentration of break-ins in the commercial zone, which are less prevalent in the more mixed-use area, but more frequent in the fringe of the area which reverts to mono-use. Domestic burglary (not shown) mapped against residential property, not surprisingly ('supply-led'), also shows a higher concentration in the housing-only area, but is less evident in the mixed ('living above the shop') properties. This contradicts the received wisdom that mixed-use areas are more vulnerable and mono-use safer – the reverse seems to be the case here. Resident surveys confirmed a low level of 'fear of crime', but greater concern for anti-social behaviour, particularly environmental (litter/rubbish, noise). On the other hand, robbery ('street crime') mapped against evening activity such as bars, clubs and restaurants highlights key crime hotspots (Plate 2), in this case focused on specific 'café culture' streets, where pickpocketing, snatch theft and vehicle crime (bike theft, car break-ins) are very high. These few partially permeable streets present too many open-access points for pedestrians and bikes, and have poor surveillance (a conclusion shared by the local police).

Finally, the key analysis of how mixed and 'safe' an area is, can be drawn from the visualizations and correlation of land uses and activity in 2D and 3D format (Plate 1). This is represented in Figure 10.1 in terms of both activity and economic mix. This is based on analysis of new 'points of interest' (POI) Ordnance Survey data, showing the density of the mixed-use area with a range of commercial, leisure and visitor amenities, in contrast to the less diverse zones which also attract higher street and vehicle crime. This includes cases where ground-floor use is dominated by night-time or consumption activity.

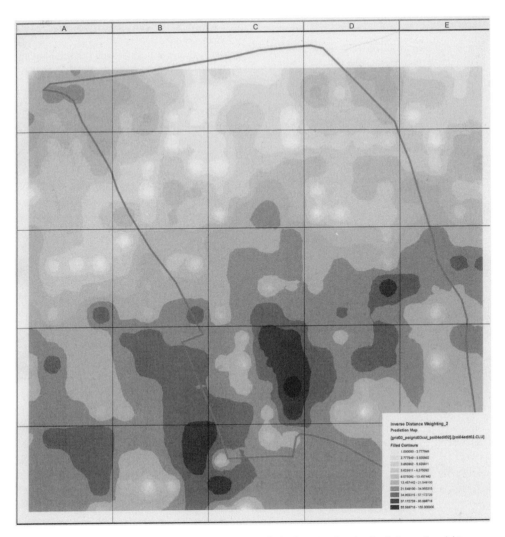

10.2 Points of interest data showing areas of multiple activity and mixed-use premises density. © Crown Copyright. Ordnance Survey. All Rights Reserved.

Conclusion

By synthesizing detailed land-use, economic and socio-environmental data in this way, presumptions in favour of mixed use as providing animated, naturally surveilled and diverse economic/social spaces are confirmed at the sub-ward scale. 'Urban villages' do appear to evolve and require separate activity and land-use areas within a larger mixed-use neighbourhood. However, overdominant activity and land use – whether residential, office or entertainment – exhibit greater environmental and social problems and are thus less sustainable.

The GIS data analysis and synthesis techniques summarized here serve therefore as both an analytical and an interrogatory tool, to which other layers of social, economic and environmental data can be applied and visualized, and more sophisticated spatial modelling undertaken.

Acknowledgement

Thank you to Vanessa Newton for her contribution to the chapter.

References

Aiesha, R. and Evans, G.L. (2007) 'VivaCity: mixed-use and urban tourism', in Smith, M. (ed.) *Tourism, Culture and Regeneration*, Wallingford, CAB International.

Aiesha, R. and Perdikogianni, I. (2005) 'Decoding urban diversity in "mixed-use" neighbourhoods', Proceedings of Sustainable Urban Environments, 'Vision into Action' Conference, Birmingham.

Aldous, T. (1992) *Urban Villages: A Concept for Creating Mixed-Use Urban Developments on a Sustainable Scale*, Urban Villages Group, London.

Brundtland, G. *et al.* (1987) *Our Common Future. Report of the 1987 World Commission on Environment and Development*, Oxford University Press, Oxford.

Cooper, R., Evans, G.L., *et al.* (eds.) (2008) *VivaCity-2020: Urban Sustainability for the 24-Hour City*, Blackwell's, Oxford.

DETR (2000) *Our Towns and Cities: The Future*, HMSO, London.

Department of the Environment (1995) *PPG13: A Guide to Better Practice*, HMSO, London.

Evans, G.L. (2005) 'Mixed-use or mixed messages?', *Planning in London*, 54: 26–29.

Rowley, A. (1996) 'Mixed-use development: ambiguous concept, simplistic analysis and wishful thinking?', *Planning Practice and Research*, 11(1): 87–99.

11 Multiple centrality assessment: mapping centrality in networks of urban spaces

Sergio Porta and Vito Latora

Introduction

Centrality is a key factor in shaping both urban space and urban life. Places that are *perceived* as central in respect to all others in the system of reference are assigned more value, are easier to reach and are more clearly conceptualized. Apart from such *cognitive* prominence (Conroy-Dalton and Zimring, 2003), places can be actually *located* in a more central position in the system of city spaces: in this case, they exhibit a *geographic* prominence. The two dimensions of centrality of a place, cognitive and geographic, are strictly interwoven in a complex dance, a subtle balance which plays a crucial role in contributing to the performance of that place in terms of many relevant urban dynamics.

Central places tend to be more *popular*, in that everyone knows where they are located and can drive you there with simple, straightforward directions; they also are more popular in the sense that they are very often crowded with people moving around for a lot of different reasons and taking advantage of the environmental and human diversity. Because of that, central places are usually *safer from criminality* because they are more efficiently self-surveilled (Newman 1973): more people on the street means more eyes on it (Jacobs 1961), more social control and more informal collective management of problematic situations, cases and needs. Also, central places are *richer in secondary activities and services* of all kinds that exist in the daily, ordinary exchange with other people in movement: grocers, pharmacies, libra-ries, wine-bars and cafés, butchers and greengrocers, music and clothes stores and the like, which in turn attract more and more people to a public space which makes it safer and safer again. In turn, this favours the introduction of *other primary land uses* like theatres, opera houses, city halls, secondary schools and institutions for education and research, major libraries and special activities like civic aquariums, outdoor markets and exhibition centres. Primary activities in turn attract other people again, which further reinforces the virtual loop towards the making of a lively, vibrant, diverse, popular and safe urban centre.

Why was multiple centrality assessment created?

Because the creation of such urban centres is a priority for any policy of sustainable urban planning and design aimed at the realization of the nodal/information city of the future (Newman and Kenworthy 1999), whatever may help in understanding the potential of an existing place to be central, as well as that of a proposed place in alternative development designs, is very useful. The lack of the understanding of such potential, in fact, seems to have played a role in the decay and failure of many urban places and projects, especially after the advent of modern planning, such as most – if not all – large social housing estates in the Western world. After previous studies mainly anchored to an interpretation of spatial centrality which was limited to issues of transportation, regional analysis or economic geography (Wilson 2000), and after the 'configurational' approach of space syntax since the early 1980s (Hillier and Hanson 1984; Hillier 1996), multiple centrality assessment (MCA) implements to cities and open spaces concepts and tools of the network analysis of non-spatial systems in sociology (Wasserman and Faust 1994) or the physics of complex networks (Boccaletti *et al.* 2006). The MCA tool produces visually clear, intuitive maps of urban areas and regions, highlighting the centrality of streets in their global or local surroundings (Plate 3).

For what and whom was MCA created?

In any effort towards the sustainable city of the future it is important to understand which places hold the greater potential to be, or become, the 'backbone' of a neighbourhood, a district or a city. Much of the recent debate about urban sustainability at the international level, in fact, focuses the concept of compact, walkable, diverse urban centres (Jenks and Dempsey 2005) as the anchors (or 'nodes') of a metropolitan to regional territorial framework that minimizes the need of cars and private transportation while maximizing the opportunity to choose among a mix of alternative and collective means. Such centres also work as the core of a *hierarchy of community* that embodies a social perspective in a vision of sustainable cities (Frey 1999). Prerequisite to the functioning of such 'transit-oriented' centres (Calthorpe and Fulton, 2001 Cervero 2004) is their capacity to attract people, shops and services at the local level, then upwards in a *hierarchy of mobility* to the district and city levels (Urban Task Force 1999). The locational centrality of streets, as streets are the constituent part of the structure of any urban 'organism' (Marshall 2005), deeply affects this potential, which is also affected by other families of factors, like the 'constitutional' (Hillier 2004) and the functional. Therefore, in short, the *locational*, *constitutional* and *functional* dimensions of a city space contribute to its potential to be the heart of community life at different scales: MCA accounts for the locational, while formal indicators analysis (Porta

and Renne 2005) and accessibility analysis to retail and services account for the constitutional and functional.

Altogether, these models may offer a highly descriptive device for the purposes of researchers, students, practitioners, stakeholders and policy-makers in all fields related to urban studies and sustainable development in built-up areas.

How does MCA work?

MCA can be applied to different spatial systems and at different scales, using substantially different procedures. For the purposes of this chapter, we will present the core application that works on networks of streets and intersections: readers can refer to recent publications for any technical and methodological detail (Porta *et al.* 2006a, 2006b, 2006c; Cardillo *et al.* 2006; Crucitti *et al.* 2006a, 2006b; Scellato *et al.* 2006; Scheurer and Porta 2006). The road system is represented as a network of arcs and nodes, which is easily turned into a mathematical device called a graph. The kind of street-graph format that MCA uses is the most common standard worldwide for geographers, traffic planners and everyone in the field of urban analysis: it turns streets into edges and intersections into nodes. Obvious as it might appear, this point should not be taken for granted: in fact, this characteristic differentiates MCA from its closest 'competitor', space syntax, which is based on dual graphs where streets are represented as nodes and intersections as edges. The primal graph ground allows MCA to retain the geographic content of spatial systems, so that distances are computed in metric rather than topologic terms: this property makes MCA more adherent to the traditional urban planning bias in favour of the geographic dimension of space; while space syntax, which is based on topologic distance (number of turns), is more oriented to its cognitive dimension. Thus MCA, by using standard graph representations of road networks, takes advantages of the immense amount of information already available, and permanently updated, in all planning offices of cities in the developed world.

The road graph is then imported into a GIS environment and cleaned up of the many 'rumours' that are always present (in example, invisible disconnections); after the cleaning, a table of connectivity is produced over which the algorithm for the calculation of centralities is launched. Such an algorithm calculates *many different centrality indices* that account for the several different ways in which a place can be considered to be central. This results, again in GIS, in a number of maps where a colour code is applied to streets in order to represent the centrality of those streets in terms of that particular centrality index. Thus MCA does not produce one single 'solution', but instead a set of images which are never identical to each other: urban places can be central in one sense, and at the same time marginal in another sense.

MCA illustrated through an example application

MCA has been applied on many occasions for purposes of research and practice. In partnership with the Agencia de Ecologia Urbana of the city of Barcelona (Spain), MCA has been applied to identify structural properties of the urban network which shed new light on the role of historical routes and patterns that are still at work beneath the surface of the contemporary city (Plate 4). We also are working in Barcelona on a large investigation into the correlation between street centrality and the location of economic activities of all kinds – a huge effort that involves some 170,000 real activities in the metropolitan area.

MCA was also applied with the Agencia in the context of the planning process of the city of Vitoria (Spain), where it helped in defining new visions for the development of the city structure. Under the framework of City Form, a research project led by a consortium of public and private bodies in the UK which involves five universities – Oxford, Sheffield, Leicester, Edinburgh and Glasgow – MCA developed all structural analysis of city-wide and neighbourhood-wide cases: such structural measures were correlated to other sustainability indicators, from environmental to economic, from social to educational, from cultural to institutional. The correlation between street centrality and the location of services and shops is still the subject of an ongoing investigation.

This correlation has already been established through a first case study in Bologna, Italy (Table 11.1). Here the centrality of streets as a result of an in-depth MCA analysis turned out to exhibit a significant correlation with the density of shops and services: such correlation was especially relevant for betweenness centrality, which is a confirmation of the leading role that

Table 11.1 Linear correlation (Pearson index) between kernel density of street centrality and kernel density of ground-floor activities in Bologna: first 15 positions in ranking.

Rank no.	Correlated variables		KDE bandwidth	Linear correlation
	Centralities	Activites	Metres	Pearson index
1	C^B_{Glob}	Comm + Serv	300	0.727
2	C^B_{Glob}	Comm	300	0.704
3	C^B_{Glob}	Comm + Serv	200	0.673
4	C^B_{Glob}	Comm	200	0.653
5	C^C_{Glob}	Comm	300	0.641
6	C^S_{800}	Comm + Serv	300	0.620
7	C^S_{Glob}	Comm + Serv	300	0.615
8	C^C_{Glob}	Comm + Serv	300	0.608
9	C^C_{Glob}	Comm + Serv	200	0.583
10	C^C_{Glob}	Comm + Serv	100	0.567
11	C^B_{Glob}	Comm + Serv	300	0.565
12	C^B_{Glob}	Comm	100	0.555
13	C^C_{Glob}	Comm	200	0.547
14	C^S_{Glob}	Comm + Serv	200	0.546
15	C^C_{Glob}	Comm	300	0.533

the 'passing-through' factor holds in driving the movement economy in a city context.

An application of MCA in an urban design process was developed in Parma, Italy, where the model made it possible to distinguish the potential of open spaces among different project alternatives and finally to identify the best solution for the revitalization of pedestrian paths and green areas (Plate 5).

Notes

1   The *betweenness centrality* (C^B) of a node (intersection) measures the number of shortest paths connecting every couple of nodes in the network that cross that node; therefore, C^B captures the extent to which one space in the city is likely to be passed through while going from each place to each other place.

2   The *closeness centrality* (C^C) of a node measures the overall metric distance that separates that node from every other node in the network; in so doing, C^C captures the simplest notion of a place's spatial centrality as its proximity to all other spaces in the city.

3   The *straightness centrality* (C^S) of a node measures how straight (or linear) is the shortest path that connects that node to every other node in the city, thus giving an idea of the 'searchability' of a place in the cognitive practices for orienteering in the complexity of the city's labyrinth.

4   *All indices can be computed globally or locally*: in this latter case, the local centrality (say: C^C_{1600}) of a node is no more referred to all other nodes in the network, but rather just to those nodes located within a certain distance from it (in this case, 1,600 metres). Local measures give an idea of how centrality changes when changes occur to the geographical territory of reference of the users: for instance, users of ordinary services and activities like grocery stores or corner shops are likely to refer to much narrower portions of the urban area (the neighbourhood) than users of highly specialized functions like large malls, airports, hospitals or financial districts. In this sense, a place which is *locally* central offers potential in terms of the development of urban sub-centres and residential communities.

5   The kernel density estimation is a statistical probability means that visualizes the density of locations of a certain class of features (for example, shops of a certain kind) that are reachable from any point in the city. In this case, the kernel density has been used for correlating features of different categories (basically shops and services on one hand and weighted – by centrality – streets on the other).

References

Boccaletti, S., Latora, V., Moreno, Y., Chavez, M. and Hwang, D.U. (2006) 'Complex networks: structure and dynamics', *Physics Reports*, 424: 175–308.

Calthorpe, P. and Fulton, W. (2001) *The Regional City: Planning for the End of Sprawl*, Island Press, Washington, D.C.

Cervero, R. (2004) *Developing Around Transit: Strategies and Solutions That Work*, Urban Land Institute, Washington, D.C.

Conroy-Dalton, R. and Zimring, C. (eds.) (2003) 'Environmental cognition, space and action', *Environment and Behaviour*, Special issue, 35: 1.

Cardillo, A., Scellato, S., Latora, V. and Porta, S. (2006) 'Structural properties of planar graphs of urban street patterns', *Physical Review E, Journal of the American Physical Society*, 73: 6.

Crucitti, P., Latora, V. and Porta, S. (2006a) 'Centrality measures in spatial networks of urban streets', *Physical Review E, Journal of the American Physical Society*, 73: 3.

Crucitti, P., Latora, V. and Porta, S. (2006b) 'Centrality in networks of urban streets', *Chaos, Quarterly of the American Institute of Physics*, 16: 1.

Frey, H. (1999) *Designing the City: Towards a More Sustainable Urban Form*, Routledge, London.

Hillier, B. and Hanson, J. (1984) *The Social Logic of Space*, Cambridge University Press, Cambridge.

Hillier, B. (1996) *Space is the Machine: A Configurational Theory of Architecture*, Cambridge University Press, Cambridge.

Hillier, B. (2004) 'Can streets be made safe?', *Urban Design International*, 9(1): 31–54.

Jacobs, J. (1961) *The Death and Life of Great American Cities*, Random House, New York.

Jenks, M. and Dempsey, N. (2005) *Future Forms and Design for Sustainable Cities*, Architectural Press, Oxford.

Marshall, S. (2005) *Streets & Patterns*, Spon Press, London.

Newman, O. (1973) *Defensible Space; Crime Prevention Through Urban Design*, Macmillan, London.

Newman, P. and Kenworthy, J. (1999) *Sustainability and Cities: Overcoming Automobile Dependence*, Island Press, Washington, D.C.

Porta, S., Crucitti, P. and Latora, V. (2006a) 'The network analysis of urban streets: a dual approach', *Physica A, Statistical Mechanics and its Applications*, 369: 2.

Porta, S., Crucitti, P. and Latora, V. (2006b) 'The network analysis of urban streets: a primal approach', *Environment and Planning B: Planning and Design*, 33: 5.

Porta, S., Crucitti, P. and Latora, V. (2006c) 'Analyse du réseau des voiries urbaines: une approche directe', *Géomatique Expert*, 53: 56–71.

Porta, S. and Renne, J. (2005) 'Linking urban design to sustaibability: formal indicators of social urban sustainability field research in Perth, Western Australia', *Urban Design International*, 10(1): 51–64.

Scellato, S., Cardillo, A., Latora, V. and Porta, S. (2006) 'The backbone of a city', *The European Physical Journal B*, 50: 1–2.

Scheurer, J. and Porta, S. (2006) 'Centrality and connectivity in public transport networks and their significance for transport sustainability in cities', paper presented at the World Planning Schools Congress, 13–16 July 2006, Mexico DF.

Urban Task Force (1999) *Towards an Urban Renaissance*, DETR/E & F.N., Spon Press, London.

Wasserman, S. and Faust, K. (1994) *Social Networks Analysis*, Cambridge University Press, Cambridge.

Wilson, G.A. (2000) *Complex Spatial Systems: The Modelling Foundations of Urban and Regional Analysis*, Prentice Hall, Upper Saddle River, NJ.

12 Measuring the success of transit-oriented development using a sustainability framework: TOD outcome analysis

John L. Renne

Introduction

Planners and urban designers are promoting transit-oriented development (TOD) to encourage sustainable urban development around public transport nodes. TODs are compact, mixed-use developments that facilitate walking, bicycling and the use of public transport through urban design (see Plate 6). TODs include both greenfield and redevelopment projects, typically around rail stations, although there are several examples at bus and ferry terminals. This style of development was most prevalent before the proliferation of the automobile during the twentieth century. As cities are trying to find solutions to urban problems, such as traffic congestion and sprawl, this old concept is promising to offer a new opportunity to solve complex issues. This chapter summarizes a new tool – TOD outcome analysis – to determine if TODs are, in fact, leading to sustainable outcomes.

A theoretical framework for evaluating sustainable development: why TOD outcome analysis was created

Before developing a tool to measure TOD, it is necessary to understand how sustainable development relates to urban policies and development. Figure 12.1 presents a framework for evaluating sustainable development. Government policies, such as zoning regulations, design guidelines and site development regula-

tions, shape urban development. Implicit in every policy are economic, environmental and social goals. If economic, environmental and social outcomes could be accurately measured, policies could be reformulated to produce more sustainable outcomes. The feedback loop shows that this process is iterative and existing policies are constantly in need of updating to ensure outcomes have more benefits and fewer negative externalities.

Current TOD literature focuses mainly on impacts upon travel behaviour and property values surrounding train stations (Cervero *et al.* 2004; Boarnet and Crane 2001). A growing breadth of literature discusses TOD as a tool to encourage sustainable development and smart growth, which has economic, social and environmental implications (Porter 2002; Calthorpe 1993; Calthorpe and Fulton 2001; Bernick and Cervero 1996; Newman and Kenworthy 1999). The tool presented here uses a sustainability framework to measure TOD success in holistic terms – economically, environmentally and socially. A primary goal of TOD is to integrate land use and transportation to create successful and sustainable urban environments that overcome automobile dependence. Sustainable development occurs at the intersection of economic development, environmental stewardship and community development, thus any attempt to measure the success of TOD should reflect this holistic view. In 2005, Renne and Wells first presented a tool to measure the holistic benefits

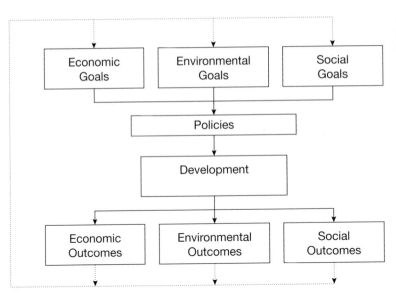

12.1 Theoretical framework for evaluating sustainable development and TOD

of TOD. This chapter builds upon that work by refining indicators used to measure TOD as well as discussing the application of TOD outcome analysis in Perth, Western Australia.

Cities across the globe, especially in auto-dependent countries such as Australia and the USA, are looking to TOD as a tool to create a more sustainable form of development and facilitate smart growth. TOD is a specific application of sustainable development. It seeks to integrate land use with transportation. As more compact and mixed land uses support walking, bicycling and public transport, per capita energy consumption and carbon dioxide emissions decrease, thus creating more sustainable neighbourhoods and cities (Newman and Kenworthy 1999).

Governments have high hopes that TOD will fulfil a variety of objectives. A study of transit agencies in the USA found that the most important goals included increased transit ridership, promoting economic development, generating revenues, enhancing liveability and widening housing choice (Cervero et al. 2004). Renne (2005) surveyed local government planners across Perth, Australia, and also found similarly wide-ranging goals, including increasing transit ridership, stimulating economic development, expanding housing options, reducing traffic congestion, diminishing sprawl, creating a milieu for diverse communities, improving the quality of neighbourhoods and bolstering political support for transit.

One of the challenges facing TOD is varied expectations. More research is needed to determine if its outcomes meet the goals set for it. 'The literature is replete with platitudes that have been heaped upon the TOD concept; however, relatively few serious studies have been carried out that assign benefits to TOD in any quantitative or monetary sense' (Cervero et al. 2004: 119). Identifying a need for a tool to measure the effectiveness of TOD holistically, Wells and Renne (2004) developed a set of indicators to evaluate the success of Transit Villages in New Jersey.[1] They recommended a TOD evaluation framework that looks at measuring economic activity, environmental and transportation activity, institutional changes and community perception. Due to data availability, they found that economic activity, travel behaviour, and public perception were the easiest categories for which to find measurable indicators.

The findings in New Jersey prompted a national study, funded by the National Cooperative Highway Research Program of the Transportation Research Board (TRB), to evaluate what local, county and state governments and transit agencies across the USA reported as benefits and measures of TOD. The study found 56 indicators that were grouped into five categories: travel behaviour, economic performance, environmental performance, the built environment and social benefits. However, the research found that half of the agencies surveyed had access to five or fewer indicators to measure these criteria. The study also sought to determine which indicators were most useful and easiest to collect. However, the project did not include actual data collection (Renne and Wells 2005). It recommended the following indicators as the most essential for a TOD evaluation framework:

- transit ridership;
- density – population/housing;
- quality of streetscape design;
- quantity of mixed-use structures;
- pedestrian activity/pedestrian safety;
- increase in property value/tax revenue;
- public perception—resident and merchant surveys;
- mode connections at the transit station;
- parking configuration—for commuters, for residents, and shared.

How does TOD outcome analysis work: measuring TOD success – lessons from Western Australia

TOD is a core strategy of Western Australia's Network City strategy, which calls for 60 per cent of future growth to occur as infill development (Government of Western Australia 2004). The Network City planning strategy is part of the overall state goal to encourage sustainable development (Government of Western Australia 2003). Building upon the New Jersey and TRB studies, the State of Western Australia commissioned a study to measure the performance of TOD. The State of Western Australia's Department for Planning and Infrastructure (DPI) and the Public Transport Authority (PTA), two members of the Western Australian TOD Committee, funded this study[2].

The TOD Committee has also created a TOD assessment tool, which is used to determine which stations are ripest for TOD (Government of Western Australia 2006). Once selected,

station precincts receive special funding and technical planning assistance to facilitate TOD. The study's mandate was to develop a tool to establish baseline data and measure future performance.

Based on lessons learned from the work cited above, as well as input from planners, the researchers created six categories of indicators:

- travel behaviour;
- the economy;
- the natural environment;
- the built environment;
- the social environment;
- the policy context.

For each category, measures were identified using indicators developed in both the New Jersey and TRB studies and discussions among planners in Western Australia. Five pilot station precincts in Perth were then selected to determine either the ease or difficulty in collecting indicators to measure TOD success. Each selected TOD included the train station and the surrounding 800-metre area. The study then sought to find as much as possible from secondary data sources, including data from the DPI, PTA, TransPerth, Australian Bureau of Statistics (Census data), local government and other sources (see Table 12.1 for specific indicators collected from each source).

Based upon this research, secondary data sources provided a wealth of information but lacked some important indicators. Therefore, site visits and a household-based survey were conducted to collect additional indicators, as reported in Table 12.2.[3]

After analysing all indicators available from primary (site visits and surveys) and secondary sources, few indicators were found which directly related to the natural environment. As discussed above, planners often promote TOD for its environmental benefits, citing reductions of traffic congestion, sprawl, energy use and carbon dioxide emissions. Environmental proxy variables, created using travel behaviour and built environment indicators, can show impacts on the natural environment. The state of California provides a precedent for this in a 2002 study that uses vehicle miles travelled to

Table 12.1 TOD indicators collected in Western Australia – secondary data

Indicator	Category
Data collected from the Department for Planning and Infrastructure, State of Western Australia	
Average VKT per household (per day)	Travel behaviour
Number of trips per day, by mode, per household	Travel behaviour
Method of journey to work (residents)	Travel behaviour
Method of journey to work (employees)	Travel behaviour
Method of other journey (visitors)	Travel behaviour
Trip lengths (residents)	Travel behaviour
Trip lengths (employees)	Travel behaviour
Number of vehicles per household	Travel behaviour
Ped-shed	Travel behaviour
Number of retail, commercial and industrial businesses	Economic
Number of vacant buildings (floorspace)	Economic
Number of jobs in the area (by type)	Economic
Number of residential units (houses/flats/apartments)	Economic
Number of rental and owner-occupied residences	Economic
Resident population (density)	Built environment
Pedestrian activity	Built environment
Area/number of vacant land parcels	Built environment
Number of mixed-use buildings	Built environment
Housing density	Built environment
Area of plazas and parks	Built environment
Bicycle parking spaces	Built environment
Presence of bike/pedestrian paths and on-street bicycle lanes	Built environment
Number of libraries, theatres, galleries, etc.	Social
Data collected from the Public Transport Authority and TransPerth	
Number of services available (train and bus)	Travel behaviour
Timetable coordination	Travel behaviour
Customer satisfaction with station	Travel behaviour
Passengers boarding	Travel behaviour
Security at railway stations	Built environment
Facilities (including retail) at railway station	Built environment
Data collected from the Australian Bureau of Statistics (Census data)	
Rent/mortgage payments	Economic
Breakdown of household by income level	Economic
Household size	Social
Data collected from local government	
Property taxes	Economic
Traffic volumes	Built environment
Crime rates	Social
Number of libraries, theatres, galleries, etc.	Social
Number of other community facilities	Social
Festivals	Social
Is the precinct zoned for TOD-supportive land uses by local government?	Policy
Is there a specific TOD precinct plan?	Policy
Is there an implementation body?	Policy
Are there public subsidies?	Policy
Is there active public-private partnership to encourage TOD?	Policy
Data collected from other sources	
Property values (Real Estate Institute of Western Australia, State's Valuer General)	Economic
Heritage listed buildings (State Heritage Register)	Built environment

Table 12.2 TOD indicators collected in Western Australia – primary data

Indicator	Category
Data collected from site visits	
Retail breakdown	Economic
Vacant land parcels	Built environment
Streetscape/public art	Built environment
Pedestrian amenity	Built environment
Safe design – street-facing buildings	Built environment
Area/number of auto-oriented land uses	Built environment
Area/number of pedestrian-oriented land uses	Built environment
Bicycle parking spaces	Built environment
Traffic-calming features	Built environment
Number of parking spaces (surface, on-street and parking structures)	Built environment
Educational facilities	Social
Data collected from household survey	
Number of people in home-based employment	Economic
Income spend on housing and transport	Economic
Perceptions of noise levels	Natural environment
Perception of overall TOD 'quality'	Built environment
Desirable elements of TOD/neighbourhood centre	Built environment
Public perception of the neighbourhood, crime, pedestrian and bicycle safety	Social
Public perception of community	Social
Perceived quality of retail environment	Social
Community support for further (re)development	Social
Perceived quality of community facilities	Social
Perceived quality of events	Social

estimate energy conservation and climate change benefits for TOD (California Department of Transportation 2002). The creation of the proxy variables should aim to calculate, at a minimum, how TODs impact on air quality, energy use and carbon dioxide emissions.

Applying TOD outcome analysis to any city or region

Because travel behavior, the built environment and the policy context are multi-dimensional with respect to sustainability, TOD outcome analysis provides a refined version of a 'triple bottom line'[4] analysis that has applications for real and proposed projects. As in the case in Western Australia, the goal is to establish a baseline to measure future progress of actual station precincts and compare that to changes, over time, within the surrounding region. Another application could entail the modelling of different proposed development scenarios to determine the most sustainable alternative.

As TOD becomes more widespread and adopted as a strategy to encourage sustainable development and smart growth, TOD outcome analysis provides a flexible tool for measuring performance over time. This method does not prescribe a calculated balance of economic, environmental or social priorities because true sustainability necessitates that decision-making remains in the hands of local and regional communities.

Notes

1   An intra-state agency task force in New Jersey designates transit villages for the purpose of encouraging TOD around transit stations. Local governments designated as transit villages receive special funding and technical assistance from the state. For more information about this program and its evaluation, see: http://policy.rutgers.edu/vtc/tod/.

2   In order to encourage TOD in Perth, the State established the TOD Committee, an intra-state agency committee consisting of the DPI, PTA, Transperth (operator of transit services), the Department of

Housing and Works, Main Roads, the Midland Redevelopment Authority, the East Perth Redevelopment Authority, LandCorp (a public sector developer) and the Western Australian Local Government Association. The TOD Committee meets on a monthly basis and has examined the potential for TOD at every major public transport node in Perth.

3   Due to financial constraints on the project, no merchant-based or user-based surveys were conducted. If more resources were available, surveys of these groups would have been conducted to have data from all groups in TODs – residents, employees and users (shoppers and/or people enjoying themselves).

4   The triple bottom line refers to economic, environmental and social goals, rather than just having a single bottom line using cost-benefit analysis.

References and bibliography

Bernick, M. and Cervero, R. (1996) *Transit Villages in the 21st Century*, McGraw-Hill, New York.

Boarnet, M.G. and Crane, R. (2001) *Travel by Design: The Influence of Urban Form on Travel, Spatial Information Systems*, Oxford University Press, Oxford and New York.

California Department of Transportation (2002) 'Statewide transit-oriented development study: factors for success in California, technical appendix', California Department of Transportation, Sacramento, California.

Calthorpe, P. (1993) *The Next American Metropolis: Ecology, Community, and the American Dream*, Princeton Architectural Press, New York.

Calthorpe, P. and Fulton, W.B. (2001) *The Regional City: Planning for the End of Sprawl*, Island Press, Washington, D.C. and London.

Cervero, R., Arrington, G.B., Smith-Heimer, J., Dunphy, R., Murphy, S., Ferrell, C., Goguts, N., Yu-Hsin, T., Boroski, J., Golem, R., Peninger, P.,

Nakajima, E., Chui, E., Meyers, M., McKay, S., and Witenstein, N. (2004) *Transit Oriented Development in America: Experiences, Challenges, and Prospects, TCRP Report 102*, National Academy Press, Washington, D.C.

Government of Western Australia (2003) *Hope for the Future: The Western Australian State Sustainability Strategy*, Department of the Premier and Cabinet, Perth, Western Australia.

—— (2004) *Network City: Community Planning Strategy for Perth and Peel*, Western Australian Planning Commission, Perth, Western Australia.

—— (2006) *Transit Oriented Development Assessment Tool*, Department for Planning and Infrastructure, Perth, Western Australia.

Newman, P. and Kenworthy, J.R. (1999) *Sustainability and Cities: Overcoming Automobile Dependence*, Island Press, Washington, D.C.

Porter, D.R. (2002) *Making Smart Growth Work*, The Urban Land Institute, Washington, D.C.

Renne, J. (2005) *Transit-Oriented Development in Western Australia: Attitudes, Obstacles, and Opportunities*, Planning and Transport Research Centre, Perth, Western Australia.

Renne, J. and Wells, J.S. (2005) 'Transit-oriented development: developing a strategy to measure success', *Research Results Digest*, Vol. 294, Transportation Research Board of the National Academies, National Cooperative Highway Research Program, Washington, D.C.

Wells, J.S. and Renne, J. (2004) *Implementation of the Assessment Tool: Measuring Economic Activity, Assessing the Impacts of the New Jersey Transit Village Initiative*. Alan M. Voorhees Transportation Center, Edward J. Bloustein School of Planning and Public Policy, Rutgers University, New Brunswick, NJ.

13 Accessibility and user needs in transport: street audit toolkit

Nastaran Azmin-Fouladi

Introduction

'Accessibility and User Needs in Transport' (AUNT-SUE) is one of a cluster of research projects supported under the UK Engineering and Physical Sciences Research Council's Sustainable Urban Environment (SUE) programme. The project responds to the theme of transport, social inclusion and urban design, in particular the relationship between access and mobility and the whole journey environment – see Figure 13.1.

Why was the tool created? Rationale and scope

There are several challenges to achieving inclusive transport in both policy and operational terms. On the one hand there is the absence of transport accessibility in social inclusion policy and official measures of deprivation (Lucas 2004; Solomon and Titheridge 2006), and a narrow focus on physical 'disability access' barriers, such as step-free stations, as a proxy for 'accessibility'. This is manifested in standardized transport planning guidance and benchmarks as used in local transport planning and in measuring public transport accessibility levels. These presume equal pedestrian journey times, walking speeds and catchments served by transport provision (e.g. bus stops), but take no account of variable environmental conditions or perceptual restrictions, notably risk and safety (Crime Concern 2002). Benchmarks also do not reflect the wider

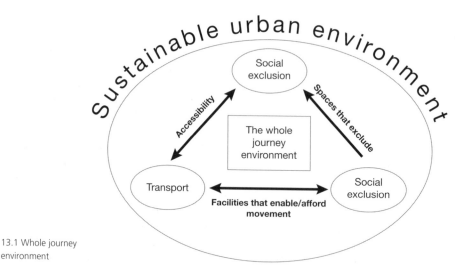

13.1 Whole journey environment

range of abilities and needs of more vulnerable groups.

On the other hand, responsibility for the urban environment and movement therein is highly fragmented between traffic and street engineering, house-building regulations and town planning – which traditionally lack a design knowledge base – and architecture and urban design (including communication, product and industrial design of vehicles and information systems), which focus on buildings and facilities to the exclusion of users, pedestrians and their interaction (Azmin-Fouladi and Evans, 2005). An inclusive design approach and the development of tools to assist design, planning and transport intermediaries and the travelling public are therefore required.

AUNT-SUE has structured its research and toolkit development around three interlocking themes (see www.londonmet.ac.uk/aunt-sue).

- *Benchmarking needs*: macro-level – GIS-based policy model for target groups and local transport planning.
- *Urban design*: meso level – GIS-based street audit, community safety and design quality assessment.
- *Design for all*: micro-level – CAD-based capability modelling and ergonomics.

The development of a street audit index and mapping toolkit (the meso level) is the subject of this chapter. The overall project integration (from macro to micro levels) will incorporate CAD modelling, urban design and guidance, and transport policy benchmarking – supported by a GIS platform.

User-led GIS tool

The application of geographical information systems (GIS) has widened from physical to human geography, driven in the UK by the promotion of e-governance, the availability of national statistics and the need for improved measurement of interventions and change effects through evidence-based policy evaluation (Evans 2006). The availability of mapping services such as GoogleEarth and Cities Revealed and web-based visualization software

has increased awareness and demand for spatial analysis (Batty *et al*. 1998). However, there is a skills and capacity deficit, and fragmentation in the access to and usability of data in the public and private realm, requiring modelling that can draw on appropriate data analysis and presentation formats in order to meet the needs of professionals, intermediaries and, ultimately, the public.

In the urban design and transport context, the whole journey environment also cuts across a number of engineering, design and planning professions and disciplines, as well as service providers – including housing, the police, health, social and education services. Local authority planning (including transport) also demands greater community consultation, e.g. community strategies, and methods by which local quality of life can be measured. In areas of development change – new-build, brownfield sites subject to densification and new and upgraded transport facilities – the opportunity for inclusive design requires a more informed and responsive system to support greater transport use. In terms of the most excluded groups, barriers to access start literally in the home and immediate environs, with most journeys taken within the neighbourhood and local area. Piloting the street audit toolkit has therefore been undertaken in local areas with above-average levels of deprivation, but in proximity to public transport provision.

Mapping the territory

Defining the area in which to pilot the research tool firstly required setting the characteristics and data needs which met the research question and case study of accessibility, transport and urban design. This selection process was also carried out in consultation with the local authority and other collaborating partners, and the community development and planning agendas. Partners are key, both in contributing to the scope and governance issues and in accessing land-use, facility and other environmental data. As well as local authority planning, transport, housing and street engineering officers, local community organizations (e.g. pensioners and cultural groups), tenants'/residents' associations, schools and youth centres also have local knowledge and, of course, daily experience of their urban environment. Other stakeholders include the police, whose 'Safer Neighbourhoods' and crime prevention initiatives also contribute to the quality and accessibility of the journey environment. This includes interventions such as 'Crime Prevention through Environmental Design' (CPTED) which have been used to reduce street crime and burglary in the pilot areas, i.e. 'alley-gating' (reducing access to alleyways and rear access to housing), reducing setbacks (alcove entrances to buildings) and the introduction of CCTV surveillance. It is clear, however, that some of these physical design 'solutions' also create barriers and environmental problems, and can actually engender fear of crime.

Location selection and delineation criteria were therefore informed by local authority consultation and GIS mapping of the road network (layout, access, transport routes) and land use (housing/blocks, morphology, mixed use, community facilities – see Plate 7). This was supplemented with spatial analysis of socio-economic data providing a rich source of community characteristics which help define areas of social exclusion. Key sources include the Census of population and indices of multiple deprivation (ODPM 2004), datasets available online via central government neighbourhood statistics portals. These can be analysed at lower levels of geography or 'output areas', which in high-density locations represent a cluster of houses or part of a small street. Data from the police also provides recorded crime by geo-location, including the time and type (e.g. street robbery, vehicle damage, burglary), over a specified period, thus giving time-series data and density analysis ('hotspots'). Locally provided geodata include traffic movement, transport points, pollution (air, noise) and street facilities (lighting, bollards, seating, crossings, etc.). However, official spatial data do not provide perceptual or qualitative information which reflects the actual experience of the journey chain, barriers to access and the 'feel' of the street and neighbourhood from the perspective of residents and other users. This includes sense of place and identity, natural surveillance and travel aspirations. For example, community safety is a universal issue, but for more vulnerable groups it can be a critical barrier to pedestrian and transport usage. The UK Department for Transport, for instance estimated that over 11 per cent of the public would travel more if they felt safer on the transport system (DfT 2004).

Street audit

GIS mapping of the first test-bed area designated for the street audit therefore defined a bounded area by which local and national administrative data could be analysed, and providing a discrete morphology and street network in which to conduct primary research and data collection. The assessment is conducted in two stages. Firstly the macro-elements are audited, as shown in Table 13.1.

The detailed features (Table 13.2), are captured by observation recorded by annotating hard-copy maps (scale 1:500) and measurement

Table 13.1 Main elements and features

Feature	Element
Land use – floor Windows Active frontage	Office, residential, commercial, community, leisure; occupation/usage/vacancies/voids, temporal use (evening economy), mixed use *Reflecting natural surveillance*
Walls/boundaries Set-backs	*Reflecting territoriality/sense of ownership/access control*
Public space management	Graffiti, vandalism, fly-tipping, litter, other physical incivilities
Street furniture	Seats, bins, trees/ grilles, railings and 'clutter'

Table 13.2 Categorization of urban design elements for street auditing

Concepts/aspects	Elements/Variables/Cases/Values	Attributes
Natural surveillance		
Windows (*eye on the street*)	Both sides (numbers) One side (numbers) No windows/blank walls/bushes and green areas	Lots of windows, some windows, no windows, no ground-floor windows
Activities on the footway	Shops, places of business (frontage)	Curtilage – narrow <1.5m, absolute 1.5m, accepted 1.8m, desired 2m
	Gathering places (benches/children's play area)	Public park, as part of walking environment, communal, front garden
	Street market (occasional activities)	
General image		
Broken windows	Graffiti /vandalism Boarded-up buildings/broken windows Rubbish/general cleanliness	
Territoriality	Set-backs	Front garden, parking curtilage, access to lower ground, planter>10m wide
	Demarcation of public/semi-public/ private	<1.5m, >1.5m
	Enclosure/continuous building frontage, proper height-width ratio	<1.5m, >1.5m height
Fear-based route configuration	Entrapment (width of the footway) Blocked prospect/open sightline Bushes and grown-up plantation	<1.5m, >1.5m (bushy), planter
Special features	Local characteristics/identity Landmarks and historical buildings/features	Listed building, conservation area
Physical barriers		
Accessibility to buildings	Level entry Ramp Step(s)	Level entry, ramp, step, steps Change of surface, change of level

– for instance, pavement and crossing width – and photographs. The latter are geocoded by location, providing hyperlinks to the final GIS maps. Attributes are noted, totalling 30 indicators representing the prime elements of the street audit index. A relational database is used to record qualitative measurements and features which are coded for transfer to digital maps and visualized as colour-coded line or block (polygons) and layered with land-use, transport and street audit information, and contextual data outlined above.

As is emphasized in *Better Places to Live* (CABE 2001) the individual elements of buildings, landscapes and their interface have a key role in determining the overall quality of an area. However, auditing all of these elements for a wide area is time-consuming and impractical. Thus, after identifying sections of public spaces and routes within our test-bed area which exhibit negative qualities, micro-elements such as the design of railings, treatment of boundaries and appearance of shopfronts are examined more thoroughly. Some of the features considered to be most influential include:

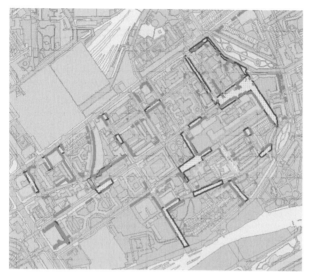

13.2 Areas with negative qualities for personal safety and recorded street and vehicle crime density

- design and arrangement of boundary walls/railings/plantings;
- planting (trees, planters, grassed areas, flowers and borders);
- banners and signs (interpretative, instructive, informative and directional);
- lighting (pavement, pedestrian, highway, security, building and feature);
- public art and features (permanent and temporary works, fountains and graphics);
- shop fronts (thresholds, glazing, stall risers, signs, banners and shutters);
- advertisements (hoardings, kiosks and banners, signage);
- safety and security (emergency equipment, CCTV, gates and grilles);
- elements that signify identity and character.

Case study pilot

These elements were captured in a test-bed area of Somerstown in the London borough of Camden (St Pancras ward). This is a deprived neighbourhood, with low car ownership and economic activity, a high number of school-age children and a mixed, multicultural community (e.g. Bangladeshi, Irish) living in predominantly social housing estates. Ironically – given high accessibility barriers and incidence of social exclusion – the neighbourhood is bounded by major transport interchanges (Euston and King's Cross). However, from local resident surveys it is clear that journey horizons are very limited, and fundamental barriers to transport access start at the front door and the immediate external environment – both for the physically impaired and other mobility-impaired, and also for those for whom safety is a particular concern (e.g. the elderly, visible ethnic minorities, women with young children, unemployed seeking work).

Following the mapping of community profile and land use, using OS data and observation to capture vertical premises mix and open space (Figure 13.2), primary data collected from the test-bed area were entered into (Arc)GIS as 'shape files'. In order to analyse the quality of the public realm for the inclusive journey environment, attributes of each element were ranked with negative and positive values. For example, routes that have a low level of natural surveillance are drawn based on the combination of the following six variables:

- no window;
- no ground floor window;
- blank walls;
- high fences;
- boundary wall/plantation >1.50m;
- set-backs of >10.00m.

Layers of spatial data are thus combined to determine areas with potential personal security problems (Figure 13.2). Comparing street analysis with recorded crime, it is evident that robbery/theft is concentrated on the fringe of the area, adjacent to the main routes and proximity to major transport facilities, not in the internal streets where insecurity is felt (fear of crime versus recorded crime). In terms of vehicle crime (damage, theft, including bicycles), this is more widely spread and correlates more with the street audit observation

While some housing blocks are outward-facing and street-oriented, most have a 'defensible space' estate layout, with a lack of direct access from individual buildings to the footway and limited numbers of doors opening to public spaces. This implies a low level of interaction between the walking environment and buildings, as well as a high level of inactive building frontage. Streets with this characteristic are shown in Plate 8. The layout of a neighbourhood can also dictate how people move around: 'providing for the optimum variety of journeys means creating open-ended, well-connected layouts. Introverted, dead-end layouts limit people's choice of how to travel, especially if they want to walk, cycle or use the bus' (CABE, 2001: 3). As is shown in Figure 13.3, the streets are generally formed of small blocks, with the distance between any dwelling and bus stops and train stations under 800 metres. However such permeability does not always translate into accessibility.

The GIS-based visualizations presented here draw together primary and secondary data and qualitative evidence, but represent a very small proportion of the spatial analysis and features

which can be captured through this technique. Other aspects of the whole journey environment assessed with the street audit index include continuity and enclosure, and accessibility from the view and behaviour of residents. Digitizing annotated maps and correlating these with spatial data for feedback in an iterative design process can be used for assessing street design improvements as well as interventions such as extended transport routes.

A toolkit which provides a menu of spatial factors and visualizations, layered to produce combinations of linear and cluster analysis in both 2D and 3D, thus offers a powerful tool which can be used in community consultation and planning, urban design modelling and scenario-building, and in creating an interactive spatial database as a resource for the wide range of users and decision-makers in the urban environment and transport fields.

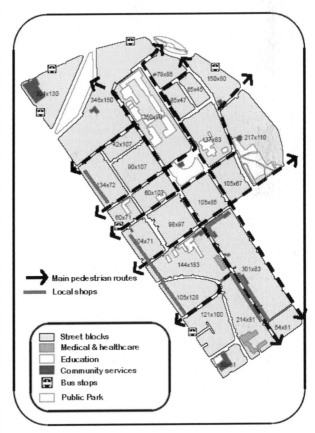

13.3 Permeability and ease of movement to local transport and amenities.

References

Azmin-Fouladi, N. and Evans, G.L. (2005) *Accessibility and User Needs in Transport Design*, Proceedings of INCLUDE 2005, Royal College of Art, London.

Batty, M., Dodge, M., Jiang, B. and Smith, A. (1998) *GIS and Urban Design*, Paper 3, Centre for Advanced Spatial Analysis, UCL (CASA), London.

CABE (2001) *Better Places to Live: By Design – A Companion Guide to PPG*, Thomas Telford, London.

Clarkson, J., Coleman, R., Keates, S. and Lebbon, C. (eds.) (2003) *Inclusive Design. Design for the Whole Population*, Springer, Vienna.

Crime Concern (2002) *People's Perceptions of Personal Security and Their Concerns About Crime on Public Transport: Literature Review*, Department for Transport, London.

DfT (2004) *Tackling Crime on Public Transport*, Department for Transport, London.

Evans, G.L. (2006) *Evidence-based or Instrumentalist: Urban Policy and Wicked Problems*, September, Royal Geographic Society Conference, London.

Lucas, K. (2004) *Running on Empty: Transport, Social Exclusion and Environmental Justice*, Bristol Policy Press, Bristol.

ODPM (2004) *The English Indices of Deprivation 2004: Summary (revised)*, Office of the Deputy Prime Minister, London.

Solomon, J. and Titheridge, H. (2006) 'Benchmarking transport social exclusion among older and disabled persons', TRANSED: 11th International Conference on Mobility and Transport for Elderly and Disabled Persons, June 18–21, Montreal.

14 Raster cities: image-processing techniques for environmental urban analysis

Eugenio Morello and Carlo Ratti

Introduction

Aspects concerning the well-being of people in both outdoor and indoor spaces are relevant in trying to enhance the environmental quality of urban spaces. In fact, the delicate relationship existing between the assessment of the urban fabric and the design of open spaces defines the urban environmental quality and assesses the success of a city. This careful balance inside the urban form is surprisingly tangible in numerous historical city centres, and was generated through a long process of transformations over time. Today, cities evolve rapidly and the slow process of adaptation of urban shape to meet human needs and sustain ecological diversity is no longer feasible.

Why was the technique created?

The proposed set of tools is presented as an alternative way to manage the complex set of environmental variables in the frame of rapid urban change. It allows us to investigate simultaneously different environmental aspects, such as solar access, cross-ventilation, energy consumption, etc., in relation to the arrangement of the urban fabric. Algorithms defined in the Matlab environment and derived from image-processing can work with very simple raster images of the urban texture stored in bitmap format. Potential users might simply use the proposed set of tools, or implement new algorithms to meet their needs and compare different design solutions from the environmental and morphological viewpoints. In fact,

using this set of tools, a new paradigm for assessing the environmental consequences generated by the urban texture is investigated. This is centred on the relationship existing between environmental indicators and urban morphology: the question is if – and in what measure – the correct arrangement and the shape of the urban fabric alone might improve the environmental behaviour of the city. With the aim of creating effective environmental quality starting just from morphology, several design tools can be developed, assessing new potentialities related to the form of human settlements. For instance, the energy-based morphogenesis of the built environment could be intended as the first step towards the improvement of the sustainability of cities with no additional cost due to the application of complex technologies.

The technique revealed itself to be useful for simulations on alternative design schemes over large-scale masterplans and for extensive and complex urban areas, helping to make decisions supported by measured quantification. In particular, the technique demonstrates the potential of digital urban models based on raster images for the analysis of the city, which brings with it many advantages such as fast computability, flexibility, precision and comparability of results obtained from several algorithms.

The tools were initially created to compare the environmental behaviour of different urban configurations. In fact, the technique might be desirable in comparative studies, whereby environmental indicators can be mapped and visualized for different design projects, and consequently critical situations can easily emerge. Especially in a case of limited resources, the identification and quantification of environmental deficiencies on the urban texture could help in programming intervention phases more efficiently. In fact, the rapid measurability of several environmental indicators on each point of the urban space is simply based on the same digital support as the unique input, which is analysed and processed through a series of imposed algorithms.

We focus on the city and its development scenarios for the future. Further work and applications of the proposed technique might promote a new concept of urban environmental architecture, based on new design strategies and generative rules for the prediction of innovative morpho-typological solutions derived by environmental indicators.

For whom was the tool created?

An optimal site or design solution is almost unachievable. Often, requirements for different environmental issues are in opposition. For instance, the exigencies of indoor spaces and outdoor spaces differ, since good exposure to the sun can reduce energy consumption inside buildings, but at the same time this action can limit the environmental quality of the resulting shaded open spaces, which suffer from the reduction of the sky-view factor. Also, a higher level of compactness reduces heat losses, but also reduces gratuitous gains from solar irradiation and does not encourage natural ventilation.

In spite of the impossibility of achieving the optimal urban design scheme from the environmental viewpoint, urban designers should not give up looking for best practice in relation to the aim of sustainability. The intention is to propose a technique which enables the analysis of the many aspects involved in the assessment of urban environmental quality, in the belief that only a wide spectrum of environmental indicators can support conscious design choices.

The technique described here was created in an effort to provide quick but reliable tools for academic and research purposes in the field of environmental design, with the aim of making them accessible to both public administrators and practitioners. On the one hand, decision-makers and public administrators could use them in evaluating the impact of different design solutions on the urban fabric and finding more sustainable design alternatives; on the other hand, urban designers could make use of the proposed tools at the initial design process, in order to take advantage of local environmental opportunities. At the least, the proposed analyses, based on the comparison of alternative design solutions from the viewpoint of urban environmental quality in the heuristic phase, could mean a significant improvement in terms of energy efficiency and environmental comfort.

Urban design students could also benefit from the diffusion of the low-cost library of functions, which might integrate traditional approaches to urban planning with a higher consciousness in the field of urban environmental sustainability. In fact, an open-source initiative could diffuse, ameliorate and increase the now available set of tools, making the technique become more sophisticated.

How does it work?

The methodology is based on the use of very simple raster models of cities, called digital elevation models (DEMs). DEMs reproduce the geometry of the urban fabric and are produced by regularly spaced matrices of elevation values, which contain 3D information on 2D digital support, stored in bitmap format. Implementing software algorithms derived from image-processing, it is possible to develop efficient strategic tools for analysing and planning the sustainable urban form, measuring geometric parameters and assessing radiation exchange, energy consumption, wind porosity, visibility, spatial analyses, etc. Results are extremely fast and accurate. However, their application to architecture and urban studies has not yet been fully explored. The first application of DEMs in architecture originated at the Martin Centre, University of Cambridge (P. Richens, C. Ratti and K. Steemers), and explored the potentialities of this low-cost and powerful technique.

Today, through the increased availability of DEMs from LIDAR (laser imaging detection and ranging, i.e. a technology that determines distance to an object using laser pulses), the proposed technique could open the way to new low-cost raster-based urban models for planning and design.

In the absence of satellite imagery, the DEM can be derived from the digital 3D model produced with CAD and rendered with software such as 3D Studio Max that enables a view from the top and from infinite distance to be generated and at the same time differentiates the elevations of buildings on a grey-scale map. Once the plan with the heights of the objects is created in a bitmap format, the latter can be easily processed by the proposed algorithms that read the image as a square matrix. Environmental indicators are the subject of the algorithms defined in the Matlab environment.

An application of the technique

The tools reveal themselves to be a feasible way to assess the environmental quality of urban spaces. Under the broad definition of environmental quality, aspects related to both energy efficiency and human comfort are taken into account: on the one hand, the aim is to quantify the potential energy efficiency derived from the capacity of the urban fabric to take advantage of passive gains at the city scale; on the other hand, aspects of perceived comfort in urban open spaces are investigated, among others or through visual preference analyses, through the definition of thermal conditions.

Environmental parameters include solar access (solar paths, mean shadow density, solar gain through solar envelopes, sky-view factors), energy consumption (surface-to-volume ratio and passive/non-passive zones), cross-ventilation, wind porosity, urban canyon height-to-width, pedestrian accessibility and visual perception of open spaces through isovist fields.

For instance, algorithms explore rules based on natural rhythms that define the morphogenesis of buildable volumes in the city and encourage the solar access of the urban fabric (for temperate climates) through an energy-based reinterpretation of the 'solar envelope'

concept ('iso solar surfaces'), first introduced by R. L. Knowles (1974, 1981) (Plate 9).

Not just the sun, but other natural forces as well help in modelling the urban environment: the urban metabolism, in particular the thermal exchanges and the natural ventilation occurring over cities, generates macro- and micro-climates, influencing the perceived comfort and the environmental quality in general.

Moreover, algorithms based on the calculation of 'sky-view factors' over extensive urban portions enable the urban form to be linked with the generation of the urban heat island. In fact, the phenomenon of the urban heat island is related to those environmental indicators which profoundly depend on design choices, such as urban materials on horizontal and vertical surfaces, the vegetation density on open spaces and the shape coefficient of street canyons. Maps containing the identification of critical situations are produced, in order to define strategies of intervention in large urban areas.

Furthermore, the broader definition of environmental quality considers human well-being in open spaces, in particular the psycho-physiological aspects related to the perceived experience of the urban form. Useful tools for measuring pedestrian accessibility, visual perception and visibility of open and built spaces through isovist fields and the reinterpretation of Lynch's (1960) visual elements are presented. Isovists describe the field of vision of the observer located at a specific point in space, and represent for instance the base unit for the construction of the model. Starting from the analysis of the geometrical characteristics of these figures, and from the sequence along a visual path, it is possible to draw a conclusion on the visibility analysis of the built urban fabric (Plate 10).

References and further reading

Knowles, R.L. (1974) *Energy and Form*, The MIT Press, Cambridge, MA.

Knowles, R.L. (1981) *Sun Rhythm Form*, The MIT Press, Cambridge, MA.

Lynch, K. (1960) *The Image of the City*, The MIT Press, Cambridge, MA.

Ratti, C. (2001) *Urban analysis for environmental prediction*, unpublished PhD dissertation, University of Cambridge, Cambridge, UK.

Ratti, C. and Richens, P. (2004) 'Raster analysis of urban form', *Environment and Planning B: Planning and Design*, 31(2): 297–309.

Ratti, C., Baker, N. and Steemers, K. (2005) 'Energy consumption and urban texture', *Energy and Buildings*, 37(7): 762–776.

Ratti, C. and Morello, E. (2005) 'SunScapes: extending the "solar envelopes" concept through "iso-solar surfaces"', Proceedings of the 22nd International Conference on Passive and Low Energy Architecture, Beirut, Lebanon.

15 The Communities in Action Handbook

Ombretta Romice and Hildebrand Frey

Introduction

The multi-method strategy (MMS), which is summarized and translated in a clear and user-friendly manual entitled the *Communities in Action* (CIA) *Handbook* (Frey and Romice 2003), is a hands-on instrument for site analysis and development of programmes, frameworks and briefs. It should ideally be used to carry out these activities by community groups in collaboration with designers/planners, but it is suited to be used in a number of scenarios and for a number of purposes. It distinguishes itself from other community planning handbooks in that it is underpinned by a combination of investigative methods borrowed from the field of psychology; this combination stems from a criticism of the limiting scope of the diffuse use of single methods for the study of complex urban problems. Underpinning belief of the handbook is that the image people have of a place is complex, being built over time, through experience and affected by a multitude of factors – formal, social, economic and environmental. Understanding such a complex image is paramount for urban transformation, and must be understood through the innovative use of a number of combined assessment procedures.

Why was this tool created?

Urban scenarios are challenging citizens with problems of increasing complexity: the revitalization of communities is one of them, and requires major changes in the physical as well as the social and political levels. Those affected by such change are increasingly advancing the right to have a say on the transformation process, to prevent the mistakes of the past, to identify, reinforce and stabilize new roles, to become 'doers' rather than 'done-to', to create responsive environments and, as a result, achieve a higher level of satisfaction for communities. Despite good intentions, community-building does not produce good results if it is not well prepared. The risk of communities being disregarded and left aside in the decision-making process, involved in distorted communication, always exists (Romice 2000a). Playing a role in urban democracy asks for more, for preparation and practice. The MMS, through the *CIA Handbook*, aims to allow more and more groups to claim their stake in enjoying urban democracy by developing an informed and proactive vision for development. It is based on the belief that architecture, planning and urban design are in need of intellectual instruments, which can strengthen them and make them less arbitrary. The MMS is based on the belief that the principles which can put architecture and planning at the real service of people are, currently, in large part available, and that these principles ought to be better formalized and transmitted for effective change.

The essence of public participation advocated by the MMS is dual. On the one side, it is contextual, because it centres on places and people. On the other, it is a form of communication. The MMS, through the *Handbook*, has the goal of developing 'topics' for this communication and syntax for its practice.

The principles of this form of participation, at the base of the MMS, are simple (Sanoff 2000: 13).

- There is no best solution to a design problem.
- Expert decisions are not necessarily better than 'lay decisions'.
- Design and planning tasks can be made transparent.
- The process is continuous and ever changing.

Space design can encourage social formations and relationships (Sanoff 2000), and the study of people's relationship in the environment must be granted a say in policy-making. When participation means getting users involved in understanding the use of space and place, it becomes an integral part of the policy-making process. In this sense, participation assumes a more determinant role: community-building. This assigns a new role to communities that want and have developed the skills to make a mark in the development of their environment because they are using new forms of communication and developing better visions of what their neighbourhood should become and how to get there.

How does the tool work?

The *Handbook* contains a concrete proposal on how to explore these potentials further, bringing in the now conventional and well-known practice of involving groups in design, new tools, frameworks and approaches, to redefine and reinvent the role that the public, as stakeholders of the urban development process, could and should take in policies for urban regeneration.

It has long been argued that this process can be optimized through the establishment of connections between disciplines and fields of research that have experience in observing and analysing environment-behaviour relations (Gifford 2002). A way to develop architecture more comprehensively such that it responds to its limitations is for it to engage in a dialogue with other fields by means of an equal and not subservient relationship. Environmental psychology is an ideal partner for designers and the *Handbook* is built upon shared ground between urban design and environmental psychology, the latter being the one providing much of the knowledge on how people perceive, understand, evaluate and consequently use space.

The contents and structure of the *Handbook* are based on the understanding of two principles. Firstly, people's evaluative image of the city is hierarchical (Nasar 1998) – they have images of their region, city, neighbourhoods, roads and houses; to each of these images corresponds a level of detail, which expands with familiarity of the place. Time and movement also play a role in perceiving places: changes within the day, seasons, age of perceivers and purposes can have significant repercussions on the images constructed. Secondly, that environmental experience – how we perceive, get to know, adapt and react to space – is a continuous and complex process. The knowledge that derives from both these principles is very important for decision-making about space because it explains how people use, appreciate and behave in it, and hence it needs to be voiced, but also enriched by communication between different groups of stakeholders.

Several evaluative methods are available to study the processes of environmental experience, and are commonly used in public consultation to gain information on immediate space perception, the formation of symbolic, functional and spatial hierarchies, the criteria that observers consider more important in a space, actual preferences for design alternatives, etc. Each of these methods focuses on just one part of such a complex experience, however – none of them on its own can generate a complete assessment of an area's qualities and deficiencies, and therefore when used in isolation can only partially assist in generating comprehensive actions for (urban) areas.

The *Handbook* combines the hierarchical and temporal processes of environmental experiences and study methods for each of these methods, to try and generate a comprehensive and gradual set of criteria, values and judgements that can effectively explain appreciation and ambitions for spaces. These can then be used for several scenarios, such as the production of a design brief, area regeneration proposals, etc.

In total, seven methods/techniques/procedures have been selected.

- *Goal setting*: to establish contacts among those interested in environmental change, raise awareness, share visions, build consensus, set goals, define objectives and attribute roles. The method suggested is a visioning process which requires a short, energetic session of discussion and contributes to building a neighbourhood vision where any information, goals and decisions are related; participants' roles are clear and every step belongs to a broader picture that is progressively refined. Goal setting is a process made of several exercises, among which are introduction, statement of options, organize information, individual brainstorming, P.A.R.K., summarize and present. Each is described in detail: tools and materials required, time needed, people to involve and means to do so are explained through examples and ready-to-

use equipment (forms, letters, etc.) included in the *Handbook* (Figure 15.1).

- *Mental/behavioural maps*: to identify non-traditional perceptions of a place by overcoming preconceived ideas and studying genuine experiences, habits, aspirations; to identify areas where action and improvement is needed.
- *Awareness walks*: what happens when the environment plays a role for us that is traditionally neglected by designers' investigations? This is a method to learn more about what spaces do to us, how we use them and why, where they are lacking and where they are supportive for us, what they need and what they have.
- *Photographic surveys*: to provoke discussion in a community about issues and concerns that we do not see or share or are aware of, but which play a role in how we use our environment.
- *Design criteria selection (multiple sorting tasks)*: to guarantee that any improvement or change taking place in users' area is carried out to respond to your own ideas and needs; to challenge designers on

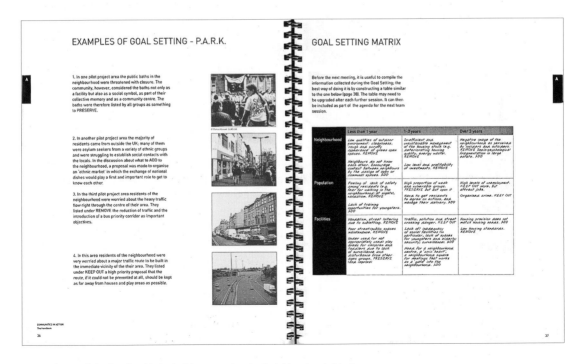

15.1 Each step of the *Handbook* helps build a comprehensive 'neighbourhood vision'

concerns other than the traditional ones. Multiple sorting tasks are very efficient ways to identify what people find important, interesting, captivating, offensive or simply significant in relation to 'something'. It is an exercise that can be used in any context and for any group of people, no matter their age, status, etc. It is conducted here using images, breaking verbal barriers which very often prevent people from expressing views. It is a fairly straight-forward process, with detailed indications on how to select images, conduct the exercise and interpret the answers, translating them in usable assessment criteria for space design (Figure 15.2).

- *Environmental assessment (semantic diffe-rential)*: to ensure that actions are evalu-

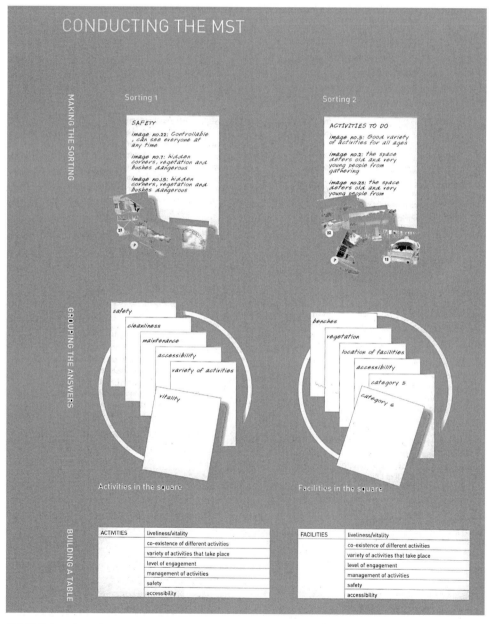

15.2 Multiple sorting tasks

ated and assessed on criteria that matter to users, and that such assessment matters when change is brought about.

- *Post-occupancy evaluation*: to measure the efficacy and responsiveness of any action taken; to guarantee constant monitoring of change and ensure commitment to design performance.

Before identifying these seven techniques, a much more complex variety of methods was considered (Romice 2000b; Frey and Romice 2003); their selective study and comparison suggested that those identified are sufficiently capable of assisting community groups in the development of comprehensive views/impressions of their environment, and helping them to use such views to collaborate with professionals in the realization of change.

The idea of combining methods has another rationale: each individual method has potential as well as faults. Perhaps the most interesting case is the use of semantic scales to assess people's rating (preference/attractiveness. . . you name it) of a feature. Semantic scales have long been used for their simplicity, speed of application and assessment. Equally, they have long been criticized for not being representative of the respondents' evaluative parameters, but of the researchers'. Semantic scales depend on the pre-definition of assessment criteria that will form the basis of the polar lists and of the resulting value judgements. If these criteria are generated by persons beyond the direct users, e.g. by a designer or a facilitator alone, there is the danger that these imported criteria will 'contaminate' the exercises by representing (imposing) views and interests of outsiders. It is therefore paramount that criteria are generated first inside the user group before it confronts the views and concepts of outsiders. All this necessitates a structured approach – the MMS as a series of linked steps – to the gradual elaboration of criteria, values and value judgements that lead to an area regeneration brief.

Potential applications

MMS can be applied to a variety of problems and goals. Once one becomes familiar with it,

one can learn to use it in different circumstances and adapt it to specific purposes. Variations are useful, but the overall structure and principle should stay the same. The MMS consists of two phases focusing on the study of the built environment. The first phase involves, in an intense commitment, a working team. In a target area, a small group of representatives of users and designers is assembled to take part in a process of collection, confrontation, analysis and organization of information on the built environment. This phase is 'issue specific' and uses steps 1 to 5: once having identified an area of action and the major issues of concern regarding urban features, the team attempts to identify criteria, parameters and priorities for their evaluation. The outcome is a tool to carry out an environmental evaluation of the issues identified (step 6). The second step, the 'contextual phase', uses this tool to capture broader views of the community or in general of a broader audience who for practical reasons cannot undertake the intensive 'issue-specific' process. The two phases together seek to identify existing conditions, potential transformations and their degree of acceptability in a community.

The *Handbook* is designed in a very hands-on manner, with simple and clear instructions for each step listed, and an explanation of how to use the combination of steps, building on the knowledge progressively gained. Each step is presented in a standardized format, including a description of:

- the remit of competence (where and for what purpose the step can be used);
- how to use the step in practice;
- how to evaluate and make sense of the information acquired;
- some technical details to solve practical difficulties, and examples of application.

The *Handbook* has been used by the authors in three pilot projects and also for several years in studio work with students of architecture/urban design and community groups. It has been distributed to several housing associations/community groups in Glasgow and beyond.

References

Frey, H.W. and Romice, O. (2003) *Communities in Action: The Handbook*, Scottish Arts Council, Edinburgh University & University of Strathclyde, Glasgow.

Gifford, R. (2002 3edn.) *The Handbook of Environmental Psychology*, Optimal Books, Canada.

Nasar, J. (1998) *The Evaluative Image of the City*, Sage Publications, London.

Romice, O. (2000a) *Visual literacy and environmental evaluation: a programme for the participation of community groups in design*, Doctoral Thesis, Glasgow, University of Strathclyde.

Romice, O. (2000b) 'New developments and final reflections on the use of visual literacy and environmental evaluation for the participation of community groups in design', *GeoJournal. An International Journal on Human Geography and Environmental Sciences*, 51(4): 311–319.

Sanoff, H. (2000) *Community Participation Methods in Design and Planning*, John Wiley & Sons, New York.

16 Collaborative planning and design for a sustainable neighbourhood on Quebec City's university campus

Geneviève Vachon, Carole Després, Aurore Nembrini, Florent Joerin, Andrée Fortin and GianPiero Moretti

Introduction

This chapter presents a collaborative planning process elaborated to design a new neighbourhood on the Laval University campus in Quebec City. The process consisted of an original sequence of focus groups, workshops and a design charrette, along with an internet consultation of the entire university community. The case presented here is context-specific. However, the series of activities and participatory tools used to achieve consensus around the challenges, orientations and design of a sustainable mixed-use neighbourhood provide insight as to the 'transferability' of the process to other contexts.

The context: why was the consultative tool set up?

The main 1952 campus follows modern planning principles: a highly formal composition of axes and individualized pavilions dotting large mega-blocks interspersed with parking and wooded areas. Planned and developed independently in what was a rural area at the time, the campus is weakly connected to the surrounding neighbourhoods and services. In 2004, faced with a predicted demographic decline for the metropolitan region as well as an oversized campus compared to its expected long-term growth, Laval University appointed a planning commission to conduct public hearings on the future of the institution's development. In the end, the commission proposed a new master-plan to develop its underutilized fringes with a view to consolidating this strategic area of Quebec City. The idea was to better integrate the campus better with the rest of the urban fabric while also generating more responsive environments, better services and appropriate residential accommodation to serve the changing needs of the university community (www. cameo.ulaval.ca).

Laval University's planning commission (CAMEO) delineated a 24-hectare site at the fringe of the campus for the development of a new mixed-use neighbourhood. This area is bordered by a post-war suburban neighbourhood with a not-so-thriving high street, private student accommodations in poorly maintained 1960s' three-storey apartment buildings, the university sports pavilion and a boulevard marking an anonymous campus entrance. Since it was argued during the hearings that the university should favour collaborative planning methods for the redesign of its campus, the Interdisciplinary Research Group on Suburbs (GIRBa[1]) was mandated in November 2005 to initiate, structure and orchestrate a participative process to design the new neighbourhood. The planning commission included a few guidelines to frame the intervention, one being that the university retains ownership of the land but will sell rights-to-build to private developers through long-term leaseholds.

By whom and for who was the tool created? GIRBa's research and action agenda

For almost ten years GIRBa's work has been driven by a locally grounded research and action agenda aiming at controlling urban sprawl while contributing to retrofit ageing post-war suburbs (Fortin et al. 2002). In this agenda, empirical research (urban morphology, uses and meanings of housing and neighbourhoods), design research (urban and architectural projects) and action research (collaborative planning and participatory design) should nurture each other through iterative cycles.

GIRBa's transdisciplinary approach to action research through participation is inspired by Habermas's communicative action theory (1984, 1987), acknowledging the importance of stakeholders sharing their different knowledge and experience to solve complex planning problems. Four categories of knowledge are used simultaneously: scientific knowledge, held by academics and consultants, and most often produced through empirical research; instrumental knowledge, held by planning technicians or municipal officers, which refers to practicality and experience about possible means of action; ethical knowledge, held by citizens and elected officials, which corresponds to the values, beliefs and other experiences that help stakeholders decide whether a planning solution suits their needs; and finally aesthetic knowledge, held by citizens, designers and artists, which alludes to aesthetic judgement, experience, tastes and preferences about the built environment (Després et al. 2004).

GIRBa's strategy in collaborative planning and participatory design is to provide opportunities for representatives of each type of knowledge to initiate face-to-face communication so that consensual solutions derived from

reflective thinking can emerge. The back-and-forth process of negotiating a consensus among stakeholders derives from different modes (or tools) of verbal and image-based communication within the participatory process. As put by Innes and Booher (1996), 'making sense together' is achieved by participants who are willing to reflect upon the information presented and shared, while allowing their own assumptions and interpretations to be questioned by others. Gradually, agreements and dissents emerge and are collectively resolved (Després et al. 2004; Fortin et al. 2005).

How does the tool work? The collaborative process

Defining the collaborative strategy

GIRBa prepared and orchestrated the design process over a six-month period to reach 38,000 community members. This task involved three challenges.

- Getting the attention of the university community and other interest groups and mobilizing a few of their representatives to become active participants throughout the process.
- Defining an efficient collaborative strategy through a sequence of participatory activities and tools.
- Validating the planning orientations and objectives defined during the process by the participants with the broader university community.

The first challenge consisted of having both university and local communities identify with the collaborative process. The choice of an acronym – the PACT project, which stands in French for 'Campus Participatory Planning Project' – appropriately referred to the idea of making a 'deal' among members of the community and the mandated researchers and designers. To get the attention of the local community (namely, residents and shopkeepers from the adjoining neighbourhood), the City of Quebec agreed to lend a room in a local community centre where all of the meetings would take place. A website was immediately put in place to announce and explain the project while a press release alerted the local papers. As the process evolved, all meeting minutes, validated by participants, were put on the website to be readily accessible to the broader community, as were all Powerpoint presentations, resulting data, drawings and reports (www.pacte.ulaval.ca).

According to its transdisciplinary theoretical framework, GIRBa then proceeded to identify the various groups of stakeholders who could bring different types of knowledge into the process. About 120 out of 200 invited participants agreed to take part in the process, among them students and members of the university community (professors, lecturers, administrative officers, etc.), home-owners and high-street shopkeepers from the adjoining residential area, members of non-profit and 'green' organizations, employees of public and semi-public planning agencies (including Quebec City planning officers), design professionals (architects, planners, designers, etc.) and developers.

The next challenge was to come up with a sequence of meetings, workshops and associated tools and techniques to activate the participatory process. Drawing on GIRBa members' individual and shared implications in previous collaborative processes, this sequence proposed an array of participatory tools: some adapted from GIRBa's past experiences, others borrowed from relevant cases elsewhere, and a few specifically designed for the occasion. Each tool was selected as part of a broader strategy to achieve the best consensual project possible within the time frame.

The collaborative process in three steps

The collaborative process followed three main stages: identifying the stakeholders and challenges; defining a shared vision for the neighbourhood as well as objectives and means of action; and finally designing the actual neighbourhood plan (Figure 16.1).

Step 1. Challenges and issues: stakeholders' points of view

The initial phase was meant to inform and consult members of different interest groups about the project. It involved 12 meetings with different groups of 10 to 20 stakeholders and identified 128 challenges and issues, later categorized by GIRBa into ten planning themes.

Step 2. Prospective outlook: priorities and visions

GIRBa's past participatory experience has confirmed that building a consensus around a 'diagnosis' is easier to do collectively than defining a common vision and general orientations to underlie a plan. For this purpose, a series of four one-day meetings were planned: one innovation and three consensus workshops to which all 120 members of the interest groups were invited. Between 40 and 60 participants showed up to each of these meetings.

The main objective of the innovation workshop was to envision the participants' 'ideal' neighbourhood through collective mapping exercises (Vodoz and Monteventi 2005). Each team of eight to ten participants was asked to develop and draw a shared vision using markers and a selection of images illustrating the planning issues previously identified. Then they were asked to transpose their vision on to an actual aerial photo of the site, thereby drawing a schematic plan. These image-based communication techniques, combined with a ranking exercise of the previously pinpointed planning issues, helped translate thoughts and priorities into spatial arrangements that echoed a forming consensus about key ideas: the conservation of wooded areas, better connections between campus and surrounding neighbourhoods, a concern for affordable housing and an overall ecological planning agenda. At the end of the day, participants voted for favoured ideas (Figure 16.2).

A smaller group of 40 stakeholders' representatives attended three one-day consensus workshops to identify pragmatic neighbourhood design objectives and means of action to make the vision attainable. Each workshop focused on

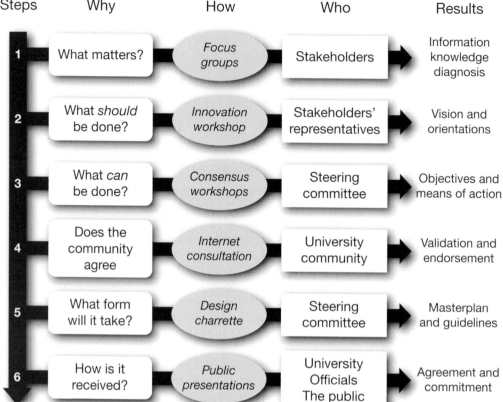

Steps	Why	How	Who	Results
1	What matters?	*Focus groups*	Stakeholders	Information knowledge diagnosis
2	What *should* be done?	*Innovation workshop*	Stakeholders' representatives	Vision and orientations
3	What *can* be done?	*Consensus workshops*	Steering committee	Objectives and means of action
4	Does the community agree	*Internet consultation*	University community	Validation and endorsement
5	What form will it take?	*Design charrette*	Steering committee	Masterplan and guidelines
6	How is it received?	*Public presentations*	University Officials The public	Agreement and commitment

16.1 Sequence of meeting and participatory tools used during the collaborative planning and design of the new university neighbourhood

16.2 Innovation workshop – participants envision the future neighbourhood and vote for what they consider to be the best idea and solutions

specific planning themes that posed sensitive challenges, such as urban diversity and density, streets, infrastructure and transportation.

Different participatory tools and techniques were used to activate communication during the three workshops. For instance, the first workshop broached the complex issue of diversity: what proportions should be allocated to different categories of residents, buildings, dwellings, tenure modes, public spaces, etc. During the second workshop, four sub-teams created scaled models of the neighbourhood from kits of wood blocks (representing housing types), ribbons and cutouts (for streets, bicycle and pedestrian paths, sports fields, public spaces, etc.) (Figure 16.3). The last workshop proposed an ambitious synthesis of all design objectives, criteria and means of action that had progressively emerged. Each of those was validated by vote during a plenary session (using green, yellow and red flashcards). The few remaining dissensions were discussed and, most of the time, resolved.

The internet consultation of the entire university community was designed to gather more information regarding the profile and aspirations of potential residents (mainly students and employees), and to validate the preliminary visions and intents so far expressed by the PACT participants. The 119-queries semi-structured questionnaire was sent via e-mail to the 38,000 university members. A total of 721 questionnaires were returned, which were analysed quantitatively and qualitatively by GIRBa; the results were presented on the PACT website. This tool proved extremely useful in informing the larger university community about the future development, and also in appreciating the high level of agreement with most of the decisions so far taken during the PACT process.

Step 3. Making a plan together: design charrette

The last phase of the process proposed actually to design the neighbourhood during an intensive two-day workshop. Day one of the charrette amounted, first, to presenting the results of the internet consultation to the returning group of about 40 participants. Two teams with mixed competencies were then asked to design a proposal for the neighbourhood plan. At the end of the day, both schemes were discussed during a plenary session in order to identify their most agreed-upon features. During the evening, GIRBa team members redrew one 'consolidated' version of the plan that best illustrated the consensus. Day two started with a presentation of the plan for validation, after which several groups were formed: one to adjust and draw

16.3 Participants creating scaled models of the neighbourhood during the second consensus workshop

the final version of the neighbourhood plan, and three others to detail housing types for selected blocks. Each team consulted the others for constant readjustments. At the end of the day, the neighbourhood plan and its detailed housing blocks were discussed in one last plenary session aiming to validate clearly the resulting neighbourhood plan.

Assessment and prospective outlook

The collaborative design process reported in this chapter and its resulting 1,500-unit neighbourhood plan fit into strong, sustainable and democratic planning agendas.[2] The 'co-design' approach, based on gradually building a consensus, relied upon the active participation of stakeholders with multiple and varied interests. A 'bricolage' of participatory tools and simulation techniques, some previously tested and others not, aimed to respect and emphasize different types of knowledge while activating communication and negotiation. The diversity of tools used in the different steps of the process is a condition allowing each participant to take part (Joerin and Nembrini 2005) according to their attitudes and values.

Despite initial tensions and fears from all sides involved, the collaboration worked well: participants with different expectations were able to listen and learn from each other, to construct a comprehensive understanding of the issues at stake and to reach a consensus on a vision for the future neighbourhood. Most importantly, participants in the PACT process unanimously expressed their satisfaction with the resulting masterplan and are acting as ambassadors for its implementation. This kind of 'endorsement' by advocates for the plan and the collaborative process should translate into more trust in (and less conflict among) all of the actors involved in the actual development, and especially the university.[3]

Notes

1   GIRBa is composed of five professors/co-directors, two associate professors, two research professionals and a dozen graduate and undergraduate students in the fields of architecture, urban design, planning, sociology, environmental psychology and geomatics. GIRBa's

activities routinely involve thesis work and studio projects funded by public research grants, and also by contracts with various government offices and institutions (www.girba.crad.ulaval.ca).

2   Reaching an average net density of about 100 dwellings per hectare, the neighbourhood project endorses sustainable principles in terms of reduction of car dependency through a reduction of parking standards, car-sharing solutions, public transportation facilities and pedestrian and bicycle paths; conservation of the natural environment (water retention, wooded areas); eco-housing (green roofs, energy efficiency, passive solar heating); affordable housing and innovative modes of tenure for students and also for other members of the university community and neighbours; quality and variety of open public spaces (parks, sports fields, squares, community gardens, commercial area); and overall economic viability thanks, in part, to a more efficient link between the campus and its surrounding neighbourhoods to capitalize on both the revitalization of the nearby high street and the existing infrastructure. The plan is available for download at www.girba.crad. ulaval.ca/articles/PACTE_Planquartier_Rapportfinal.pdf

3   At the time of writing, the collaborative process report has just been endorsed by Laval University's high officials who, it is hoped, will publicly add their voice to those of the participants in order to sustain the stakeholders' enthusiasm and commitment.

References

Després, C., Brais, N. and Avellan, S. (2004) 'Collaborative planning for retrofitting suburbs: transdisciplinarity and intersubjectivity in action', in Lawrence, R.J. and Després, C. (eds.) 'Transdisciplinarity', Futures, Special Issue, 36(4): 471–486.

Després, C., Fortin, A., Joerin, F., Vachon, G. and Gatti, E. (In press) 'Retrofitting post-war suburbs: a transdisciplinary research and planning process', in Hoffmann-Riem, H., Hirsch Hadorn, G., Biber-Klemm, S., Grossenbacher-Mansuy, W., Joye, D., Pohl, C., Wiesmann, U. and Zemp, E. (eds.) Handbook of Transdisciplinary Research, London.

Fortin, A., Després, C. and Vachon, G. (eds.) (2002) La Banlieue Revisitée, Nota Bene, Quebec.

Fortin, A., Després, C. and Vachon, G. (2006) 'Design urbain en collaboration: bilan et enjeux', 'Géocarrefour', Revue de Geographie de Lyon, Special Issue, 80(2): 145–154.

GIRBa (2006a) Démarche Participative pour l'Aménagement d'un Nouveau Quartier Universitaire sur le Campus de l'Université Laval: Recueil des Présentations et Comptes Rendus. Volume I, École d'architecture, Faculté d'aménagement, d'architecture et des arts visuels, Université Laval, Québec.

GIRBa (2006b) *Démarche Participative pour l'Aménagement d'un Nouveau Quartier Universitaire sur le Campus de l'Université Laval: Analyse des Résultats de l'Enquête Internet. Volume II*, École d'architecture, Faculté d'aménagement, d'architecture et des arts visuels, Université Laval, Québec, available at: www.girba.crad.ulaval.ca/articles/PACTE_rapportenqueteinternet.pdf.

GIRBa (2006c) *Démarche Participative pour l'Aménagement d'un Nouveau Quartier Universitaire sur le Campus de l'Université Laval: Plan de Quartier. Volume III*, École d'architecture, Faculté d'aménagement, d'architecture et des arts visuel, Université Laval, Québec, available at: www.girba.crad.ulaval.ca/articles/PACTE_Planquartier_Rapportfinal.pdf.

Habermas, J. (1984) *The Theory of Communicative Action, Volume 1. Reason and the Rationalization of Society*, Beacon Press, Boston.

Habermas, J. (1987) *The Theory of Communicative Action, Volume 2. Lifeworld and System. A Critique of Functionalist Reason*, Beacon Press, Boston.

Innes, J.E. and Booher, D. (1996) 'Consensus building and complex adaptive systems. A framework for evaluating collaborative planning', *Journal of the American Planning Association*, 65(4): 412–423.

Joerin, F. and Nembrini, A. (2005) 'Post-evaluation of the use of geographic information in a public participatory processes', *URISA Journal*, 17(1): 15–26.

Vodoz, L. and Monteventi, L. (2005) 'Opportunités et limites de l'agenda 21 Local. À L'exemple de Quartiers 21, Démarche Participative pour un Développement Durable à Lausanne', *Colloque International 'Développement Urbain Durable, Gestion des Ressources et Gouvernance'*, Université de Lausanne, 21–23 septembre.

17 GIS behaviour mapping for provision of interactive empirical knowledge, vital monitoring and better place design

Barbara Goličnik

Introduction

GIS behaviour mapping is an analytical tool which draws on a combination of behaviour mapping and GIS techniques to reveal common patterns of behaviour that appear to be correlated with particular layouts and details. This study was devised to assist designers in creating urban squares or parks for contemporary use. It concentrates on the relationship between the spatial characteristics of a place and the dynamic of its use, which is a field where the empirical basis for the design decision-making process is lacking and new techniques offering more reliable ways of predicting and understanding use are therefore valuable tools. The approach described in this chapter is an attempt to fill some of this gap. It draws on research methods that combine well-established techniques such as environment-behaviour observations and behaviour mapping but combines them with technologies such as GIS to take advantage of emerging ICTs, thereby linking users and their behaviour to places using a medium with which designers and planners are familiar.

The challenge of this analytical approach is to confront spatial and human dimensions, and to find compatible scales and comparable accuracies between the physicality of spaces and the use pattern. It is based on a 'bottom-up' approach, studying a usage-spatial relationship in a defined spatial unit, a place like a square or park. In doing so, it addresses three main issues: the potential and effectiveness of different environments for spatial occupancy; the appropriate formats of information and research tools as well as their appropriate implementation in the design process; and the validity and insights of an empirical knowledge and its reflection on decision making, evaluation and the design of urban open public spaces.

Empirical knowledge for design research

The subject of the discussion arises from a designer's interest in urban settings and their users. The main scope is to identify relevant and convenient empirical knowledge for urban designers, and an effective research tool for researchers and decision-makers, to improve efficiency in their communication with designers, landscape architects and architects. Accordingly, both direct observation of actual usage of places and the designers' tacit knowledge and perception about usage-spatial relationship have been used.

Theoretical issues and challenges involved in making better places for people have not yet been adequately resolved through the detailed examination of the distribution and physical dimensions of behavioural patterns in actual places. According to Carmona *et al.* (2003), who see urban design as a means of manipulating the probabilities of certain actions or behaviours, this should be an activity that *provides* people with choice, rather than *denying* it to them, and urban designers should be professionals who can master increasing space potential to create a meaningful, significant and desirable place. Although not all designers have these explicit aims, nonetheless many would be challenged by them. If we accept that the goal of urban design is to provide 'potential places', then potential behavioural patterns in such places and their inner structure and organization become a subject of interest and importance. Therefore, the empirical knowledge about the usage-spatial potentials of places becomes a crucial challenge in design (research).

This calls for a responsible and sensitive provision of research about the physicality of spaces, which uses the language of the patterns of use(r)s. The demand for appropriate analytical tools which address a justification and rationale for the integration of research in the design process is more than ever valid, and the so-called 'applicability gap' and incompatibilities between environment-behaviour researches and design are still very evident. Mitchell (1993), for example, emphasizes the conflict between the nature of the research and design tasks themselves. This chapter argues that the successful application of the interactive research-design relationship in an integrative framework is reflected in the quality of conversion of research data into design; and thus that the data format is crucial and, likewise, the preparation of data for conversion and the understanding of how to move from different sources on spatial reality to visual data and final design images. Consequently tools which enable such operations and designers familiarity with them are essential.

The direct contribution of GIS behaviour mapping to the design practice itself is both challenging and promising: designers are often asked to solve other people's problems, and the efficiency of their solutions depends on the degree of 'wondering about' these problems or even more fundamentally, the capability of recognizing and addressing them inclusively and correctly. This reflects the importance of knowledge which contains appropriate information about social aspects of design, i.e. the potential usage of/within a particular designed place. Activities form their own spaces and through them shape places, therefore reasoning about patterns of spatial occupancies, as elements of spatial definitions, may become essential when addressing design practice which aims to create an inclusive and responsive environment.

The tool presented in this chapter, GIS behaviour mapping, aims to benefit the practical fields of landscape architecture and architecture when addressing design projects about urban open public spaces. Generally, it enables the examination of real usage-spatial relationships (in scale 1:1); the lessons learned can contribute to both urban design theory and practice. Specifically, as shown in the following section, it can provide information and insight into the dynamics of the design and development of urban space; it can offer coherent perspectives and platforms for debating research and design for urban landscape; and it can promote better understanding, planning and design in order to respond to social inclusion and well-being in urban open public spaces.

GIS behaviour mapping as a tool for vital monitoring and better design

Behavioural maps provide a shorthand description of the distribution of behaviours throughout a place. The major value of behavioural maps, as a research tool, lies in the possibility of developing general principles regarding the use of space that apply in a variety of settings. GIS behaviour maps extract behavioural evidence into layers of spatial information to give a better understanding of the individual and collective patterns of use that emerge in a place. The overlap of behaviour maps can show characteristics and changes in using chosen open spaces in terms of activities, number of people engaged, gender and all the other variables that are explored. GIS is a tool to visualize, manipulate, analyse and display spatial data; this discussion is based on observation of several public parks and squares in two European cities, Edinburgh (Scotland, UK) and Ljubljana (Slovenia).

This analytical tool is significant for its tripartite process: data collection, database creation and analysis or evaluation. All three phases are necessary when, for example, questions such as 'Who is doing what, where and with whom?' or 'Where and for how long is what taking place?' are addressed for one or more places or, for example, post-occupancy evaluation for a certain place is being studied. Beside this original and primary purpose, the tool can also be applied in comparative studies such as, for example, the study of certain uses in certain physical settings or under specific weather conditions: if data are already available for similar places to the one in question, these can be used and any initial data collection might not be needed. The first two phases (data collection, and database creation) represent the preparation for actual analysis. However, their preciseness is crucial for the quality and richness of the final analysis and results.

In reality, data collection is fieldwork which requires a thorough preparation. This means that before any recording it is necessary to obtain an accurate scale map of the area to be observed, define the entire observation period, schedule specific times and their repetitions for observation, decide clearly on the types and details of behaviours to be observed, and provide a list of anticipated activities, their related symbols and additional coding (age groups, duration of an activity, etc.). It is important, during the observation, to stay open-ended for any possible new activity to be added, and to be prepared for the definition of attached symbols for such unexpected or infrequent activities.

There are always more or less obvious relationships presented on the maps. Some are recognizable at first glance, others become evident when the data are manipulated. As there is obviously more underlying information embedded in collected data than could be presented at once, to prevent data being left aside, blocked out or even overlooked there is a need for more transparent techniques in creating summaries and assembling collections. It is possible to create a transparent database in a digital environment, which enables interrelated layered-image presentations to be supported with lists of attached information. A GIS[1] application seems valuable in studies of usage-spatial relationships, where positions and dimensions of behavioural patterns in places are of key importance. Although the emerging ICTs (PDA, Tablet PC) may support a simultaneous coding in the future, data from every observation are usually originally recorded and mapped by hand, and then later recorded in digital form on to a GIS map system. ArcView (ESRI), for example, a GIS-supported software, offers an effective way to connect these collected data and their sources of origin, such as spatial settings, into comprehensive and interactive databases. It enables data to be organized in thematic layers in which information is listed in attached tables. Such a rich, spatially explicit database of observations could be explored in a number of different ways, e.g. according to type of activities, age of people observed, weather conditions, etc. (Plates 11 and 12).

In this context GIS is a successful practical tool to build, develop and maintain a body of empirical knowledge using GIS interactive maps as its scripts. With regards to the latter, it can provide and/or assure an exchange with data addressing the same, similar or new aspects of interest in the same environmental setting. It makes it clear and easy to arrange a selection of relevant variables of a usage-spatial relationship, and as such is a convenient tool for monitoring as well as updating designers' tacit knowledge about changes and trends in usage of places. Thus it builds empirical knowledge about both stimulating and inhibitive environments for single and multiple occupancies and users. Concerning the implementation of such knowledge in urban open public space design, operationally, a visualization of research findings and the related concerns in decision-making, evaluation and management is of key importance. To sum up, the practical value of this tool lies in helping designers to be confident that the layouts proposed for intended use will in practice serve those uses (and users) well and be likely to be used as predicted. Figures 17.1 and 17.2 show gained empirical knowledge about skateboarding. The former shows the inner structures of skateboarders' behavioural patterns revealed as the 'event', 'supplementary', 'effective' and 'latent' environments for skateboarding in Trg Republike, Ljubljana, and Bristo Square,

Edinburgh (Goličnik, 2005a: 88). The latter shows dimensions of supportive and disruptive environments for skateboarders, exemplified from the cumulative evidence on assembly behavioural maps in Trg Republike and Bistro Square (Goličnik 2005a: 90).

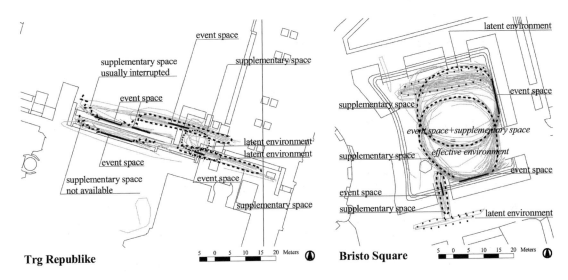

17.1 Inner structure of skateboarders' behaviour patterns

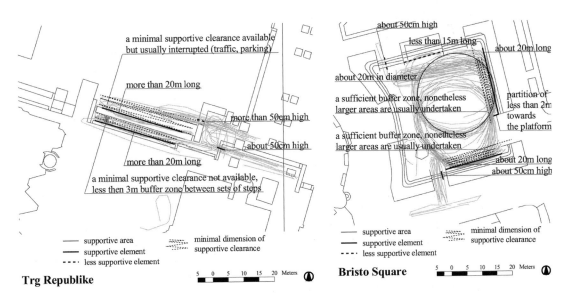

17.2 Dimensions of supportive and disruptive environments for skateboarders

Conclusion

GIS behaviour maps are recognized as an effective tool to represent and interpret behavioural patterns as visual data. They also translate recorded evidence into a body of empirical knowledge and preserve the connection of related non-spatial data (age, gender, type of an activity, etc.) to the material place. By such an association of behaviour with a certain environment, it is possible to ask questions and draw conclusions about the behaviour and its relationship to a place, and from such reasoning move towards a reconciliation between design and research in the field of urban (open space) design. Mapping physical dimensions of uses is thus seen as a potential way of negotiating (urban) landscape (design) forms.

Notes

1   ESRI's definition of geographic information systems (GIS) is that they are systems of computer software, hardware, data and personnel for visualization, manipulation, analysis and presentation of information, which concern spatial location. ESRI is a world leader in GIS data supply, software and technology. (www. esri.com).

References and further reading

Bechtel, R.B., Marans, R. and Michelson, W. (1987) *Methods in Environmental and Behavioural Research*, Van Nostranel Reinhold, New York.

Carmona, M., Heath, T., Oc, T. and Tiesdell, S. (2003) *Public Places – Urban Spaces: The Dimensions of Urban Design*, Architectureal Press, Oxford.

Goličnik, B. (2005a) *People in place: A configuration of physical form and the dynamic patterns of spatial occupancy in urban open public space*, PhD thesis, Edinburgh College of Art, Heriot Watt University, Edinburgh.

Goličnik, B. (2005b) 'Public urban open spaces and patterns of users: exploring behavioural data using GIS', in Martens, B. and Keul, A.G. (eds.) *Designing Social Innovation: Planning, Building, Evaluating*, Hogrefe & Huber, Göttingen.

Mitchell, C.T. (1993) *Redefining Design: From Form to Experience*, Van Nostrand Reinhold, New York.

18 Experiential landscape: revealing hidden dimensions of people-place relations

Kevin Thwaites and Ian Simkins

Introduction

According to phenomenological interpretations, places are not simply material receptacles containing human experiences but are partly defined by them (Canter 1977; Tuan 1980; Proshansky 1983). Space becomes place when material and spatial elements of environment are given life by the meanings, associations and experiences people inject into them during daily life. Accepting places as experiential as well as material and spatial entities challenges those who design them: the tangibility of the built environment that allows us to sculpt and order our settings does not readily hold for the fluid subjectivity of human emotional expression. Place as spatial and experiential fusion implies embracing a different indeterminate form of order, which Jane Jacobs likens to the dynamism of dance.

> This order is all composed of movement and change, and although it is life, not art, we may fancifully call it the art form of the city and liken it to the dance – not to a simple-minded precision dance with everyone kicking up at the same time, twirling in unison and bowing off en-masse, but to an intricate ballet in which the individual dancers and ensembles all have distinctive parts which miraculously reinforce each other and compose an orderly whole. (Jacobs 1961:50).

This is a form of order constantly present but less visible to conventional processes of environmental analysis and design. How we reveal such hidden order is the topic of this chapter.

Why was experiential landscape created?

Revealing the order to which Jane Jacobs alludes depends on appreciating that human functioning and its spatial context cannot be decoupled. We therefore see the experiential landscape as a spatial and experiential whole constituted from the incidental spaces and features which through regular encounter come to mean something to people. It is the mundane landscape of everyday experience: a landscape made from the often overlooked totality of building edges and doorways, streets, yards and alcoves, alleys and squares, for example, which through use and association form the life patterns of people as they move about. Experiential landscape makes these life patterns visible by means of a range of mapping and participatory tools which draw together spatial and experiential dimensions of place perception in ways relevant to environmental design professions. It provides a way of seeing the outdoor environment in primarily experiential terms, and relates this to spatial arrangement to help designers make places more responsive to human functioning (Thwaites and Simkins 2006).

How it works

Experiential landscape correlates conceptually with theories of place which argue that aspects of human experience have particular spatial implications important to achieving and sustaining fulfilled lives (Norberg-Schulz 1971; Canter 1977; Cullen 1971; Hillier and Hanson 1984; Gehl 2001; Alexander 2001). It emphasizes spatial experiences that encourage place attachment in people, strengthen orientation and stimulate a sense of neighbourhood. These experiential categories are interpreted spatially by developing Norberg-Schulz's (1971) interpretation of space as a dimension of human existence where people are assumed to possess an innate tendency to externalize locations in the environment as points of reference from which to locate themselves. Field exploration of models built from this consolidated development of a spatial language, defining human sense of place as awareness of spatial sensations called centre, direction, transition and area (CDTA), representing different facets of place experience. Centre relates to experience of location; direction to continuity and extent; transition to sense of change; and area to the sense of environmental coordination that might influence perception of neighbourhood or distinguishable city quarter, for example. We group these in the acronym CDTA to represent that they must be understood as distinctive sensations within an indivisible whole. CDTA is a vocabulary that ties experiential and spatial dimensions of place perception together, defining experiential landscape in terms of their holistic relationship.

Graphical representation of CDTA makes it possible to record and map how their levels fluctuate in the subconscious as we move about.

The experiential landscape approach develops from cognitive mapping principles and owes inspiration to Lynch and Rivkin's paper, 'A walk around the block'. This was probably the first time in urban planning and design that human emotions were associated with spatial characteristics, arising from analysis of people's direct perceptions of ordinary streetscapes. One of the hypotheses to emerge from this simple study was that 'the individual must perceive his environment as an ordered pattern, and is constantly trying to inject order into his surroundings, so that all the relevant perceptions are jointed one to the other' (Lynch and Rivkin 1959). One of the aims of developing a way to operationalize the experiential landscape concept is to try to make this hidden form of order visible. Figure 18.1 symbolizes a range of ways to obtain information about different aspects of the relationship between people and the places they use. The experiential landscape is only that which emerges from the information derived from those who participate at a partucular time. Clarity of resolution and stability of image will grow the higher up the figure one is able to get.

Operationalizing experiential landscape involves applying a multi-method approach to make experiential landscape maps recording the distribution of CDTA for settings as they are

semi-structured
interviewing

conversation

role play

anthropological tracking

non-participant
observation

professional reading
of site

18.1 The experiential landscape increases in resolution by gathering and layering information in different ways

perceived by individuals and groups. This is an important response to the intrinsic subjectivity involved in place perception and can be compared with gradually increasing visual resolution in a pixellated image (Figure 18.1). Using a single method to obtain information about people's experience of places will produce data related only to that specific method of enquiry: the resulting experiential landscape image is necessarily partial. Layering together information gathered from a range of methods, synthesizing perceptions of environmental design professionals and users of the setting brings the experiential landscape into sharper focus, gradually revealing a more authentic image of experiential order.

Professional reading

Professional reading equates with site investigations that conventionally precede development projects, in that it involves those with specialist training observing spatial and material properties of site. Findings are coded to establish a distribution of CDTA across the site. No site-user information is involved, and so the experiential landscape revealed is partial and in essence represents a set of theoretical principles projected on to the site via the interpretative skills of specialists. Its value lies in providing a provisional impression of patterns of experiential character, and this can provide guidance for subsequent user-group studies.

Non-participant observation

This stage involves moving beyond spatial observations by layering in information gained from passively observing people using the site. This gives an impression of practices, interactions and events which occur in a specific context by watching naturally occurring events and behaviour. It provides access to the cultural mechanisms of a place as well as the spatial relationship that the site users have with their surroundings. Observations are coded according to the CDTA framework and symbolized graphically, adding a further layer of experiential detail and sharpening the resolution of the experiential landscape.

Anthropological tracking

Another kind of observational approach involves watching for traces of people, rather than people themselves. The so-called desire lines that tend to develop in soft surfaces provide a familiar example of this as visible evidence that patterns of pedestrian movement do not correspond with design intention. More subtle traces, such as accumulations of discarded gum, cigarette-stubs, take-out drinks' cartons, etc. in alcoves and corners, are evidence of temporary occupation, suggesting that, while the physicality of the location may be unremarkable, locally it may be an important vantage point to pause and wait for friends, to watch, to smoke, chew and drink. In terms of CDTA this is interpreted as evidence of centred sensations at that place for some of the local population.

Conversation

The value of casual conversation as a means to gain insight into how public places are used is easily overlooked as unstructured or scientifically haphazard. It is not always possible to explore observations arising from the methods detailed above by more systematic participant interviews, but it is usually possible to ask someone. As eminent geographer Yi Fu Tuan observed, local anecdote and idiosyncrasy play a part in how places become activated in the lives of inhabitants. Anthropological studies suggest processes of communication sustain a sense of place so that places become stabilized by groups through shared activities and common language. 'City people are constantly making and unmaking places by talking about them. A network of gossip can elevate one shop to prominence and consign another to oblivion. . . in a sense, a place is its reputation.' (Tuan 1980:6).

Role play

Role play is an effective way to supplement the theory-led place perceptions of professionals that mainly tend to be influenced by what the setting looks like: role play gives a local or lay perspective. Although there are obvious limitations, role-playing adds considerably to the detail and depth of local place awareness because it forces a situation in which participants have to look at the setting through the eyes of someone likely to use it, raising to the forefront of consciousness an attitude to the setting that would most likely have otherwise been overlooked.

Semi-structured interviewing

This type of interviewing is used in qualitative research to allow participants to range freely in their responses to questions while maintaining some underlying structure. Predetermined topics guide conversation, allowing new questions or insights to evolve as the discussion develops. We have developed an approach to interviewing that tunes in with how people move about their surroundings, conducted as a themed conversation enabling participants to recreate mentally what they did and felt in as natural a way as possible.

Revealing the identity of Kirby Hill

A combination of the above methods underpinned an investigation of identity in Kirby Hill, a residential village in North Yorkshire, UK. Kirby Hill's inhabitants value their physical independence from neighbouring Boroughbridge, and are uneasy about future development on intervening agricultural land that might threaten their sense of Kirby Hill as a separate community. The parish council decided to develop a Village Design Statement to define the village's identity and help development control mechanisms to take steps to preserve it. This proved difficult because the proliferation of suburban-style residential development had all but removed the vernacular quality and historical meandering of village political boundaries had over the years clouded local views about where the village began and ended. Against this was a powerful sense of social cohesion emanating from the individual and collective lives of its people, a hidden dimension of village order hard to see in physical form but nonetheless valuable and highly sensitive to change.

Revealing Kirby Hill's experiential landscape brought this into sharper focus by making explicit patterns of routine experience implicit in the way inhabitants used and felt about the village environment, and identifying components of the village's spatial fabric that sustained it. Extensive public consultation and observational tools built up layers of individual place perceptions into a collective view. Approximately forty percent of the resident population participated in semi-structured interviews around themes determined by an initial scoping study carried out by a research team. Transcripts were coded to identify the distribution of CDTA for each individual, enabling an experiential landscape map to be generated in each case. GIS computer software layered the maps to produce a composite map representing the experiential landscape for the participant group (Plate 13).

The Kirby Hill analysis helped to illuminate dimensions of village life, crucially relevant to the sense of village identity, that transcend its superficial visual appearance. These dimensions are rooted in the way inhabitants experience village life, often subconsciously, through the places they come into contact with routinely, and the meanings and associations they hold both at the scale of the whole village and in relation to places within and around it that have particular significance. Revealing Kirby Hill's experiential landscape has given this a spatial expression through mapping patterns of open-space experience. These help to explain the complex and elastic nature of the village boundaries, where the essence of Kirby Hill is felt most intensely, and reveal that the village core is a composite of several distinguishable components working together to form its heart. It shows how the habits and emotions of individuals become embedded into the village landscape, how these aggregate into a picture of Kirby Hill's collective social identity and how this is expressed through its buildings and open spaces. It provides a benchmark from which to examine Kirby Hill's strengths and weaknesses in terms of how its spatial organization might sustain the future evolution of its community (Plate 14).

Conclusions

In this chapter we have presented a particular theoretical perspective on people-space relations and shown how this can be applied to reveal experiential potential in open-space settings. The central hypothesis is that a range of fundamental human experience is intimately woven together with certain types of spatial configuration which can be read in the physical fabric of a built environment. By using a simple spatial language (CDTA), environmental design professionals and researchers can quickly record and map the distribution of spatial types and then read the experiential characteristics of a setting from patterns that emerge as mosaics of integrated symbols. Such mosaics constitute the experiential landscape of that particular setting, and this can help augment conventional survey and analysis techniques by revealing experiential characteristics that otherwise remain hidden from view. We have shown in the Kirby Hill village identity project that experiential landscape mapping methods can underpin a significant process of public participation to map experiential components of the psyche of a resident population. By this means the lives and habits of people living in and using a setting in routine life can be integrated with spatial analysis to make explicit the spatial implications of what their place of residence means to them and what aspects of it are significant and why. This presents an important means by which a phenomenological perspective on people-space relations can be operationalized in various ways to bring an explicitly human dimension to the way that residential settings are developed and adapted.

References

Alexander, C. (2001) *The Nature of Order: An Essay on the Art of Building and the Nature of the Universe. Book One, The Phenomenon of Life*, Oxford University Press, New York.

Canter, D. (1977) *The Psychology of Place*, The Architectural Press, London.

Cullen, G. (1971) *The Concise Townscape*, Architectural Press, Oxford.

Gehl, J. (2001 4edn.) *Life Between Buildings*, The Danish Architectural Press.

Hillier, B. and Hanson, J. (1984) *The Social Logic of Space*, Cambridge University Press, Cambridge.

Jacobs, J. (1961) *The Death and Life of Great American Cities*, Jonathan Cape, London.

Lynch, K. and Rivkin, M. (1959) 'A walk around the block', *Landscape*, 8: 24–34.

Norberg-Schulz, C. (1971) *Existence, Space, and Architecture*, Praeger, New York.

Proshansky, H.M., Fabian, A.K. and Kaminoff, R. (1983) 'Place-identity: Physical world socialisation of the Self', *Journal of Environmental Psychology*, 3: 57–83.

Thwaites, K. and Simkins, I.M. (2006) *Experiential Landscape: An Approach to People, Place and Space*, Taylor and Francis, London.

Tuan, Y.F. (1980) 'Rootedness versus sense of place', *Landscape*, 24: 3–8.

19 Listening to and understanding the voices of people with learning disabilities in the planning and design process

Alice Mathers

Introduction

There is a growing impetus promoting the view that participation and social inclusion should play a pivotal role in the arrangement and content of everyday spatial realms. If we accept this, how do we ensure that the process is truly inclusive? This chapter and the following one by Ian Simkins present two examples of approaches to inclusivity. They summarise longitudinal doctoral studies that are developing tools and techniques for working with two groups in society that are often marginalized or absent from processes of change to places they use: specifically, people with learning disabilities and primary school children. In different ways they show how to facilitate understanding of place as an essential component of individual and social development. They demonstrate in particular how the techniques developed reveal the unique ways in which these groups understand their neighbourhood experiences and place perceptions and what the implications are for planning and design decision making-processes.

At the most restricted end of the communication spectrum, people with learning disabilities are often forgotten as silent, hidden members of their communities whose label, 'learning disabled', often causes confusion and fear. The white paper Valuing People (Department of Health 2001) defined individuals who display a learning disability as those with 'a significantly reduced ability to understand new or complex information, to learn new skills (impaired intelligence), with a reduced ability to

cope independently (impaired social functioning); which started before adulthood, with a lasting effect on development' (Department of Health 2001:14).

With a growing body of disability researchers arguing that it is attitudes and interactions in the person-environment relationship that have allowed our 'disablist' society to label and segregate members of the community as 'disabled', this research explores the development and evolution of a visual communication toolkit which unlocks the experience of public open spaces by people with learning disabilities. The research follows a longitudinal study working with participants supported by the British charity Mencap at two research sites in Yorkshire and the north east of England. Research methodologies trialled and developed encompass photo-elicitation, participant drawings and semi-structured interviews.

Disabled by design: why and for whom was the toolkit designed?

In the UK provisions made by the Disability Discrimination Act (DDA) 1995, enforced in October 2004, have ensured 'reasonable' adjustments must be made to environments and buildings so they are accessible to all. The DDA legislation has remained primarily a physical-access issue, with greater attention focused on the built environment, and little interest given to the experience of place or external environments. It enforces the stereotype of disabled people primarily as wheelchair users (who have been the most vocal regarding their rights), ignoring the needs of people with sensory impairments, learning disabilities or mental health problems. The Disability Rights Commission, set up in April 2000, aimed to implement the DDA. However, with a definition of inclusive designs 'the goal of creating beautiful and functional environments that can be used equally by everyone, irrespective of age, gender or disability' (Disability Rights Commission 2001) which excluded the experiential dimension of place, designers were not encouraged to understand truly the needs of their clients.

Professor Rob Imrie's work into the professional interpretation of inclusive design has shown how architects (and landscape architects) implementing the DDA continue this legacy through limited understanding and experiential neglect:

> the types of design features for disabled people which tend to be incorporated into buildings include accessible toilets, ramps and level entry or access points. Little or nothing which addresses the needs of people with learning difficulties is incorporated into much contemporary building and design processes. (Imrie and Hall 2001: 97).

To remedy this lack of understanding and information, a communication toolkit was evolved to facilitate the exchange of ideas and experiences between designers and the community they serve, thereby ensuring landscapes of genuine accessibility. The Urban Green Spaces Taskforce (2002) foresaw that these could only be achieved by engaging the local community throughout the design process, understanding and meeting their aspirations.

The field research: what is the toolkit and how does it work?

A communication toolkit emerged from an ongoing collaboration between the researcher and a group of learning-disability participants attending a Yorkshire day service centre. Day service centres aim to provide activities for adults with learning disabilities (ALD's) who do not undertake paid employment. In August 2004 a research team was created under the moniker 'Our Parks and Gardens', comprising ten participants, one member of support staff, volunteers and the researcher. The participants have a range of communication needs and abilities (including those without speech or written language). Project development occurred over several years as the researcher gained understanding of a spectrum of visual communication methods that could include all members of the group. Implementation of the toolkit is now discussed in the context of a 14-week study trial during the spring and summer of 2006. The participants in this study were five male students with learning disabilities from a further education college in the north-east of England. The toolkit was used to elicit landscape experiences during the course of a taught module.

Informed consent

Previous research studies with ALDs have encountered severe problems in identifying and recruiting participants (Siegel and Ellis 1985; Lee 1993; Lennox et al. 2005). Barriers to research co-operation included obtaining consent and the restrictive nature of organizational policies and procedures (caution is justified, as people with learning disabilities are among society's most vulnerable citizens). Prior to commencement of the study, the researcher produced two formats of project information (one for support staff/carers and one for participants). Information in the participants' pack relied heavily on photographs and drawings produced with pilot-study participants, and explained the nature of the project using simple language in large font. During the first session at the college the researcher read through the information with participants and staff, and showed a short digital presentation of the process developed during the pilot study. All potential participants and their supporters gave consent to the project and the use of their words and images in the researcher's work.

Site visits

The project began with a drawing workshop (exploring understanding of the word 'park', and its positive and negative connotations) and the distribution of individual record books, where participants were encouraged to keep their drawings, photographs and notes. Seven different landscapes (including coastal, city, formal garden, moors and wetlands) were visited during the course of the project. On each visit the researcher and participants were accompanied by a college tutor and a residential support staff member. While on site digital cameras were used in several ways.

- By the researcher/staff member to capture the participants interacting with the landscape.
- By the researcher/staff member at a participant's request to capture elements of interest for the participant.
- By the participant aided by the researcher/staff member to capture elements of interest.
- By the participant unaided to capture items of personal interest.

An example of a photograph taken by the researcher on a visit to a formal garden, to capture participant and environmental interaction is shown in Plate 15.

Drawing workshop

On return to the college the participants chose photographs that held specific meaning for them, to use as a visual prompts for drawings in their record books illustrating individual experiences on site.

Individual canvas workshop

To increase focus and encourage project ownership each participant constructed and painted a personal canvas depicting the landscape, real or imagined, that held most resonance for them. Students used a combination of sketches and photographs from their record books to produce landscape paintings that demonstrated their aspirations for employment, social inclusion, memories of family, happiness in leisure time and association with experience. Figure 19.1 shows the construction of these canvases under support staff guidance.

Photo-elicitation interviews

Photo-elicitation involves using photographs to invoke comments, memory and discussion in the course of a semi-structured interview (Banks 2001). The merits of using photographs within the interview context have been strongly supported in recent publications by visual researchers such as Gemma Orobitg Canal (2004: 38), who citing Collier and Collier (1992) says:

> both photographic content and the narratives photographs evoke offer anthropologists routes to knowledge that cannot be achieved by verbal communication. Using photographs in an interview brings anthropologists to understand reality in new ways and can act as an important prompt when the anthropologist does not know how to set out a question. (Orobitg Canal 2004: 38).

During interviews, researcher and participant sat in front of a computer watching a digital slideshow of photographs taken on site. The researcher prompted questions around themes developed in the pilot study. In addition to photographic images, participants were asked to elaborate on work produced in their record books and, in later stages of the project, their individual canvases. Interviews were recorded and transcribed with the participant's consent, and further themes relevant to this particular participant group elicited.

Staff questionnaire

When working with people with learning disabilities, the views of their support staff should also be taken into account. These people provide 24-hour care and often know participants in both residential and edification capacities. A questionnaire developed through the pilot study, but with specific reference to the sites

19.1 Warren constructing his canvas with a college tutor

and individual participants' work in the north-east, was given to the tutor who had supported the project. Feedback from this source has two aims: to highlight methodological successes and limitations, and to confirm experiential information provided by participants in their work.

Public exhibition

Creating a clear end-point for participants, knowledge transfer, project transparency and inclusive dissemination are all key objects of this longitudinal study. Through collaboration with Mencap, dissemination is not restricted to the academic arena but includes the general public, policy-makers and the learning-disability community. Pilot-study participants have orchestrated a visual communication seminar day at the 'People's Parliament' (the Yorkshire monthly meeting of ALDs, support agencies, academics, policy-makers and those in practice) and two annual exhibitions at the Showroom Cinema, Sheffield. In the north-east the project ended with an exhibition at the local arts centre in Hexham, covered by the local press.

Conclusions on participant experience

Project feedback from staff and participants was overwhelmingly positive. The project introduced participants to new environments, gave them confidence and tools to communicate their reactions eloquently to a wider audience.

Using the example of one student Warren (not his real name) the project first revealed his fear of the countryside as an unknown experience, and his preference to urban environments of which he had knowledge. He was unable to imagine himself interacting with the countryside: 'Oh, I don't think I could cope with the beach.' However, when asked to describe his ideal trip out, he replied, 'Oh, oh, could it be somewhere like Blackpool. . . the Pleasure Beach and go to all the different things you can do.' This response demonstrated how he disassociated the imagined coastal landscape from actual coastal environments of entertainment he had experienced. Through site experience later in the project, after visiting the rural coast and reflecting on photographs, Warren declared, 'Well, I sort of changed my mind.' The coast became a place of possibilities where Warren imagined how the boats at the beach would take him to different countries, where he could socialize freely with people he aspired to be like: 'Maybe go visit some Goths over there.' Warren's experiences of landscape became more joyful and thoughtful as the project progressed. Plate 15 shows Warren on the final site visit, which in his subsequent interview he excitedly explained as 'I like all of that, it's just like it's Welsh noise. . . yeah, because I'm a devil!' The canvas produced by Warren for the exhibition (Plate 16) brought all of these factors together. He painted a green park landscape, where he could skateboard with people like himself, a large open space free from judgement.

Warren's changing attitude towards landscape illustrates the emancipation aspect of the toolkit. Most of the participants at both study sites had little prior experience of the variety of environments visited during the project. Many people with learning disabilities must rely upon parents and carers to facilitate leisure activities. As a result of financial, time and access constraints, ALDs' experience of, and potential views upon, matters of public space remain hidden and unexplored. For designers, use of this toolkit reveals them, and the social issues that have yet to be addressed.

References

Banks, M. (2001) *Visual Methods in Social Research*, Sage Publications, London.

Collier, J. Jr and Collier, M. (1992 [1967]) *Visual Anthropology. Photographs as a Research Method*, University of Mexico Press, Albuquerque.

Department of Health (2001) *Valuing People: A New Strategy for Learning Disability for the 21st Century*, The Stationery Office, London.

Disability Discrimination Act (1995) HMSO, London.

Disability Rights Commission (2001) *Creating an Inclusive Environment – Report on Improving the Built Environment*, Disability Rights Commission.

Imrie, R. and Hall, P. (2001) *Inclusive Design – Designing and Developing Accessible Environments*, Spon Press, London.

Lee, R.M. (1993) *Doing Research on Sensitive Topics*, Sage Publications, London.

Lennox, N., Taylor, M., Rey-Conde, T., Bain, C., Purdie, D.M. and Boyle, F. (2005) 'Beating the barriers: recruitment of people with intellectual disability to participate in research', *Journal of Intellectual Disability Research*, 49(4): 296–305.

Orobitg Canal, G. (2004) 'Photography in the field: word and image in ethnographic research', in Pink, S., Kürti, L. and Afonso, A.I. (eds.) *Working Images: Visual Research and Representation in Ethnography*, Routledge, London.

Siegel, P.E. and Ellis, N.R. (1985) 'Note on the recruitment of subjects for mental retardation research', *American Journal of Mental Deficiency*, 89: 431–3.

The Urban Green Spaces Taskforce (2002) *Green Spaces, Better Places*, Department for Transport, Local Government and the Regions, London.

20 Listening to and understanding the voices of young children in the planning and design process

Ian Simkins

Introduction: the need to study children's perception of space

The everyday local environment or incidental spaces routinely encountered by children is increasingly highlighted as an important contributor to their social development and general health and well-being (Thomas and Thompson 2004; DTLR 2002). Evidence suggests, however, that there remains a significant loss of connection between children and outdoor settings, and that this may have long-term implications (Worpole 2003). Ken Worpole, author and commentator on open space and social issues, highlights this by synthesizing current government and community initiatives in this field, placing the importance of providing for, and giving voice to, children in policy, planning, design and management of public open space within the urban renaissance agenda. His report, No Particular Place to Go 'seeks to make clear that planning for play, and the need to create safe street networks and spaces for young people and children, is a precondition of a healthy community life and 'liveability''' (Worpole 2003:4). Issues that appear to emerge from this aspiration especially include the notion that it is the environment routinely encountered by children which should receive particular attention, because this is the realm of a vision of the 'walkable community' advocated by, for example, the DTLR (2002).

A sequence of tools for the investigation

This research aspires to give voice to children by means of a range of participatory tools to facilitate exploration and analysis of the spatial experiences of primary school age children, with particular reference to their notions of place perception. The research emphasizes that it is experience of place that matters most, rather than what it looks like, for example, and for this reason significance is given to specific experiences that are central to the development of a person's awareness of where they are in relation to their surroundings and what this means to them.

The Field Research

Three primary schools were involved in a doctoral research study in which children from years three (seven and eight years old) and six (ten and eleven years old) engaged in a range of activities that collectively aimed to reveal in detail how they used, understood and felt about places they came into routine contact with in their local neighbourhood. The schools were in the Yorkshire and north-eastern England regions of the UK and sited in rural, suburban and urban locations. Following scrutiny of ethical considerations, an informed-consent process took place and a total of 68 children engaged in a longitudinal study adopting a multi-method approach employing various participative techniques. The overall research paradigm was highly qualitative, reflecting the subjective nature of place experience, and having roots in grounded theory – identifying the components of a structured way to develop new concepts and theory from the sequential coding of data derived from direct observation (Strauss and Corbin 1998), allowing research methodology to evolve and be informed by previous phases in the study following evaluation and reflection.

First phase: semi-structured interviews

Early pilot studies relied on the use of semi-structured interviews, organized around themes categorized into three areas of interest: physical objects and features, human experience and place making. These were conducted as part of a number of school grounds improvement projects, and refined in a public consultation planning project about the place perception of the inhabitants of a village in North Yorkshire, UK. This provided an opportunity to develop themes relevant to a wider neighbourhood context. In this pilot, the children were initially engaged in a game to find their home on a base plan of their neighbourhood and then mark it with a model house; this was partly an attempt to put them at their ease. This technique helped to give the subsequent interview a sense of orientation focused on a known and familiar place. This was developed for the first phase of the doctoral research by extending the game so that, in addition to identifying their home, children also marked their school and indicated their typical mode of transport between the two places, and whether they were alone or with others, for example. This extension to the original pilot was made to recognize the likelihood that social issues as well as method of travel might play a significant part in the children's perceptions of place. The interviews for this first phase were conducted on a one-to-one basis in the company or proximity of a known adult.

Predetermined themes led to discussions centred on routine activity and an 'imagine and remember' game to establish what was noticed on emerging from their home and along the route to school. Other discussion took place to establish at what point the children felt they were near to school and then had arrived, as well as establishing patterns of spatial experi-

ence and place preference in the wider neighbourhood. The sessions were all voice recorded for the purpose of subsequent evaluation. An important characteristic of the approach adopted in engaging with the children was that it should be empathetic. This is variously described in the context of student centred approaches to teaching as 'a mode of human contact' (Egan 1990: 123), 'putting yourself in their shoes' (Wheeler and Birtle 1993: 34) and being understood from their own viewpoint rather than being evaluated (Kirschenbaum and Henderson 1990). This was fundamental to building trust between the researcher and children in the study group, and generally worked well. Reflecting upon the first phase, it was decided that the second phase would take place in pairs or small groups to provide an element of familiarity and mutual support for the more reticent of the children.

Second phase: cognitive mapping and drawing

Cognitive mapping and drawing techniques had previously been used in the field trials as an effective way of finding out how the children experience and use places. The significance of people being able to understand their environment and able to map it mentally is a prominent component in the development of place perception (Downs and Stea 1973). The maps can be particularly effective where there are cultural or communication problems, which can be the case with employing conventional methodologies due to the age and limitations of understanding of the study group (Wates 2000). It was also evident from the first phase that, because of the diversity of the group, account should be taken not only of ability to communicate thoughts but also of preferences for expressing them. This draws from work examining preference of learning styles, and in particular the work on experiential learning by Kolb (1984) and Honey and Mumford's (1992) version of the learning cycle, both of which identify individual preferences in engaging with learning experiences.

The children were asked to complete two drawings. The first was to map their existing neighbourhood experiences in response to 'this is what it is like outside, where I live, on the way to school and at my school'. By way of personalizing the work, the children were also asked to draw themselves in the picture doing what they liked doing best outside at a preferred location. While the children drew they were engaged in conversation to discern what they were drawing and why. The second picture was to draw an aspiration for their neighbourhood. This involved a technique we called a 'wish picture', a development from a synthesis of two methodologies. The first of these is known as a 'word picture' (Alexander *et al.* 1995), a technique used as a means of revealing experiential dimensions of place by describing something of the quality of sensations and experience that places would deliver in advance of thinking about the physical structure and spatial arrangement in detail. Because of the word picture's limitations in its application with younger chil-

dren, due to the potential diverseness in the development of their written communication skills (highlighted by some parents' responses to the initial participation invitation information), an adaptation was developed to combine this methodology with a 'wish poem', a visual variation of the semi-structured interview (Sanoff 2000a, Sanoff 2000b). Perhaps inevitably the outcomes were biased towards drawings of objects and features, but with the use of semi-structured interview techniques a richer picture was able to be revealed about the experiential qualities of the places they had visually created (Figure 20.1).

Concluding phase: adaptive photo-elicitation

As part of the grounded approach, the formative methods were evaluated and a set of provisional themes began to emerge as signifi-

20.1 Jack draws himself in his wish picture and includes an expression on his face

cant from the data collected; these were sub-sequently tabulated into a *leitmotif* code. As a consequence it was possible to identify broad categories within which the emergent place perceptions of the children involved could be grouped, giving a structure to the final phase of the work. The themes identified related to place or object-specific experiences; feelings and emotional significance; social networks; and imagination and temporal aspects. These emerging themes appeared consistent with those cited by Aitken and Wingate (1993), who define a code from a self-directed photography study to include the built environment; natural environment; dynamic/action; and social rela-tions. The resulting code and themes from the earlier phases were tested using adaptive photo-elicitation techniques to ascertain preferences and the conceptual relationship between pre-ferred images and the code. Image sets were compiled from data derived from the *leitmotif* code which informed the choice of a number of settings to test. These settings were photo-graphed by the researcher from a child's height in order that the places would appear from their perspective as much as an image can represent such.

The first exercise of this phase was con-ducted in two parts. The aim of the first part was to present an image set to explore issues of social networks; the children were asked to stick a silhouette on to a preferred image where they would most like to be in three different social situations – with their family, with a friend and lastly if they were alone. In each case a different silhouette could be chosen to represent each scenario.

The second part used a technique designed to explore dynamic actions, imagination and temporal aspects, and a second image set was added to the first. The children were asked to choose a place they would most like to go to, in order to engage in a range of scenarios that had emerged from the code. In each case they stuck a silhouette representing themselves in a picture of their choice from either the first or second image sets and wrote a reference num-ber next to the image relating to the scenario. The children were also requested to consider not only which image they preferred but also the

positioning of the silhouette in the preferred image.

The second exercise tested aspects of feelings and emotions – from second-phase work it was apparent that when the children drew themselves in their cognitive map, some expressed how they felt about places by includ-ing an expression on their face in the picture. From this construct a Likert scale of expressive faces was developed. An image set was then selected to test scenarios of feelings and emotions. The children were asked to tick a face or faces that showed how they would feel if they were in the picture, and if there was not a face that represented how they felt then they could draw one (Figure 20.2).

The last exercise was conceived from the previous phases where some children had talked about or drawn their constructivism charac-teristics – engaging in virtually or physically building places. This was adapted into a tech-nique for the children to design a neighbour-hood using a number of place images. The children were asked to select images of places they would like in their neighbourhood and stick them on to a blank A3 piece of paper, con-sidering the inclusion in this neighbourhood of houses, streets, places to play, different types of boundaries, alleyways, pathways, places to rest and places to go to. A range of 62 images were offered, developed from the *leitmotif*. The children were asked to arrange as many or as few of the images as they desired on the paper and stick them down relative to how they wanted their neighbourhood to be. They were also asked to include home, represented by a picture with the text 'home', and their school, and then arrange their selected images in relation to these. To complete their picture they stuck a silhouette representing themselves and placed it where they would most like to be. They were then encouraged to explain the choices they had made and the composition of what had now become a poster of their con-structed neighbourhood (Plate 17).

Finally the children were asked to partake in a methodological evaluation of the whole study, asking them which parts they enjoyed or disliked the most, if they noticed anything different about their neighbourhood, had they discussed

20.2 Amy draws her own expressive face to show how she would feel in the alleyway

taking part with anybody else and if they were asked would they do it again.

Mapping the children's experiential landscape

A conceptual framework has been developed to help reveal the experiential dimensions of open-space use by translating categories of place experience into spatial themes called centre, direction, transition and area (CDTA) (Simkins and Thwaites 2004; Thwaites and Simkins 2006). A method has been developed to map these by plotting the distribution of symbols representing different kinds of place experience, and by using this technique the participants' existing experience of the place in the context of these categories can be mapped. This method of mapping spatial experience has been developed and refined from a number of pilot studies, and produces a map or series of overlays of existing

contextual activity and experiential characteristics together with their spatial location using GIS.

Conclusions

The research employs a variety of qualitative participative techniques. The value of the longitudinal study and grounded approach enables reflection and refinement at each phase of data collection while maintaining a consistency across the study groups at each phase. The reflective process of evaluating the methods allows for development and refinement to test assertions from the previous phases. The multi-method approach is important in research of this kind to respond to the intrinsic subjectivity involved in place perception. Using only a single method to obtain information about people's experience of places they use will produce data related only to that specific method of enquiry. The variety of techniques also attempts to engage with the children as individuals with preferences and individual needs rather than a collective whole. The evolving themes demonstrate a complexity and fine grain of place perception that is often experienced by adults subliminally but would appear more significant to children's daily encounters with their local environment. If we are to appreciate this 'realness of place' from the perspective of children then we not only need to give them a voice, but we also need to listen to the voices and understand them.

References

Aitken, S.C. and Wingate, J. (1993) 'A preliminary study of the self-directed photography of middle-class, homeless, and mobility-impaired children', *Professional Geographer*, 45(1): 65–72.

Alexander, C., Black, G. and Tsutsui, M. (1995) *The Mary Rose Museum*, Oxford University Press, Oxford.

Downs, R. and Stea, D. (eds.) (1973) *Image and Environment, Cognitive Mapping and Spatial Behaviour*, Edward Arnold, London.

DTLR (2002) *Green Spaces, Better Places, London, Department of Transport*, Local Government and the Regions.

Egan, G. (1990) *The Skilled Helper: A Systematic Approach to Effective Helping*, Brooks Cole, California.

Honey, P. and Mumford, A. (1992) *The Manual of Learning Styles*, Peter Honey, Berkshire.

Kirschenbaum, H. and Henderson, V. (eds.) (1990) *The Carl Rogers Reader*, Constable, London.

Kolb, D.A. (1984) *Experiential Learning: Experience as the Source of Learning and Development*, Prentice Hall, New Jersey.

Sanoff, H. (2000a) *Designing with Communities 2000 Conference*, Collection of Abstracts and Biographies, University of Strathclyde, Glasgow.

Sanoff, H. (2000b) *Community Participation Methods in Design and Planning*, John Wiley & Sons, New York.

Simkins, I.M. and Thwaites, K. (2004) 'The spatial experience of primary school aged children: the development of an open space design language', paper and conference presentation at the International Open Space: People Space conference, 27–29 October 2004, Edinburgh.

Strauss, A. and Corbin, J. (1998 2edn.) *Basics of Qualitative Research*, Sage Publications, California.

Thomas, G. and Thompson, G. (2004) *A Child's Place: Why Environment Matters to Children*, Green Alliance/DEMOS.

Thwaites, K. and Simkins, I.M. (2006) *Experiential Landscape Place: An Approach to People, Place and Space*, Taylor and Francis, London.

Wates, N. (2000) *The Community Planning Handbook*, Earthscan Publications, London.

Wheeler, S. and Birtle, J. (1993) *A Handbook for Personal Tutors*, SRHE, Buckingham.

Worpole, K. (2003) *No Particular Place to Go: Children, Young People and Public Space*, Groundwork, West Midlands.

PART III
CONCLUSION

21 Conclusion

This book is the outcome of a process of discussion among the authors, a consequence of a realization that although they belonged to different disciplinary backgrounds with different approaches to research and professional practice, they shared a common background of values about the urban environment and its inhabitants. Central to all is a concern to think about how to understand, make and shape urban environments that are above all for people. Why is it that sometimes our towns and cities can look impressive, stunning even, and yet feel to us like vacuous deserts, sterile and devoid of emotional and experiential value? There seems to be a gradually creeping chasm between how we understand the aesthetic of city spaces and their liveability: their potential to be successful places to raise children, run businesses, find new solutions, exchange ideas, move around efficiently and feel safe at home.

As the process went on, the author became increasingly aware that the work was not going to be one characterized by answers but rather by questions. A successful urban place is much more of a miracle than a goal, with numerous contributing factors – social, economic, environmental, cultural. What role does urban design play in the realization of this miracle, and how can we be sure that the approaches we adopt deliver to our clients and society a heaven rather than a hell? What does it mean, for our thinking and our working practices if we accept, as Lucien Kroll and Christopher Alexander evidently do, for example, that our responsibility as professionals is to deliver fulfilled lives rather than simply a physical infrastructure of buildings, open spaces, transport networks and the like? Step by step, as the author's and contributors' personal reflection and research began to converge, there was a feeling of approaching a somehow radical point of view.

A first realization was a growing sense of dissatisfaction with the results of a neo-traditional 'compact' city movement in urban design. Although this remains by far the best thing to have happened in the discipline in recent times, there seemed to be something missing: are we just doing the same that our modernist predecessors did, although behind a different mask? Are we simply continuing to speak in obscure, pseudo-technical jargons that are legible only to a limited circle of peer scientists and professionals? Are we producing cataclysmic projects that do not take into account the resources that have been developed through time in biological, spatial, social and economic environments? Are we excluding substantial parts of the human community? Are we producing 'solutions' without a previous serious attempt to understand and define the problem properly?

The modernist culture has permeated the Western world so deeply that many of the predominant ways of urban development we see are still arguably simply a different visual manifestation of the towers and slabs or the low-density sprawl of the modernist conventional heritage. Compared to this mass activity, recent realizations of the compact city movement's avant-garde in urban design show a substantial change of attitude and much better results in terms of environmental quality, transportation balance, pedestrian accessibility to urban opportunities, support to social cohesion and public life and so forth. Progress this certainly is, but at least in part it can also sometimes reveal a certain élitism in architectural style and insufficient investigation of urban resources and problems, especially the human experiential ones, to which the protagonists aspire to respond. Repopulating towns and cities with eye-catching, rapidly constructed and let apartment blocks will certainly fill the human vacuums in cities left by de-industrialization and migration to the suburbs. Yet this is surely short-term thinking unless we realize and can effectively respond to the reality that bringing 90,000 or more people, usually of a limited demographic, into one place in less than five years is just a big crowd and not a community. How sustainable, socially and otherwise, is this approach?

The authors began to believe that the missing ingredient, the concept that might make a beneficial difference, could be the notion of *time* itself. Perhaps, they thought, the most profound and comprehensive key to the understanding of the problem is not really the design, in a strictly physical sense, of those urban developments, but the whole process that produces them. Hardly ever, in the race to capitalize on urban regeneration, is such development 'time-conscious'. After the realization of this point, the book came out rapidly as a reflection in two directions. On one hand, the authors tried to summarize the foundations for the reconstruction of a place-responsive perspective in urban design, investigating where some of what we take for granted as the ordinary approach to our daily work of designers comes from. Much of value in this respect was found by drawing from environmental psychology, epistemology and the specific history of urban and architectural design. These intellectual resources are not all new to urban design by any means: in many cases they are cornerstones of its development and identity. Yet it seems that some of the core messages have been left behind, misunderstood or simply marginalized by much of the mainstream of practice. Building from this the authors tried to move towards an understanding of what time-conscious urban design might actually mean, arriving at the conclusion that a time-conscious realization of urban design is one based on a respect for architectural and urban cultural heritage, a respect for and reuse of ordinary old buildings and urban fabrics, and incremental multi-actorial change.

Here is where questions, rather than answers, take the foreground. One can easily outline how to undertake the first two issues, as they are part of well-established disciplines such as architectural conservation or cultural and urban anthropology, but the third and most crucial one still remains largely obscure. Incremental multi-actorial change has to do with re-establishing a framing in space (e.g. by fragmenting large parcels of land in smaller units of development), in time (e.g. by favouring piecemeal processes of transformation) and in decision-making (e.g. making the universe of 'stakeholders' involved in the process of change wider and more representative of the community as a whole). Accepting this inevitably involves the realization that its impact on current practices would be strong and radical. Current approaches are, in fact, increasingly enlarging the spatial units of developments following the growing level of financial investment, compressing the duration of the process and generally limiting admission to the lowest possible number of persons and organizations under firmly structured legal, temporal and political frameworks. There are strong impediments to any idea of incremental multi-actorial change well rooted at the heart of the organizational, cultural, political, economic and even technical assets that support the process of urban transformation.

However, no matter how radical the idea, the main message of this book is that time-conscious urban design is key to the achievement of social sustainability, visual attractiveness, responsiveness to change and evolution and the implementation of a deeper human-environment relationship. Moreover, time-conscious urban design can be anchored to several well-established traditions in disciplines as diverse as urban design, urban sociology and anthropology, governmental studies and the sciences of complexity. For example, there is a tradition of research in urban design that has been dealing with the project for evolution and change since the early 1960s, while a more recent area has been trying to devise and manage 'inner codes' for emerging – not predetermined – formal solutions, and finally a third one has been dealing at various levels with the idea of participatory or 'community' design. New techniques of spatial analysis allow a much deeper understanding of some of the fundamental properties that appear to rule the relationship between the urban structure and the emerging, self-organized collective behaviours while others allow us to comprehend better the collective association of values and meanings to the visual aspects of the built environment. Also, there are many examples of large projects that consciously focus just on several common rules, leaving to successive steps and different actors the definition of more detailed solutions: this poses the problem of the urban design code, a central issue in the contemporary international debate on the constitution of the 'masterplan' as an urban design document.

At least there is now a growing culture of place-responsive urban design that may help in the interpretation of what really counts for making better places for human beings, a culture that increasingly relies on interdisciplinary visions, approaches and tools. It is that culture that we as architects and urban designers should practise and contribute to in order to enhance the idea of time-conscious transformations in the urban environment. One way of doing that is to stratify practical methodologies of urban analysis, like those outlined in the last part of this book, aimed at overcoming disciplinary boundaries, building different representations of problems, involving citizens, in short constructing many 'sections' of complexity as contributions not to the best solution, but rather to the richest possible episteme-diversity of the process.

It is not so difficult, therefore, to imagine how a more time-conscious process of urban design should be shaped or what technical cultures should be put at work to achieve it. Nevertheless, we are far from even imagining a real shift in current practices of urban change in such a direction. Notwithstanding the existence of many single achievements, many cases of good practices and many specific technical and scientific resources that may indicate the way, we still miss a general framework where all those contributions can find their way into a new mainstream perspective. Such a framework cannot be realized without a significant cultural shift in the discipline of urban design itself: one that can not only reverse the destructive aspects of the culture of modern urban design, but that can recognize and respond to the need for urban development to harmonize more than is currently evident with how neighbourhoods and communities establish, grow, adapt and ultimately survive. Revealing the form of such development, and more especially the processes that can bring it into being, may be one of our most important intellectual and professional challenges.

Index